SOL
CAMPBELL

THE AUTHORISED BIOGRAPHY

SIMON ASTAIRE

'I chose Simon as my biographer because I knew he'd produce something different to the usual type of sports biography,' says Sol Campbell.

Simon Astaire is the author of four novels, the latest of which, *The Last Photograph*, was published in November 2013. This is his first biography. He divides his time between London and Los Angeles.

SOL
CAMPBELL

THE AUTHORISED BIOGRAPHY

SIMON ASTAIRE

SPELLBINDING
M E D I A
LONDON

Also by Simon Astaire

Private Privilege
And You Are...?
Mr Coles
The Last Photograph

Published by Spellbinding Media 2014

1 3 5 7 9 10 8 6 4 2

First published in Great Britain in 2014 by

Spellbinding Media
17 Empress Place
London SW6 1TT
www.spellbindingmedia.co.uk

Spellbinding Media Ltd Reg. No. 08482364

A CIP catalogue record for this book is available
from the British Library.

ISBN 978-1-9099-6408-2

Printed and bound by
TJ International Ltd, Padstow, Cornwall.

CONTENTS

'No wonder I sigh for the days gone by, the times
that should come no more.'

JOSÉ HERNÁNDEZ

PROLOGUE

Saturday 17 November 2001, White Hart Lane

It is different today. Even the man from the Salvation Army shouting out for donations isn't smiling. On the corner, a street vendor is doing a roaring trade selling t-shirts with what the uneducated would perceive as the world's biggest villain since Hitler printed on the front. Here comes a group with their teeth biting so tightly that their jawbones may crack. 'Come on!' shouts the tallest, 'let's get in there!' He coughs one of those long phlegmy spasms that you hear in the next-door room through thin walls in cheap hotels, before a spit to the pavement.

A crowd is huddled outside the burger stand. It is nothing more than a one-sided caravan with a stove, on which burgers and onions fry. The owner, an enthusiastic raconteur not unlike those we hear on Speakers' Corner, has a queue of punters. He sweats a lot as he serves, his hair rather wet from the steam; each customer receiving a special quip as they hand over their cash. Although there is hate in the air, it does not seem to have spoiled the crowd's appetite. There is nothing better than to have a full stomach before a battle.

'Keep up!' the father calls to his son, the boy's blue and white scarf tied tightly around his neck. The father takes hold of his hand. Today, of all days, even without the bigger story hanging over them, would be one to hold firmly on to little hands. For today is the great derby match between Tottenham and Arsenal.

It's ten minutes to three. Time to get in. The father passes over their season tickets to a woman who tears off the paper in the booklet. 'She's our lucky charm!' the father once said to his son, and since then the boy has always whispered the word 'lucky' into his ear. They walk through the click of the turnstiles, beyond the milling hordes and up the steep stone stairway, out into the open again, the green grass of the battleground brilliant to the eyes. It feels like the Coliseum today. The crowd is singing, no, yelling.

Traitor! Traitor!

There is a sense of madness spreading through the ground. A flicker in the faces of apprehension, of anticipation, of bafflement.

Why did you do this to us?

Yes, how quickly things can change in life. Our one-time hero has transformed himself into our everlasting villain.

It's five to three. The crowd jumps up and down, sways. Sections fall over each other in cascades of tribal bonding; a mass of humanity stacked so close together, even though they have their our own seats you feel you could gauge the tone of each individual breath.

Then, in slow motion, they see a flurry of activity at the head of the tunnel. Thirty-seven thousand people inside the ground, and millions watching back home on television, rise to look in that direction. Down below on God's turf, stewards so eager to turn round have to watch the crowd to make sure there is no trouble. Trouble? Some have never felt so close to war, to hatred. 'Judas!' yells the man in front; the rest of the row join in. The photographers are squeezed together, their index fingers twitching with excitement; today they know where and who their money shot is. They know what their editor wants, what the public wants. The snappers step forward. The teams are on their way: the good angels and the evil angels. Soon the reason for the home supporters' anguish will emerge. Very soon. Here they come. Yes, I see them! The teams walking side by side. Where is he? Where is the man? 'We Hate You Because We Loved You' is written on one banner.

Do you understand, do you realise that?

It's one of those love affairs we can never forgive because of the way it ended. The crowd release four thousand white balloons with the word 'Judas' etched in blue. They fill the grey sky for a moment but soon disappear from view, an act of defiance that would be completely forgotten if it wasn't for what comes next. Finally, he's in sight. Here he comes: Judas into the Garden of Gethsemane. He looks straight ahead and immediately picks up his pace. Spellbound or terrified? There he is, the man the crowd have been waiting for: Sol Campbell, the home team's former skipper, in red shirt with white sleeves with a number 23 on his back. The man who said he'd stay at White Hart Lane and sign a new contact when his original deal ran out. He said that he loved Tottenham.

Really? Did you really say that, Sol? Well then, why did you leave the club and break a thousand, no, tens of thousands of hearts? Why on earth did you do that? And why did you, to cap it all, sign for Arsenal, the North London neighbours and sworn enemy? Answer that, Sol.

He is the seventh man out. It's a cliché but he looks the calmest person on the field. He doesn't give a clue that he is being threatened by the onslaught of venom. Enjoying it even? Perhaps, deep down, he is terrified. But no-one can truly tell. The crowd begins to whistle like a freight train exploding through the station. The man to the father's right wrings his hands. 'Boooooooooo!!!' howls his son standing on tiptoes. The father's instinct is to scold him. *Don't do that, don't join in the pantomime.* But he doesn't. Maybe because he is too angry. Anyway, it's not causing much harm, is it? It's just a game after all.

But no, it's more than that. For those of us who follow and appreciate its beauty, it maps our moods, shapes our days and for many adds colour to our drab uneventful lives. Such delicacy, such grace. Yes it is personal, of course it is. Watch the football. Think of all it's given us: the tales we've been able to tell, the debates, why we won, why we lost, why is our life so good, why is it so shit. Post mortem on our day, on our life.

'Loved football all his life' should be written on our obituaries, because as football fans it's true. Yes, it is true. Hands in the air. Praise be to God. Here's another tale from our beautiful game: Sulzeer Jeremiah Campbell's story, our one-time favourite son.

Then silence. The referee puts the whistle to his mouth. The game begins.

•   •   •

Eight Years Later

I'm in La Delizia, my local Italian restaurant. La Delizia sits on the corner of a precinct of shops on Chelsea Manor Street, off the Kings Road in Chelsea. This unassuming place is one long thin room with chestnut-coloured walls and a dozen tables; you could easily walk by without noticing it's a restaurant. People who find it tend to return. They like the anonymity of the place; it reflects their character.

I sipped at a latte. There was only one other customer in the restaurant. He was someone you could not easily miss. It was Sol Campbell. He certainly looked the part of one of our finest footballers in recent years: firmly angled lantern-jawed face, body of a supreme athlete, the omnipresence of a superstar that usually sounds off a vibration that unsettles anyone who comes within reach of its aura. But I could see, or rather feel immediately, that Sol was different. He merges his presence within the walls. He was there, without being there, like someone walking across snow without leaving footprints. And I was surprised my initial reaction was one of confusion; the result, I realise now, of a flashback to the days of watching him play football, and although not understanding his actions, having a liking for single-minded ambition.

He is talking with the owner Michele, who is opening his mouth wide and long, shoulders hunched, palms open, speaking to him like he's answering several telephones at once. Sol is listening, not uttering a word. His smile tells me he is enjoying the tale, his entertainment for the morning. Suddenly Michele turns and calls out, 'Simon, have you met Sol?'

'No I haven't,' I reply. I get up and walk over to introduce myself. So much for ignoring him.

'Another coffee, Sol?' a waiter asks, interrupting the flow of our introduction. He says, 'double espresso' and shakes my hand with a firm grasp and a straight look into my eyes. The way Sol struck me at first with that look was that he was shy. We exchanged a few pleasantries. He seemed a little distant. Although I think he wanted to talk, he gave the impression that opening up to someone new was not easy. But we did speak briefly about football. What else? Every famous footballer has to go through the barrage of overexcited eager fan questions before any further connection can be made. I thought I would start with an easy one: 'Why did you leave Tottenham?' Nothing too testing, then. I half-expected him to say, 'Leave me alone ... You ask too many questions ...' But no, he was nothing like that. He was cordial, respectful even. Our conversation lasted a few minutes. Before leaving, I confessed I was a Spurs fan. When I told him, I felt sure he already knew. I think it's obvious. I think we carry it in our eyes.

After a few encounters, we begin to feel more comfortable in each other's company. He asks me over to join him. He's the one who starts the conversation, when before it was always me. He talks more freely about his mood, how he is feeling. There is still hesitation when we talk about Tottenham; I notice it is definitely there.

'Good result for Spurs at the weekend. I think they'll finish in the top four. Don't you?'

There is a pause. I change the subject, or rather the team. And he begins to talk more freely, until we reach the point where I can ask the question.

'Can I write your book?'

He doesn't reply immediately and then says, 'It's too early.'

'Too early or too painful?'

I kept prompting him about the book each time we met. And then, four years later, things changed. He had retired from football and it seemed that he was trying to fill up his days. 'The beginning of the season is very difficult,' he told me at the start of 2013-14. 'I want to be involved. *Playing!*' he emphasises. 'I mean, just watching the games is very painful. I used to be out there. Part of it.'

He authorised me to write his biography. 'It's time,' he said without hesitation. What follows is his story told through a series of text messages, talks with team-mates, managers and friends, but mainly from face-to-face conversations with Sol himself, usually held in our local Italian.

He was nearly always late for our meetings by at least fifteen minutes but would send word by text. When he arrived he would apologise and greet me with a firm handshake. He did not once refuse to answer a question, however tough the question might be. Sometimes he would stare at me with a seriously blank expression when I asked something difficult, but he would eventually open up.

I've listened carefully to Sol and although you might imagine you've heard it all before from a footballer, in numerous keys and orchestrations, I believe he will surprise you.

Sometimes there may be slight discrepancies in events, but as the saying goes, if two or more people recall an incident in exactly the same way, you can be almost certain they got together and agreed to lie...

HOME

'We shall let God decide.'

WILHELMINA CAMPBELL

The street is plain and uninspiring with a long row of semi-detached pewter grey houses on each side. Some roofs are losing tiles. It is typical of Newham, a sprawling urban community in the backwaters of London. Tree-lined East Road is quiet in the early mornings, not even a chink of light coming from behind a drawn curtain. Cars are tightly parked, some crookedly edged onto the curb. In the Sixties everyone knew everyone else here, but things have changed. Families come and go; few have stayed over the last fifty years. Yet those who have left haven't gone too far; once you live in Newham, it's hard to leave. It's as if there's an invisible cage marking its borders.

The Campbell family still live in the street and in the same house where Sol was brought up. Theirs is the most striking because of an unexpected splash of gold paint covering moulds over the door and windows. The local newsagent, Bill, an Asian with the warmest of smiles and the kindest of faces, is also still there, the cornerstone of the community.

Bill has gone out of his way to talk to me. 'I never forget a face. I have seen the children grow and now I have had the privilege to watch their children's children grow.' He knows the Campbell family and by the way he tells his tales assumes everyone else knows about them. Like many local shopkeepers he has the uncanny knack of being able to assess a man's true worth after only a brief acquaintance, even at a moment's glance. He remembers Sol's father coming in daily to pick up his *Daily Mirror* and his packet of Old Holborn tobacco with red cigarette papers. He describes Sewell as a large West Indian, courteous and always having had time to share a joke. 'I liked him,' he says, assured that he has given me an honest take on his character and has not trivialised an enquiry with a mere guess.

Sewell Campbell was a tall man, six feet four with a booming Jamaican accent. He was immaculately dressed, always seen in a black suit, white shirt, black tie and hat. He worked nights for London Transport, fixing signals. He punched in at 11.30pm and returned home by 7 o'clock the following morning. He worked there for twenty-seven years and not once did he discuss what his shift was like with his wife. Whatever is said about Sewell, he did work hard to earn a living for his family and provide a home. He bought his first house in Canning Town for three thousand, five hundred pounds. When he sold it in 1974, he immediately bought the house in Newham with his profit. 'You have one chance. Grab it!' he would repeatedly say. He is dominant in Sol's story. His father's memory envelops Sol like a tall building shadowing you on a hot day. If Sewell were alive today, he would be happy to know how much he'd defined his famous son's nature and helped to create not only a world-class athlete but also a respectful and well-mannered man.

Sulzeer Jeremiah Campbell (he changed his name to Sol when he was sixteen, after he found that people kept pronouncing Sulzeer wrong) is the youngest of twelve children, ten boys and two girls. Sewell emigrated from Jamaica in 1960 and his wife Wilhelmina came over a year later. They left five children back in Jamaica with one of Sewell's sisters; four later came over to England, with one left behind due to the immigration laws. 'The children we left behind say that we love the children who were born in England more than them, but it is not true,' says Wilhelmina. 'We love them all equally. They also say that those born here have had a better life. That might have been true at the start of their lives, but I'm not sure it's true anymore. It may have been more difficult for the ones born in England.'

Wilhelmina arrived at Heathrow Airport on a British Airways flight. She planned to meet her husband there. But on landing she couldn't find him and had to make her way by coach up to Birmingham, where she had an address for one of Sewell's sisters. 'He was waiting at the airport all along. Funny, I thought I had heard my name being called but I wasn't sure, so ignored it,' she laughs.

When Sewell reached Birmingham, he stifled his anger and together they returned the same day by coach back to London. 'Our first home was a small room in Forest Gate.' However tight the accommodation was, she never had any regrets in making the move to England. 'I don't miss Jamaica at all, no way. I'm here and will be staying here until I go for my burial. I've always been at peace [here] and so was my husband. He never said it, but I know he was glad he made his life in England and that some of our children were born here.'

Beneath Wilhelmina's sweet and calm exterior is a woman of remarkable strength. The only outward clue is her hands. They are large and strong, and look as if they have worked every day of her adult life. It's hardly surprising that as soon as she arrived in the country, she started work. Her first job was in Telford, in a meat factory making hamburgers for supermarkets, where she worked from 2pm until 10pm. When she had the twins, George and Gerald, she left and began work in Dagenham for Telephone Cables. She was with the company for nearly twenty-seven years, employed on the morning shift from 6am to 2pm, where she worked with cables, twisting them and stringing them up over a wheel. There were a lot of West Indian women who worked with her. 'There were more black people than whites because it was a hard manual job and you needed to be strong,' she pauses and chuckles. 'I was young then.' And although she was having children, her bosses were understanding and considerate. 'They always treated you well. They never minded if you had to take maternity leave. They were good people. The only thing we complained about was our bonus. You never knew how much you would get. We would go to the supervisor's office and he would sometimes be generous and sometimes not. I was first paid weekly in cash but after three years they gave me a cheque and I would deposit it into the bank. My husband and I kept our money separate. He never asked me how much I was being paid. He would pay the council rates. He paid what he wanted to pay and if we were short, I would make up the difference.'

Wilhelmina had forged a good life in England. She had convinced herself that her work was worthwhile. She was dedicated to it, to her home and to her children. She didn't have much time to herself and she had little communication with her husband. They probably didn't realise that the years were passing them by, or certainly the days. When she came back from work, he was going out. She wasn't even bothered that he was spending more and more time out at the pub. She just got on with it. Their house in East Road was orderly and well-run. Yes it was short on space, but they could manage; everything was just fine, until one day her peace was shattered by the voice of a doctor.

Wilhelmina was pregnant again. This would be her twelfth child. Her GP advised her it wouldn't be wise to have another. He suggested she terminate the pregnancy. 'You are forty-one years old,' he said. 'You have had many children and this pregnancy could seriously affect your health. I don't think you have the strength left in you, and even if you managed to have the child there could be complications.'

She left the surgery confused and angry, finding it difficult to digest what had been said. *Have an abortion? I can't do that.* She carried the weight of the doctor's words with her for days. She told no-one. There was nobody to tell. She certainly couldn't discuss it with her husband and there was nobody at work she felt at ease with to seek advice. She started to imagine the worst. What if it made her so sick she was unable to look after her living children? What if she died? What if what he said was true, and her twelfth child was born with problems?

On the Sunday, when she was in the launderette in Canning Town, she couldn't keep the doctor's conversation secret any longer. She needed to talk to someone and she opened up to a white woman in her seventies who worked there. She never understood why. She didn't normally talk to strangers about her life. She explained what the doctor had said, what she had been advised to do: to have an abortion. The woman came to sit next to Wilhelmina. She put her hands on hers. She squeezed them tight. 'You listen to me,' she said. 'I had twins when I was forty-five years old and they are the tallest, strongest lads you are ever likely to see, and you can see I still have my health. Pay no attention to what has been said. You have that child my dear, and God bless him.'

Wilhelmina was filled with warm relief, like hearing the voice of a comforting friend. It was what she needed. 'I will have the child,' she said, a hundred times if she said it once. She smiled and thanked the woman. 'I will never forget you. Never.'

The following day, she returned to her doctor and told him she was going to have her twelfth child and she never wanted to discuss the termination ever again. 'We shall let God decide,' she said pointedly.

•　　•　　•

Sol was born on 18 September 1974. On that Wednesday, it was one of those freak Indian summer days without a breath of wind, when the stifling weather took Londoners by surprise.

Wilhelmina was admitted to Newham General Hospital the night before at 11pm. Sewell was at work so she called for an ambulance. It was not going to be the easiest of births. There were times she thought about what the doctor had said but her faith was strong. She had no doubt that she and the baby would be safe. She would have a caesarian the following morning.

Sewell arrived at the hospital from work. Mother and baby were doing fine. The birth could all have been so much better. But as Wilhelmina held the baby in her arms, she knew it could have been far worse. Sewell would never know how she had given all her strength just to survive the full term of pregnancy.

'My mother is a remarkable woman,' says Sol. 'She brought up all these children and maintained a good standard of living. She raised us on a different level of comfort than most in the neighbourhood and has always been there. She has always made me feel safe.'

Mother and child returned home after nine days. He was christened at the local Baptist church three months later. 'I remember he cried a lot,' says Wilhelmina. 'His brothers were christened when they were older. Peter wasn't christened until he was five years old and I promised myself, if I had another child, I wouldn't wait so long. It depressed me not having them christened early on in their life. I thought once they were christened they would be protected, and it was proved I wasn't wrong.'

•   •   •

Wilhelmina is in the kitchen preparing food. She's alone in the house apart from Sol, now four months old, upstairs in his cot. Everything is quiet. Nothing appears out of the ordinary until she looks down and sees the black and white cat staring straight at her. She bends down. 'What are you doing? Go on outside.' She shoos it away and opens the back door but it won't move. 'Go on!' But again it won't move. All it does is utter a 'miaow', not in a sentimental way but in a way she hadn't heard before. Then silence. And suddenly the cat dashes in the opposite direction to the bottom of the stairs. She can't ignore it, so Wilhelmina starts to follow. She is drawn upstairs to her room. The cat goes up to the cot, which is next to Wilhelmina's bed. The baby has a nappy covering his head and tied tightly around his neck; his feet are kicking hysterically for freedom, for breath. She rips the nappy off. For an instant, Sol's face is an unrecognisable colour. She lifts him up and takes him into her arms. A breathless hush. Her little boy could have suffocated. He is safe now. He has an angel on his back, she thinks; he will always be safe. She strokes the cat. Our youngest has been sent by divine providence. As it purrs, Wilhelmina is convinced she sees the cat's lips open and close in a half-smile.

• • •

Sol was strong, even in those early days. 'He was a good baby, quiet,' says Wilhelmina. 'By the time he was nine months old, he was already climbing on his own into his cot. All the children were strong. Sol walked at nine months. The twins walked at seven. We never had weak kids. Maybe because us parents were both strong.'

He learnt at a very early age to be independent and to occupy himself, with his mother out at work until the early afternoon, his father fast asleep upstairs after his night's shift. He remembers he irritated his siblings; fidgety, longing to move out into the fresh air, making sounds that drew attention to himself. But the rest were too busy getting on with their lives to be bothered by the newest member of the family.

Alone, he would stare at the television and be transfixed by the ever-changing shapes and angles and the multitudinous colours. Sometimes his father would walk in, turn over the channel, sink into his chair, take one look at young Sulzeer, mumble something or other, light his roll-up cigarette and gaze at the screen. Sol would shuffle his feet, stammer in silence. Stand back. Sit back. Stand up and walk to the window and see if mum was coming down the street. Sit back. Try to talk to Dad. No answer. Then a brother would come in, say something to Dad. Sol would be left out and leave the room to entertain himself with a used tennis ball or football in the garden... Alone again with his thoughts.

'I've since tried to remember where my dad was coming from. He would say, this is my house, and what I say goes. A few times I got punched but as I was the youngest, my brothers felt more force. Sometimes there has to be discipline if you do something completely wrong. You've got to learn. I understood it.

I got a belt when I probably deserved it. I know it helped me,' he says, then pauses and gives a slight nod as if reassuring himself that what he's just said makes sense not to the listener but to himself.

•   •   •

It's early afternoon. All he can see from the front window of the house as he waits for his mother to return from work are children, playing directly opposite outside the community hall. Sol spends hours spying on them. As he watches, he plays peek-a-boo. The curtains are drawn and when the kids notice Sol's face peeking through, they half-wave and gesticulate. Sol immediately ducks and pretends not to be there. This game amuses him for hours. He laughs to himself at the enjoyment. Not such a lonely place after all, is it? No – when, suddenly, he stands up with a jolt. The thud of the front door shatters the silence and his concentration. His mother is back. He runs into his mother's arms, hugging her tightly as she is trying to take off her coat. *I'm safe now. Mum's home.* He follows her into the kitchen.

The front room was cleanliness itself, spruced up ready for an occasion, with dark heavy furniture, a television, sofa and the most importantly-placed armchair. There was the ever-present smell of cooking in a house that rarely opened its windows, but it was kept as tidy as best you can imagine for a large family whose mother was out at work all day.

What Sol loved about the sanctuary of his front room was its peace. It was the best room in the house and had to be treated with respect, like a place of worship. 'It was so silent,' Sol remembers. 'I would sit in there when I came back from school, all alone while no-one else was in the house. The calm made me happy. Since then, I've always been in search of it.'

Then, the house would become a noise again. Everyone returning from school, from work. They would pile into the kitchen and start to cook or switch on the television. The various roars drowned out any peace and quiet, so Sol would creep out of the house and head to the sanctuary of the street; his tranquility.

He would say little in the house. His silence would shadow him throughout his life and make anyone who met him feel at times uneasy, even suspicious. But, like in a great novel where there is another text being written in invisible ink between the printed lines, his other story was as full as the one he was living.

'As I was the last one, I was kind of adrift. I was the youngest by five years,' Sol says. 'When you're growing up you're none the wiser, but it's not rocket science and no surprise I spent most of my time outside, away from the others. I wanted to be in the streets or in the park. I always wanted to be out of the house.'

He was a gentle boy who, although very shy, made friends. 'Sulzeer, as he was known then, would always be respectful when he came into the shop,' says newsagent Bill. 'I remember him buying fizzy sweets and saying thank you when he left. He also kept a watch on his friends. He would scold them if they behaved badly. He was a leader among his group. His friends would listen to him. It's my most vivid memory, of how they would react when he spoke. He gained the respect of his contemporaries with his calm, respectful behaviour.'

Sol's first real memory of his childhood was a day at his nursery in Upton Lane. Before he left the house, his mother was taking extra care that her four-year-old Sulzeer was looking his best, his smartest. 'It's a special day today,' she said. He remembers the day clearly, as if the house was transfused with a new energy. Police cars were parked outside the nursery, exciting for any child, probably more exciting than anything that was about to happen. A lot of people were craning their necks to get a better view. I'm not sure what's happening, thought Sulzeer, but there is great excitement and I like it. His mother says her goodbye; she needs to get to work. Sulzeer is led into the classroom and his teacher tells everyone to be quiet. 'We have a special guest today,' she says. He remembers she then paused or maybe he has added the pause to his memory. 'Lady Diana Spencer.'

The children were told to line up. Perhaps they were told all
this the day before, but the young mind doesn't remember time
like that. They remember the moments.

The countdown is on. The teacher tells the children to get
ready. She's on her way. The door opens and the effortless
beauty of a future princess walks into their classroom surrounded by admirers. Children giggle nervously. Not Sulzeer.
He is standing to attention, upright. He knows how to behave;
his parents have taught him that. She stops and talks to a boy,
or was it to a girl, just in front? Or was it both? He thinks she
smiled at him but he may be wrong, it may just be his imagination. But her presence made the day very special. After she left
the building, they decided to record the day by taking photographs. A teacher brings out a box filled with an assortment
of toys. 'Go on Sulzeer, choose something.' Sol pulls out an
object he is most comfortable with. Snap goes the photograph.
'We'll make sure your parents get a copy,' the photographer
says. He still has that photograph today. It is of a four-year-
old Sulzeer proudly holding up a red and blue football.

•   •   •

Sol's early education took place no more than a couple of miles
from his front door. After nursery, he went to Portway Infants,
five hundred metres from his home, followed by Portway
Juniors and then onto Lister Community School.

At Portway he would always choose the desk closest to the
door. A psychologist would deduce an urge to leave the classroom as soon as the bell goes, but that would not be true in
Sol's case. He wanted to stay and wanted to learn. But he found
in class, he had so much time in which to sit and think.
'Sometimes I sit and think, and sometimes I just sit.' The class
would have up to forty kids and he found himself lost in the
numbers. Quiet and shy, he could not be heard. 'The sad thing
is, I didn't really learn anything in those years. You suffer. You
go to school each day but take away very little. I didn't start to

be properly educated until I was fourteen, when I moved up north. My grades would have been much better if someone had taken the time to recognise I had the chance to improve, but I understand it's difficult in classes of that size.'

He remembers the swimming lessons: forty kids splashing about, testing the mood of the instructor. Sulzeer would walk away from the pool frustrated that he couldn't improve his swimming. His friends couldn't understand. 'We're here to have fun, aren't we?' they'd say. Sulzeer wouldn't answer back but inside he was saying, 'No. We're here to get better.' He was just eight years old but already getting to an age when he wanted to challenge himself further, push himself harder. With everything he did, he wanted to be better than he was before. Not necessarily to be the best but to improve. Shy and quiet, sport became his language of communication. 'He was the best sportsman. Not only in football. He could jump the furthest, leap the highest,' remembers his childhood friend, Jermaine 'Winston' Barclay. 'He was never the type to say look at me.' Yet, on the sports field he found he was doing it without trying. He had found his deliverance.

The boys used to play a game called 'Wembley' where they would individually take each other on, one goal, one keeper, and the first to score went through into the next round. The eight-year-old Sulzeer was drawn against an eleven-year-old, Robert Bragg, considered one of the best players in the school. 'I did a few moves that surprised him. In the end I scored and went through,' Sol smiles at the memory. 'Strange, I remember thinking, that was good. Did I really beat him? I didn't think much more of that moment at the time, but now when I reflect back on those days, I realise I had a talent, which was budding. It was just, for a long time, no-one in authority told me I was any good. I just got on with it, enjoying my sport and being picked for the school teams.'

There was no talking about dreams when he was a child. They remained hidden. They were his secrets and weren't to be shared. His first memory was of the need to escape.

Self-respect is a required commodity, as is space, both of which Sol went in search of as early as he can remember. In a school yard game of football, an eleven-year-old bully who had been gunning for Sulzeer charged into him, so viciously he fell and banged his head against a low wall. The bully had taken aim at him because of a run-in with older brother John. Better to go for the younger brother, he must have thought. And he did. Sulzeer was hurt. 'But I shall never forget Sulzeer's reaction,' remembers his friend Jermaine. 'He got up, never said a word and walked away. You couldn't tell how he was feeling. It showed maturity way beyond his years. He's always been like that.'

•   •   •

On the way back home from Portway, Sol would make a detour. He'd hurry past his front door and cross the main road to West Ham Park. He'd head to the tennis courts in search of any lost tennis balls; the volley struck with gusto that finds itself flying off towards Canary Wharf instead of hitting the baseline. There were quite a few to choose from. He would pick the best one and play against the wall in his street. He would practise every day and every night, learning to become the master, not the servant, of the ball. Like the young boy who locks himself away in his bedroom practicing the chords on his guitar again and again and getting better without noticing it, Sol would have the same dedication, staying outside, not going back into his house until he was called for. Enjoying his solitude, he would relish his practice. Hitting the ball against the wall with his left and right foot again and again, concentrating, keeping focused. Sol: 'You don't learn how to shoot but it helps your eye coordination; watching, trapping, passing with a used tennis ball.'

Even when the temperature fell in the winter months and he shivered in the increasing cold, he would remain out on the street or in the park, with just the tennis ball as company and a crowd of spectators in his mind, created by the rustle of the trees. In the autumn, with sycamore leaves falling off the branches and spiralling like marionettes out of control, he would create other sounds in West Ham Park to be his company.

He would sometimes watch games on television and then hurry back into the park to recreate what he'd just seen. The group would consist of Sol, a tennis ball and the trees as his team-mates; kicking the tennis ball against a tree, which would then ricochet back with the perfect pass to his foot, and then *wham!* into the makeshift goal. Yes! Practice! Practice!! Practice!!! He would work so intensely that the soles of his trainers wore down and his feet could feel the pavement or the wet grass. 'I would use cardboard to fills the holes in my trainers,' Sol says. He would save up for months before being able to afford a pair of new ones. 'I was given a little bit of money from my mum and dad, sometimes my brothers, 10p or, if I was lucky, 50p. I used to have this little piggy bank, which I kept hidden behind the cot.'

The cot, which Sol slept in as a baby, was now a laundry basket and piled to the brim with clothes. When no-one was looking, he would push the cot away from the wall, open his piggy bank shoved deep in the corner, and count out his money. Slowly. Counting and recounting. Then he would return it back behind the cot and the pile of clothes, well hidden from even the most inquisitive sleuth.

Money was always tight in the household. It was something you lived with, even if Sol used to notice his father filling his pockets with notes before he went off to the pub. He was too young to understand this was wrong. It's his house, he works hard and surely he has the right to go out and enjoy himself, Sol thought. 'Sometimes I had to use soap to brush my teeth if we ran out of toothpaste. It was that bad. It would usually take days to replace it. If my trainers were virtually impossible to wear anymore and had to be used sparingly, I wouldn't go out and instead I'd play upstairs in mum's room, using the bed and its corners as the goalposts, with a wrapped-up piece of foil as the ball.'

•   •   •

'I saw a lot of things as I was growing up. I was very observant and didn't miss a trick. I could see very quickly how things would pan out. In that environment, I grew up pretty quickly but it was always tough. The main thing I learned was that I saw a lot of my brothers waste time on different things, like not really concentrating on their schoolwork. I swore I wouldn't be like that.'

Birthdays and Christmas were never easy for Sol. Beneath his calm persona laid a hotbed of unease. He rarely found a present under the Christmas tree and he rarely enjoyed a day accepted by the vast majority of the country as a time of joy and frivolity. In the Campbell household, the youngest was never spoiled. The house was full of family with underlying tensions. Sol used to sit there quietly, half-listening, waiting for something to explode, like a firework going off; his father holding court like a king, as Sol's siblings paid respect to the man who provides.

When he was sixteen and earning enough money with Tottenham Youth, he went to Dixons and bought himself a Walkman with a cassette and radio. He also treated himself to a tape: a compilation album with the Robert Palmer song 'Addicted to Love' as its opening track. He sauntered around the neighbourhood for a week listening to his music; the best, and at that time only present to himself. Two days before Christmas he wrapped it up and put it under the tree. On Christmas day, he went downstairs, looked under the tree, acted surprised and opened his one present, the Walkman. It was the first time he found a special present waiting for him.

Birthdays were no different, except on his twelfth when he received the present of all presents. It was a Mongoose bike, chrome with red pads and handlebars; more importantly it was from his dad. As with all things, beauty can be seen anywhere. And this present was, in Sol's eyes, truly beautiful. Waking up to find his dad standing by the bike; the proximity of the gift in front of the house; his father holding the handlebars ready to hand it over. But after that, he received nothing. The beauty of that day made the following birthdays even harder, for his father never repeated his generosity again.

He tried not to think of his birthday as a special day. He would urge it to go by without fanfare or celebration. Some close friends might have known but most would never have guessed. There was never a party; never were his friends invited over to sing him a happy birthday.

On one birthday, when his mother buys him a birthday cake, he dashes home from school before the rest of the family gets there. He wants to eat a piece of cake on his own and then have time to hide the rest of the cake in his one drawer in his mother's room so no-one could find it. He lights himself a candle, blows it out and sings himself a happy birthday. The cake is so tasty; he savours every single bite. And, as a treat to himself, he buys a coca-cola at the local newsagents. There's no Hollywood scene when his father suddenly wakes up from his sleep to find his youngest son eating the cake on his own and clasps him to his chest and wishes him a happy birthday. There's no moment when father tells him how much he is loved, hugs his son again and says, 'I am so proud of you.' No, his father remains asleep upstairs in his own room or at his local pub drinking a pint, having a smoke and sharing a laugh, unaware it's Sol's birthday.

The cake lasts three days. Sol goes through the same routine. He rushes back after school, creeps upstairs and puts his ear to his father's door just to check if he is in there. He does not want to be disturbed. This is his moment, no-one else's. He opens his drawer and there is the cake, waiting, neatly sliced with a knife he borrowed from the kitchen. He crosses his legs on the floor and gulps down a whole slice, but not before looking at the door to check no-one is watching. Then he pauses and eats another slice. He is tempted to have a third but resists; he wants this pleasure to last for as long as possible. He doesn't sing a happy birthday to himself again; no, that can wait for another year. But other than the bike, the cake that his mother bought is his favourite present ever.

•　　•　　•

Sol was always kicking something along the street. He would dribble, smack and juggle a football, tennis ball or a can as he walked without losing his stride. Even if he was on his bike, riding up and down the street, he would be seen holding a football under his arm as if he was never going to let it go.

His clothes were well worn but he still managed to look smart, proud and upright. His one drawer at home was filled with clothes handed down from brothers, some too stained or creased to continue wearing. But even if there was no more use for them, he was hesitant to throw them out. It was an unspoken rule in the house not to throw anything away 'just in case'; to be kept safe if worse became the very worst.

He started at Lister Community School at the age of eleven. He arrived with a reputation from the local boys that he was a good footballer, someone to watch. There's nothing better than to arrive at school with a reputation; life becomes easier when you're thought of as being a good athlete. Sol was taller, stronger than most in his year and although still very quiet, he soon became the chosen leader. These decisions are never openly discussed. They just happen. If he had known, he would not have felt comfortable. He would turn down many offers of leading a team until Gerry Francis asked him to be captain at Tottenham years later; he was more content to remain in the background, without much fuss, rather than being thrust forward on show. And yet he would tend to walk a few steps ahead of his group of friends and, if the pack were slow in following, he turned and they would pick up their pace. This was all done without any signal, visual or vocal. That would be ridiculous. His calmness demanded respect even for boys heading into their teenage years. Sol had little idea he was conveying such an influence but it was happening and it was natural. He would display an instinct to teach those not as naturally talented as him in football. Before big games, he would take friends to the park and would help prepare them and try to improve their play. It would not always be one way. He was lucky to have good players around him at the time and was never daunted to learn from others. He wanted it and he needed it too; his drive and dedication were insatiable. The competitive matches were vital in his life. He longed to be on the pitch against an opposing team, working hard, and after a game, worn out and elated, feeling the exhaustion as if he had finished a cross-country run. It was around this time that his first imagery of opposition becoming the enemy in a battlefield came into being: the courage and coolness he needed in the heart of battle; not fearing any player in the opposition. Driving them back to defend, scoring to mark the victory. He would never lose that descriptive force in his imagination; never, whether he was turning out for the local district side, or playing for England in the World Cup.

He never wanted to talk about his success on the field. There was no longing to rush home and share with his family his latest news or get approval. There was no welcome face or the thumbs-up from one of his siblings. Even with his brothers who understood, played and liked the game, there were no questions. It didn't matter. He was just having fun, loving the game. Football was thought of in the Campbell household as recreational and not something you could earn a living from. It hadn't happened for his older brother John, so why should it happen for Sulzeer? It wasn't said, but it only worked out for the few. There was no-one in his life at the time to encourage him to think otherwise, neither at home nor at school. This young man didn't think much about his future, certainly not in football. What he wasn't realising was that his strides in the game were becoming more forceful.

'He had a certain maturity even at that age. He was humble as well,' says Edwin Lavinier, a close friend and future best man. Edwin saw Sol's upright behaviour as coming straight from his home. Whenever his friends went round to pick Sol up (waiting at the door and not invited in), they would be respectful. They would address Sol's father with hands out of pockets, arms to attention at the side. 'Good morning, or good afternoon, Mr Campbell' and, before saying another word, you waited for him to answer; not unlike an exchange with royalty. 'I didn't and still don't even know his first name,' says Edwin. To the boys, he looked just like they thought he was: a dominant West Indian man with a strong exterior who always expected those in his company to behave with manners and courtesy.

•   •   •

The English teacher detects giggles from the class. They are even more exuberant than usual. The ones sitting at the back were given some strong advice a few days before that behaviour in class was not very good and they were at school to learn and not just to play. But this has had little effect; those who decide that they are going to misbehave continue to do so. That morning, they were definitely finding something very funny.

The teacher decides the best way to treat them is to simply ignore the troublemakers and concentrate on those who want to learn something. The boys start to whisper into each other's ears. The desks are so close together they are virtually squatting on the same chair. The talk and near-laughter continues until the teacher has had enough and asks them, politely at first, to 'settle down'. It works initially but then the muttering starts up again, and the class sniggering gets louder and louder. Sol is not part of the noise. He is disturbed by it and soon his conscience tells him he must do something. So he gets up and walks straight to the teacher, who looks surprised to see the sight of a concerned-looking young Mr Campbell standing by his side. He is about to chide him for walking up to him without permission, when Sol asks, 'Can I have a word?'

The teacher is about to answer when Sol beckons him down. As he whispers, the class falls silent and the titters and sneering suddenly lull. After he is finished, Sol returns to his desk and the teacher, looking very embarrassed, turns away from the class to the blackboard and pulls his zip up sharply and loudly. The teacher turns to face the class and continues as if nothing happened. 'Only Sol would have done something like that,' says Edwin. 'We would have been laughing all day, but for Sol. He had no choice but to go up to the teacher and tell him his flies were wide open and he was exposing himself. He said very little but his actions spoke volumes. He was always considerate and with the smallest amount of fuss he gained our respect.'

Sol's shyness was considered a drawback by some but not a weakness. He stuck to the set of rules put in front of him, and as he grew, stood up for its unwritten code of good behaviour. If anything, his father's heavy-handed authority and his mother's kindness taught him that you are not alone; you can revel in life's imperfections and learn from the humility and humanity of getting it right and getting it wrong.

•   •   •

Often when Sol returned from school, the front door was locked, and without a key, he would have to use his ingenuity to get himself back inside. He would at first knock on the neighbour's door and if they were in the routine was easier; he would be allowed to miss out on a couple of leaps to get through next door's back garden. Otherwise, he would have to leap over the neighbour's fence at the front and back of the house, squeeze himself through the smallest window in the bathroom, and drop down from a height onto the toilet seat. His motivation was hunger. He was always hungry in those days. He had a huge appetite. He never had enough money for the local shop and needed his bowl of cornflakes, which he would demolish very quickly. He would then do his homework alone and afterwards he'd escape to the park to play football, which was fast becoming his refuge. He was growing more and more independent; he had to, he had no choice. His mother was out during the day at work and his father had become an empty presence in the home and in his life.

He was being chosen to play football for the school side and by the time he was eleven he started playing in the district league for Newham. The school had put his name forward and without a trial he was accepted and picked to play. So this became part of his life outside school hours. It was a role he felt most comfortable with; without realising it, football was becoming the epicentre of his life. Nobody was recognising the change. His parents and siblings took little notice of their youngest's ambitions or interests. He would disappear for a few hours, play his game and come home without a mere mention of who he had played against, if he scored or if he played well. As long as he didn't get into trouble, from his parents' point of view, all was fine and nothing need be asked. For Sol, home was home in title only. He couldn't really understand what home was meant to represent. It was somewhere his dear mother lived but little else, other than it being a place to escape from.

He played in a number of positions for his school and for Newham District. First he was used as a sweeper, then centre-half, next as a forward and finally in midfield, where he stayed for the majority of his early teens. He played at Flanders Fields in East Ham and the Terence McMillan Stadium just behind Newham General Hospital where Portway and Newham District both played their cup finals. 'I played my first cup final at the Terence McMillan Stadium: Portway versus Nelson school. We won and I scored. I remember Nelson had hundreds of fans and were expecting to walk over us. They'd played us the week before and beat us in the league 4-2, so they thought they could just turn up and win the cup.' In that league game Sol had scored and played well. He was the youngest on the pitch. 'I was nine, coming up against ten or eleven-year-olds. I was at least a couple of years younger than anyone else. After the game, and I have never forgotten this, a Nelson boy who was playing in defence came up to me and said, "You know, you're a fantastic player."' It was the first time in Sol's life someone had complimented him on his football, in fact on anything, straight to his face.

In the cup final, he scored two goals. 'One was a long shot,' he remembers, 'and the other one I beat two and then went on to beat the goalkeeper. The goalkeeper actually played for Newham District. He was the best in the area but he didn't stand a chance that day.' He remembers the state of the pitch, his movement when beating the two boys before reaching the goalkeeper, the weather, the length of the blades of grass, the mud in the goal area. Every detail meticulously recalled and relished like discovering a fine bottle of wine. 'It's hard to forget our goals, isn't it?' he says, which sets off in his subconscious a deluge of other football memories which, until that moment, had remained buried.

•　　•　　•

Sol was sixteen at the time he was waiting in line at Barclays Bank in Plashet Road in Upton Park. The queue was long but he didn't mind. Queues can be good barometers of mood, and that day he was in a good one. He was called and walked forward to deposit some cash. The cashier look at his filled-out slip, read the number on the cheque and was about to stamp it, when he suddenly stopped and looked straight up at Sol.

'Sulzeer Campbell? I know that name. Weren't you once down to play for West Ham?'

'Yes.' Sol replied. He instinctively looked round to see if anyone was watching, or better still listening.

'I used to work part time at the club.' And he read out Sol's full name. 'Sulzeer Jeremiah Campbell. It's a hard name to forget.'

Sol smiled shyly.

'And you're now playing youth for Tottenham?' The cheque was from the club.

'Yeah.'

'What happened then? Why didn't it work out with West Ham?'

'Oh, nothing. You know, just one of those things.'

The cashier stamped the slip. 'Well, good luck then with Tottenham,' he said and held out his hand to shake.

Sol walked out of the bank and stopped. He thought to himself that it wasn't 'just one of those things'. No, it wasn't. It was another example of his defining character.

He trained with West Ham United in an area called Chadwell Heath. He'd been spotted by a scout and asked to join up. This part of his short West Ham story is vague. He doesn't remember where he was seen or the name of the scout. Most of us would remember the weather of that particular day: the first time a professional team showed interest. But not Sol. He saw it only as a chance to play more football. Nothing more.

He would go training twice a week after school and during his summer holidays. West Ham was the first team he went to see play live. Unable to pay for a ticket, he'd get into the ground fifteen minutes before the final whistle, when the gates opened to let the disgruntled leave early. The stewards let schoolboys in free to watch. It was Sol's first chance to experience the songs and passion of a football crowd. He would also hear the debates going on as the fans drifted home: why West Ham won; why they lost; who was good; who was bad. 'I didn't support West Ham. I never supported any particular team. Perhaps I'd say Manchester United if I was pushed, but that was because Remi Moses played for them and I naturally liked black players making their way. I was more into international football: the likes of Brazil, Holland, France.'

He trained hard at West Ham, keeping himself to himself; the shy boy with an inner determination. Who said talent without energy leaves you a pauper? Sol trained even harder. Then, after one heavy session, a coach came up to Sol as he was heading off to shower.

'Cheer up Sulzeer, you're two-one up.'

He stopped and turned to face him. 'What do you mean two-one up?'

'West Indies are beating us in the cricket, two-one. Get it?'

Sol didn't answer.

'Get it? You're winning two-one! West Indies! The Test series!'

'Yeah, I get it.' Sol replied. He walked away without another word. He didn't shower. Instead, he changed straight into his clothes, packed his kit into his bag and never returned. He had been at West Ham for six months. He had nothing more to do with his local club, nothing, and would only return there when he played for an opposing side. He didn't for one moment think he might be throwing away a chance; forget what he had heard, keep his head down and keep playing. His mind did not work like that. He knew someone was being racist and it didn't matter where he was in his life, he wouldn't stand for it.

'I didn't report him because I was young. They'd never have listened nor probably understood. Many people today might find it difficult to understand. But I knew what he meant, what he was insinuating, and I made up my mind at that very moment, I'd never return to the club.'

DELIVERANCE

'He didn't seem particularly pleased to be there.
He was sullen and I think I tried to crack a joke
but he didn't react.'

KEITH WALDON

Len Cheesewright was a small, rotund man with receding hair, cockney accent and the widest of smiles. Born in Croydon, it was in the Sixties during which he developed his gift for discovering future football stars when Alec Stock, manager of Leyton Orient, offered him a job as chief scout. After almost twenty years at Brisbane Road, he had a spell as youth coach and chief scout at Leicester City, followed by a second spell with Orient, before joining Tottenham as a schoolboy scout in 1982.

When Len spotted someone special, he would return to watch the player a number of times, just to make sure his instinct was right. Usually it was. But with Sol, his normal rules were thrown out. He saw and immediately believed. 'As soon as they touched the ball, you began to frame in your mind a picture of the player,' he said, and that is exactly what he did with Sol. 'I thought he was awesome,' he said, 'but playing out of position.'

Sol was playing centre-forward for Newham District at the Terence McMillan Stadium.

'You're John Campbell's brother, aren't you? asks Len.

Sol nods his head.

'I'd like a word,' he says, barging by the other players as they leave the pitch.

Sol keeps walking; he's never been good at small talk.

'Please stop for a minute!' Len cries out.

Again he ignores the plea, suspicious of this stranger. Len tries to catch up. He starts to lose his breath, gasping hard on his lungs. (A habit of being short of breath is something Sol remembers about Len in later years.) Sol stops all of a sudden, and turns. He looks to the ground, avoiding eye contact.

'I'm a scout for Tottenham Hotspur. I'd like to talk with them about you,' says Len.

What most boys dream of hearing doesn't seem to impress. Sol says nothing and continues to gaze at the ground. Len can see this and reverts to talking about his brother.

'I know your brother John. He's a good footballer.'

John was a midfielder and forward who had trials with Charlton and West Ham. He played around the area but generally for teams with older players. He eventually played for East Ham. 'I think that was a mistake. Perhaps he joined them because they paid more, I'm not sure,' Sol says. 'But by making that decision and not being an apprentice at a proper club, he lost touch with the main network, where you can get more easily noticed.' He kept playing for East Ham until he was eighteen, but by then it was too late. 'It's a shame, he had a chance,' says Sol. 'He was a very good player.' He shakes his head in disappointment. *Why couldn't he have been stronger and got through it all? He should have made it. He had all the skill on the pitch – the talent of a Brazilian – but his mentality and lifestyle meant he struggled to fit into the discipline of the system.*

'I'll come to watch you again then,' says Len.

Sol doesn't reply.

Len knew what he'd found, what you rarely find: a genuine talent with enormous potential. Sol's skill, his gazelle like physique, his athleticism, his discipline, dominated Len's day. How was he going to encourage this shy boy who hardly uttered a word to move forward in line with his sporting destiny?

He persisted. He didn't give up. He would pick Sol up from home and drop him back after his games if it was too late for him to catch the last train. Sometimes Sol would get back home after school and there was Len, sitting down with his dad. Sol would hardly say hello, instead drifting into the garden and starting to practise once again, hitting a ball against the wall. When he paused for a moment, he found himself counting the cracks in the wall, experiencing a strange feeling that inside they were trying to control his destiny, which made him feel uncomfortable. Wilhelmina remembers it well. 'Len wouldn't stop. He was always coming over to the house. I had seen him speaking to my husband in the past, but I remember one morning him coming over to try and persuade me. My husband was asleep or out, I can't remember, and Len started to talk to me in the kitchen. He said, "I'm asking you, in fact I'm begging you to let him come with me and have a trial for Tottenham." I just listened. I wasn't interested in football. I'd taken John to a few games but that's how I saw it, as just a game. There was no future in it. But what I do remember was, Len's continual begging had an effect on me.'

Sol remained elusive. He was the authority in his life even at the age of thirteen. He did not need or want any interference, or as he saw it, control from anyone. He had learned to take care of himself. 'I had a bad experience with West Ham, so joining another professional team didn't appeal to me. My life was so restricted growing up, I felt I was being forced into another corner.'

The dance with evasion and keeping his life simple continued; his guard held up high, like a batsman in cricket playing defensively, refusing to drop. On the outside, his exterior seemed unfriendly and difficult to understand to a stranger, but persistence worked and, two months on from their first meeting, Len picked Sol up on a Tuesday evening and took him to training at Tottenham. 'Why not?' I eventually thought, 'I have nothing to lose and I'll be playing against some new players, which would be a fresh challenge. I'd also begun to trust Len. He was a genuine man with a heart of gold. I recognised he wanted the best for me. There aren't a lot of people like him around in football anymore. He was full of life and I am always grateful for his belief in me.'

The man Len so wanted Sol to be seen by was Keith Waldon, who was Tottenham youth team manager and the ultimate decision maker on whether a player was kept on or not. 'One of the best youth team managers ever,' Sol says. Waldon was respected in the game, and his reputation for coaching the young and helping them grow into their full potential was as good as anyone who had ever coached for that age.

Sol was just one of a number of boys who were brought along that night. Keith liked Len. He rated him as a scout. He had faith in his judgement. Sometimes, he felt Len could bring in some 'really good kids and others that weren't so good,' but he knew he had a good eye and was always interested to see who he might turn up with. Keith's strict orders to his scouts were not to waste his time. The only boys he wanted to see had to be 'a little bit special'. They should be as good as or better than what he already had.

Keith remembers that day when he first met Sol for two reasons. 'First, he stood out immediately because of his physicality, and second I remember he didn't smile. He didn't seem particularly pleased to be there. He was sullen and I think I tried to crack a joke but he didn't react.'

Tottenham made a quick decision to sign him. The youth development officer, John Moncur, advised if he signed for the club they would be able to put him forward for a scholarship at the FA's School of Excellence at Lilleshall. If he didn't have a club, he was told, he wouldn't be considered. 'I'm not sure that was true,' Sol says, 'because when I got there a number of the boys weren't signed to any club.' It was probably just an extra enticement to get Sol to join the club. It was competitive to get a talented boy's signature. David Beckham, who trained with Sol at the time ('He always wore a Manchester United tracksuit, which was funny, it being Tottenham,' remembers Sol), agreed to sign for Manchester United on his fourteenth birthday. Boys could not sign to clubs before they were fourteen; in Beckham's case, Sir Alex Ferguson flew into London the night before his birthday – as legend goes, in the darkness of night – and offered his mum and dad money for his signature.

So, Beckham signed for Manchester United and Sulzeer Jeremiah Campbell signed for Tottenham Hotspur. Not for any advance in Sol's case, just a bag full of promises. 'My parents were naïve. They probably didn't think money was involved,' Sol says.

• • •

'I absolutely saw his potential,' remembers Keith Waldon. 'He physically stood out but at that point he was not the most technically proficient footballer I had seen for someone of his age.'

Tottenham recommended him for Lilleshall. There was no question he had a good chance but the process was drawn out and highly competitive. The players had regional trials with six to eight selectors under strict orders not to confer with each other. The selectors' recommendations would then be passed on to the FA, who would collate the information and select about sixty boys to go for their final trial, spending a weekend at Lilleshall. That was how the final sixteen from the hundreds of boys that started the process were chosen.

Those boys were considered to be the top young footballers in the country at that time. Sol enjoyed the process. He excelled under pressure. His father's mantra of grabbing the chance if you are given one resonated in his mind. He was focused and worked hard, making sure the next day was even better than the last. Fear didn't come into his mind. He was relaxed and the only pressure he felt was his own, which was not fear of failure but more a fear that he would not represent himself in the right way.

The key to the final decision was potential. Do you think this young boy can go and achieve great things in the game? A lot of the boys looked very good at the time of their trial but something would tell the selectors, however small, that they would not progress. This is where the coaches would use all their expertise and experience to recognise who could move through their teens to become a contender in both the top leagues and internationally. There was no doubt, even at fourteen years old, that Sol had the right physical attributes to make it as a professional sportsman. He was the finest of specimens, which made him an outstanding prospect. He may have been deficient technically and lacking an overall understanding of the game, as Keith Waldon suggests, but those were things that could be taught over time. What Sol knew, and coaches would eventually learn, was that few boys who would work harder and be so determined to improve their game. 'He was an influential player even at that age,' says Keith. 'At White Hart Lane we had a ball court indoors above a car park, forty metres long by thirty metres wide, and that is where we did most of our training. In that small environment, you need a little bit of intelligence and skill and Sol was certainly effective in those conditions where your physicality is not so important. There is no question he had ability and clearly stood out.'

•   •   •

A white envelope falls through the letterbox into the hall. It is not immediately picked up. In fact, it's there for hours before Sol notices it and sees it is addressed to him. He holds it up to the light as if he's inspecting a rare artifact.

The house is empty. Not a sound. Thank God, he thinks, I can have a bit of peace while I read the letter. He knows who it's from but it's taken time to arrive. The length of time has made him think, or rather, reach the conclusion he's been turned down. Just as he's about to rip it open, he hears the front door. It's Sewell.

'What do you have there?'

'I think it's the letter from the FA telling me whether I've been accepted for Lilleshall.'

'Let's see it. Give it to me, will you?' Sewell says, snatching it away from Sol's grasp.

His father tears it open. He wears a mock-mournful expression on his face.

'You've been accepted. They want you,' he says.

Sewell passes the letter back to his son without any congratulations. Sol reads out the words as if the letter isn't important. Little does he know or understand, these lines will be the beginning of a new life.

His father goes into the kitchen to make himself a cup of tea. Sol follows, the letter still in his hand. Not a word is said between them; the only sound, Sewell's spoon stirring the milk into the tea, followed by more silence. The moment is not being recognised as anything particularly special. Why should it be? The letter has simply invited Sol to join a football academy. He wasn't even sure he wanted it. There is no realisation for Sol, his father or anyone else who reads the letter that Sol has just been recognised as one of the best sixteen young footballers in the whole of the country and has beaten hundreds of hopefuls to get there.

•   •   •

The decision to go to Lilleshall was not immediate. For many of us there is a sense in life to allow movement, escape from where you were brought up, out of your neighbourhood, just across the river, the ocean, and the country. But for most, we will think about it and think about what the future may not bring, then cart out numerous excuses as to why it is impossible to take that step.

In the Campbell household, there was hesitancy, even though Sol had spent virtually every minute of every day trying to work out how he could escape. But he did it without really knowing what he was escaping from. He was now playing football nearly every day of the week. Training with Tottenham, playing for the district, his school and for his Sunday league side, Rippleway

Newham. He had even gone for a trial with Essex. He was loving his football, but at that time he had no aspiration (and in many ways didn't think it was possible) to make football his profession, his life, his future. The FA had taken their time to get back to Sol; by the time the letter arrived, it was no longer at the forefront of his mind. He'd let it go, started to think about other things. He also thought he was a second choice. 'They took a long time making their decision,' says Sol, but there is no proof he was a substitute for anyone, and Keith Waldon says, 'I am not sure if that's true.'

It was his parents who encouraged him to accept the offer. 'They thought it was a chance to get out of my neighbourhood. To improve my life,' says Sol. They informed Lister Community School that Sol was leaving. A new life beckoned. He didn't know it then, but within months, everything he subconsciously craved would be his.

LILLESHALL

'He's going to be a very good footballer.'
SIR BOBBY ROBSON

Sol, in dark blazer, white shirt and tie was bound for Lilleshall. His parents were going with him for the induction; Sewell in suit as always, Wilhelmina wrapped up warm, carrying a large bag. They caught the underground to Euston and changed to take the train to Stafford.

Lilleshall, the Football Association's National School of Excellence, was established in 1984 by then FA technical director, Charles Hughes. As Scott Peck, the writer of *The Road Less Travelled* said: 'The best decision makers are those who are willing to suffer the most over their decisions, but still retain their ability to be decisive.' It was set up to help produce a stream of internationals. Other than Sol, Michael Owen, Andy Cole, Joe Cole, Jermain Defoe and Gareth Barry headlined an impressive alumni from a list of 234 students. But throughout its time, there was much sniping that it was too elitist, too restrictive as the FA's boarding school for the sixteen best players in the country aged between fourteen and sixteen, and the funding of what was reported as £500,000 a year would be better served on various regional centres of excellence around the country.

You can approach Lilleshall Hall through the 'Golden Gates' (an exact replica of the gates that adorn Buckingham Palace), from the main Wolverhampton to Chester Road. For many footballers who motor up the driveway, it is not only their first sight of privilege and wealth, but also an otherworldly mixture of nature and beauty; the antithesis of their own upbringing and neighbourhood. 'When I first saw the mile long driveway, I knew I'd arrived at a proper place,' Sol says.

The coach picked Sol and his parents up at the station. The train journey had been quiet. Sewell read his *Daily Mirror* and smoked his usual Old Holborn cigarettes, gently nodding off to sleep before suddenly waking again. Sol looked out of the window, silently in communion with how he got to this moment and what was about to happen, with Wilhelmina making the occasional comments with little if any reaction from her husband or son. She wanted this for Sol. She wanted anything that would make his life better. She wasn't convinced that football was his future but it was giving him the chance to move away from his neighbourhood, and perhaps where he was going would help to define him. Football hadn't happened for her older son John and people thought he had a real talent. But she knew Sol was fundamentally different, that he had inside him a seriousness and dedication John did not possess.

The coach edges a few metres forward and Sol sees the house. He has arrived. He knows this will now be his home for two years and thinks deeply that even if it proves difficult, he believes what he was once told, that only through agonies do we grow and experience a full life. That realisation changes something inside him. He feels, without the slightest warning, a sudden peace flow through his body. He's relaxed. He looks at the others sitting near him in the coach: the parents, wide-eyed and optimistic, the majority of boys sharing the same expression. 'There were a few who didn't get it; the whole place was too much for them,' Sol says.

The headmaster Tony Pickering and his wife are waiting on the driveway to greet the new arrivals. There were sixteen new boys. It was a warm welcome, unlike the weather, which was grey; a half drizzle clouding the beauty of the grounds. Sol remained silent. His father wanted to go off immediately to explore but held himself back. Why run? We have the whole afternoon.

It was Pickering's first year on the job. 'He was kind and keen to make everyone comfortable,' says Sol. For the first week, it would be just the sixteen boys. The year above would not be returning for another week; a chance to let the new arrivals settle. So it would be just the new boys, in a large house with furniture creaking like a ship's rigging and voices echoing in empty corridors.

After the welcome, Pickering led everyone upstairs to see the sleeping quarters. Sol was shown to his first. He would be sharing one room with five others. It was a large dormitory with beds made in pristine glory, with the whitest and freshest sheets anyone was ever likely to see tucked in. You could smell the cleanliness. Sol stopped. It was the first time in his life he felt his eyes nearly pop out. He looked at the single bed. It was his bed; no-one else's. His very own bed. This would be the first time he'd sleep on his own since he was in a cot as a baby. He looked at the wardrobe. His very own wardrobe. *Can you believe it? he thought. Look how big it is. And look at those chests of drawers.* Again, his very own. No need to share. One, two, three large drawers. The miracle of it! What space! He wanted to call out, tell someone what this meant to him, but as always there was nobody to tell about what he saw as his good fortune. He couldn't express it to his parents. They wouldn't understand, or maybe they would be hurt by his overwhelming excitement. He'd only ever had one drawer to put all his clothes in. He hid his elation, hiding it again when he went to the toilet and saw the lock on the door. There was no lock to the bathroom at home. All you could do was wedge the warped door into its frame. He could be in the bath or sitting on the toilet and none of his brothers had the courtesy of even bothering to knock. They wouldn't have even thought of it. Time and space was not conducive to common courtesy. They walked in, did what they had to do and strolled out. The only ones with privacy were his mother and any females in the house. Sol vowed that when he bought himself a house, he would take as long as he liked in the shower. Fifteen minutes, half an hour, it did not matter. No-one would take away that simple privilege.

The boys were shown the pitches and given a guided tour of the grounds. The boys and parents then headed back to the house. Wilhelmina trailed behind the group and found herself next to Bobby Robson. She was not good at recognising people but she knew who Bobby Robson was. He had been the England manager.

'Are you Sulzeer's mum? he asks.

'Yes.'

'He's going to be a very good footballer.'

That must mean something if an England manager says that, she thought. It didn't labour in her mind but she took it in and wanted to tell her husband, but he had disappeared. 'He was probably giving himself his own guided tour. Looking around the house,' she says.

Soon it was time to go. The parents made their way to the coach to take them back to the station. 'I was heavy hearted when I went up to him to say my goodbye. He was my youngest...'

She hugged the young Sulzeer. His face tightened and he had a look that suggested he was about to cry. But he had the sort of face that not only demanded to be looked at, but which was constantly changing, especially when seen from different angles and in different lights.

His father dithered, probably wanted to say something but didn't, and instead gave his son a firm handshake. This was a theme of his life and had already become the same for his son.

So many words left unsaid.

The coach drove away from the house and Wilhelmina looked round one more time. Sol had turned and was walking back inside. She said nothing to Sewell. She wanted to but they didn't talk much anymore. They didn't share a word about the day; not on the train back to London, not to the family when they got back home. Nothing.

They would visit him just once more and that would be for his passing out ceremony on his last day. 'They couldn't afford it,'

Sol says in a matter-of-fact tone, and with seemingly no regret. 'Some of the other boys had money in their family; we did not.'

He returned home every three to four weeks, just like in a proper boarding school. 'I used to see him grow every time he returned home,' Wilhelmina says. 'When he had to go back on the Sunday, I used to take him to Euston to catch the train. There he was, in his Lilleshall suit looking very smart, and I noticed people staring. It made me happy that he was improving his life. I thought he was God blessed. I always did from the very beginning. Even before he was born, when I met that woman in the launderette. I knew he was a gift. He was meant to be here to share his talent.'

Sewell would hardly say goodbye to his son as he headed back to Shropshire. If he was watching the television, he wouldn't turn away from the screen. He behaved like he was busy and had too many things on his mind. He wouldn't get up. Why should he? The king doesn't have to rise. He might occasionally shake the boy's hand, but mostly it was the dismissive gesticulation of one his hands in muted resignation.

Sol was used to it. It was part of life. Whether it hurt, he maintains at the time it didn't. They wouldn't talk about how Lilleshall was going. As long as he looked okay and seemed well, there was little more to discuss. 'If someone hadn't mentioned to him in the local pub that I was captain of Spurs, he wouldn't have known. He never discussed it with me. I never told him because I wasn't asked.'

Wilhelmina would hug her son goodbye at the station and give him £50. She would always say to him, 'Don't look into other children's pockets; here's your own money.' He would then get on the train still flushed with the freshness and sense of anticipation about his new start in life. He was, and always has been, careful with money. By the end of his stay at Lilleshall, he'd saved enough to spend on his return to London.

•　　•　　•

That night, Sol would experience his first sky without light pollution, and his first smells of nature. There were no longer any streetlights giving a sense of protection, just a darkness hanging uneasily above. He would stare up at the night sky. He would notice things he had not noticed before. The sound of his name being called out when he was alone in the grounds but no-one was there. The time when he saw a half moon and noticed the other half being just visible. Is there a hazy moral to that? Are you likely to see things more clearly if you don't look too closely? Are things more likely to happen if you don't try too hard?

No, he concluded. To succeed 'you had to work hard, you *needed* to work hard'.

Having been recognised as different, a natural talent, it becomes a part of you that you sense creates a chasm. Your friends at school are happy for you because they know you have a gift they will never possess.

'We were proud of him. All of us. And wished him luck,' says his friend Edwin. And after a few months, things get better. Your new surroundings become more comfortable. You have the space you have always dreamt of; the manicured fields just outside your front door to play the game you love. Things most of us take for granted and, because of that, don't notice. You surrender to the cards that have been dealt.

•   •   •

For years Sol had waited for his own space and privacy. Here it was on offer in a large house in the middle of Staffordshire. He had spent the first fourteen years of his life sharing a bed with his mother in her room. Three brothers shared another bedroom, two more shared one downstairs. His father, acting as the misguided patriarch, was the only one to have his own room. It would never be questioned.

During his first night at Lilleshall, he wasn't sure whether it was within the context of a dream, but he had a sense of bliss;

just for an instant but he certainly felt it. It was a feeling that would drift into his consciousness at different times during his two years there.

The very next day, he walked out on his own into the deserted grounds. There was an eerie sense of solitude; the breeze seemed to sigh. The nets on the goalposts bellowed. And then quite suddenly his mood changed. He began to feel the beginning of a delicious tingling sensation that usually comes from a perfect blend of peace of mind, a slight cooling current of air and an unexpected small act of kindness on the part of someone else. It was beautiful. 'I loved the open countryside. I loved the simple things. I didn't really realise how much until I got there. I didn't really know how much I needed nor what I was looking for. And when I found it, for the first time I experienced a peace I could only imagine a few months earlier.'

He didn't suffer from homesickness. 'Not for a moment.' Some of the other boys were keen to forge their future, as were their parents, calling from the touchline at their prodigy, a true genius. 'Tackle him son!' a father would yell and the boy, instead of keeping his position, would chase frantically to do so. That chase for success, it was not part of Sol's make-up, at least not in that way. He'd work hard, listen to the coach but never panicked. In life, people have been known to swim hither and thither, to go to drastic mental lengths to extricate themselves from a situation; yet, the more they try, the further they end up from the goal intended. No, Sol decided if he worked hard enough, success would come in its own time.

•　　•　　•

Imagination and desires were growing. His ambition to buy a house had already been set for as long as he could remember. But now his vision was changing. He would delve into his local paper, the *Stratford & Newham Express*, for property prices. Seeing how low he could go pricewise to buy a house; dreaming of what lay ahead. Lilleshall was teaching him there was another world out there. Even though his first property might well be in a neighbourhood he knew, there was no harm in checking out other areas. He chose Richmond to explore.

Why Richmond? No reason, other than it was the furthest station on the underground from the family home. He asked a couple of his mates if they wanted to join him. 'They thought I was mad,' Sol says. They cackled with laughter, 'What do you want to do that for?' He wanted to explain why. That he was exploring. But they wouldn't have listened and probably wouldn't have wanted to. For them, it would've been a waste of a day.

When he reaches Richmond, he looks into the windows of each of the shops, enjoying the affluence of the area, jotting everything down in his mind to remember how comfortable he feels. It is still more like a village than the bustling high street of global brands it became later. He turns away from the main thoroughfare and walks down to the River Thames. There, he passes some of London's most beautiful houses. He stops at one, stands back and looks up at it. He takes a black and white photograph in his mind. Of its front, the living room, the hall, the stairs, the bedroom. The black and white photo changes slowly into colour, greens, reds, yellows, and the image becomes more defined, as if this house is already his.

•   •   •

The Lilleshall boys combined their football with tuition at Idsall Comprehensive in the village of Shifnal. Says Sol, 'I didn't make many friends there but felt I was being properly educated for the first time.' The boys would be woken at 7am with a knock at the door from Mr or Mrs Pickering. Some would get up immediately while others would wait until the last minute before coming down for breakfast. There was always one who had the dishevelled appearance of someone who had dressed rather more quickly than he might have wished. Sol was never like that. Even in uniform, he looked coolly dressed without effort. He would always possess that innate talent of looking good without taking the time to do it.

Breakfast was generally eaten in silence; an early morning appetite born out of youth, fresh air, a good sleep and, for that matter, good food. There followed a twenty-five minute minibus journey to Idsall, with yawns so wide you could toss a peanut into the mouth without touching the lips. Sol felt some of the students possessed a feeling of envy. This led to compromises in conversation, backing away from confrontation and debate. A retreat into a new world of insecurity, even though security for life was within touching distance.

The classes were smaller than the schools in Stratford and Sol had time to grasp what was being taught. Everything seemed less rushed; life moved at a gentler pace. As he attended his lessons he subconsciously thought: *I want this. I want to learn.* There was a breadth to his learning as well. 'I studied Science, Design and Realisation, Geography, French and English.' For a Design and Realisation project he designed and built an architect's table that tilted and swivelled. 'I remember being very proud of it.'

They would leave Idsall by three o'clock, and as soon as they arrived back at Lilleshall, they would have a cup of tea, biscuits, change and head out for training by 4.15. In winter the floodlight would be on. There would be no excuses to miss out on a full day's work. His coach was John Cartwright, the former footballer turned professional youth mentor who developed many of England's best footballers including Bobby Moore. Headlined in the *Daily Telegraph* as The Guru, he was not afraid to upset the apple cart. 'I liked him. He was an ex-pro who understood the game. He was always forward thinking with his football. He understood what we were going through.' Cartwright was especially keen on encouraging the boys to play with both feet. Sol spent hours practising on his weaker foot, his left, and was taught to concentrate on weaker skills, his shooting, his passing. It was drilled into them. 'It was a great education. I started to use my left just as much. I took more time on my left.

I was more controlled with my left. As the right was so natural, I didn't think about what I was doing, I just did it. By the time I got into the first team at Tottenham, I was very comfortable with my left. I could chip the ball, drive, cross. With the long ball (thirty to forty yards), it was more controlled. I would get my body into the correct position and the ball would generally fall at my team-mate's feet.'

But at the time it was Craig Simons, the physio, who had the biggest influence on Sol. It was Simons who was the first to say to him that he was going to make it. 'You have a long-term future in the game,' he'd say. There he was at Lilleshall, chosen ahead of thousands, thought of as being one of the top sixteen in the country, chosen to play in his school team; he'd signed forms with Tottenham, played for his district – and it wasn't until Simons said those few words that the possibility football could be his life, his living, began to be real. Before then, he was simply enjoying it. Nothing more. 'Craig understood me. He saw where I was heading and recognised my mentality.'

Sol played right side of midfield for Lilleshall XI. They would play games at the weekend, sometimes midweek against other clubs' Under-15 and Under-16 sides. Tottenham came up to play. 'It was difficult, really. Here I was, playing against my own team. I played them twice. Once at Lilleshall and then once at Mill Hill.' Nick Rust, the former Brighton and Hove Albion goalkeeper and Arsenal schoolboy who was at Lilleshall at exactly the same time as Sol, says: 'Out of all the boys who were signed to Tottenham, Sol would have been my last pick to make it. I felt at that time he seemed less comfortable than the others to be connected to Tottenham. The club didn't seem to fit his character.' At the time, Tottenham had a reputation of attracting a more brash type of personality.

In contrast to Sol, Rust's father played a major role in his football career from a young age. 'I was always encouraged by my parents. My father was in some respects more dedicated to my career than me. He was a big influence.' He was impressed by Sol's maturity, even at that age. 'I found Sol had a sense of humour and a very positive attitude to life. Although he was solitary at times, I never saw him as an outsider. He applied himself not just to football but also his academic work. While others were having fun, he would be doing his homework – he was grounded and I could see he didn't rely just on football being his career. He was covering all bases.

'On one occasion Sol was confronted by a boy in the senior year. He was goading him, trying to pick a fight. But Sol kept his cool. He refused to react. I remember he left the room and when he returned, the atmosphere had calmed. It was as if he had gone out to measure the situation. He thought before reacting.'

Rust continues: 'You never heard him complain about his background. He was more interested in what was given to him rather than what he didn't have.'

•   •   •

Sol was certainly lapping up the rigorous training schedule at Lilleshall. There was a marked difference between the club sides and the boys at Lilleshall. Those at the clubs would report two or three times a week for training, while the boys at Lilleshall were being conditioned every day. 'It was like a lab, really,' Sol says. 'We were being intensely coached on how to improve our skill. The staff watched closely to see who would come through and take their education into the professional league and international football.'

When Lilleshall first played Manchester United away at their ground The Cliff, it was the first time Sol saw Ryan Giggs play. 'I remember him scoring two goals, one was a sidekick, the other an overhead, and I thought wow, what a player!' They also went to games during the week. 'We saw Manchester United, Everton. Mostly Aston Villa though, as it was local. We would go as a group. I enjoyed it. I'd hardly been to games like that before.'

Sol made his England Under-15 debut in a Scandinavian tournament in Finland alongside the other boys from his age group at Lilleshall. England played Iceland in their opening game. 'I was on the right side of midfield,' he says proudly, 'and I scored! A left foot shot into the bottom left corner.' It was also in Finland that he changed his name from Sulzeer to Sol. When he heard the announcer 'muck up' his name for the fourth time, he thought, enough of this, and so not only did he pull on the proper Three Lions England shirt for the first time, he changed his name too.

A new chapter had truly begun. In his heart, mind, and soul.

•   •   •

Sol's parents travelled up to see their son's graduation. Sewell and Wilhelmina again took the train, and before they had passed one word to each other, they had arrived.

Sol is waiting outside the hall when the minibus bringing the parents from the station arrives. Wilhelmina sees her son as the minibus draws up and thinks immediately how smart he looks, what a kind boy he is and what a fine man he is turning into. He welcomes her with a hug. 'You look well,' she says to her son, still of an age, and seemingly he always will be, to listen to what his mother has to say. Sewell, walking just behind his wife, gives his son a grasp like a vice then immediately looks round to see what is happening, who is greeting who.

It's a bright day. The air is warm. The atmosphere is good. The sense of formality is evident. Speeches are made. The boys are sitting together in the front row; the parents and officials behind applaud enthusiastically, never in the wrong place. The legendary Don Howe, coach of Arsenal's 1971 double-winning side, makes the keynote speech. He talks about the talent sitting in front of him and his hopes for English football. He then presents the caps to the boys and handshakes to all, like he is presenting the FA Cup. Sol, still only sixteen, towers over him. He is cool and unflustered. He says thank you and hurries away. When the ceremony ends, Sol poses for photos with Howe and then with Howe and his parents.

Sewell was proud of his son that day. You can see it in the photograph. But he didn't mention it.

'It was a good day,' says Sol. 'Nice words were said about me. Yes, it's a good memory.' He lets out a laugh and a smile that loiters long, or certainly for a while after the laugh itself lights up his face.

TOTTENHAM

It was Terry Venables who gave Sol his debut for Tottenham's first team against Chelsea on 5 December 1992. He would do the same for England. Yet Sol hardly knew the man who gave him his chance. 'After my debut with Tottenham, the following season, he had gone. The same thing happened after Euro '96. I think he liked my ability and attitude. I understood he picked me for Euro '96 because he saw me conduct myself beyond my age.' As he prepared to run onto the White Hart Lane turf in the 68th minute, for a moment it seemed all the sounds around him stopped dead. There was a pause. As if time had come to a halt. He clenched his fist and said to himself, 'I'm ready for this.' Twenty minutes later, he scored. He jumped up in celebration, arms in the air. *Goal!* People were open-mouthed, rolling their heads. The White Hart Lane faithful were shouting in delight; shouting their heads off. A new hero had just been born in N17.

He remembers the goal as special even though his shot bobbled over the line after poor Chelsea defending. 'It was well executed and it was a drilled shot. Although I do remember Justin Edinburgh, doing his best to follow it through and grab the goal for himself.' The dressing room was miserable after the game. Tottenham had lost 2-1. None of the players went up to congratulate Sol for his goal. He felt not for the last time completely alone in his celebration. The twenty or so minutes on the field had taken a lot out of him. 'My chest was burning. I was sitting on the floor. The pace of the game was very different to the youth games.'

As he drove home that night in his white Ford Orion 1.31 – 'I remember the number plate, A207CUY; it was, after all, my first car' – Sol felt a certain pride wash over him. He had scored on his debut. He knew his parents would not be waiting at the door anxious to hear the result or how their son had played; proud parents revelling in pride to be shared with friends and neighbours that their youngest son, just eighteen, had played for Tottenham and scored on his debut.

No. The game would never be mentioned. Never.

When he crept back into his family's house, it was, as he expected, quiet. It didn't matter, he had by now a numbness located somewhere in his chest. No emotion, no pain because of the lack of recognition. 'It was normal that no-one took any interest,' he says simply. He walked upstairs, straining his eyes until reaching his room. He undressed silently so as not to disturb his brother Murphy and crept into bed. He needn't have bothered to be so quiet; his brother was sleeping soundly, snoring like a drunk.

As he lies in bed, he looks up to the ceiling. *What a wonderful day.* He relives his goal again and again. His lone celebration – 'I don't remember anyone else joining in' – and the surge forward of the crowd. And then he pauses.

Here I am, without even the freedom to switch on the light, play my own music. Shit. He continues to gaze up at the white ceiling. *This isn't easy. This is not easy at all. Each day the past fades a little. Time heals, but does not cure. I've grown out of this. I have to get out of here as soon as possible.* (He won't for two more years.)

He interrupts his headache and thinks again about the afternoon. *Oh, it felt so good.* Something momentous happened earlier, from which he won't fully recover, and probably never will. Things are changing. He can try now to smile his way through his days. Things aren't that bad. Are they?

In the present, Sol thinks back to his frustration: 'I could have been playing before that game; I had the skill and the temperament. The only thing I didn't have was experience.' He wouldn't be picked for the first team again that season. The following week he went back to the youth and stayed there. He would play a reserve game against Arsenal at Highbury but in his own words, 'I didn't play well. The ball deflected off me for Arsenal to score and I had an off-night. It can happen.'

It wouldn't be until returning Spurs legend Ossie Ardiles took over as manager at the end of the season that Sol would get another chance. He was called up three days after helping England win the UEFA European Under-18 Championship. There would be no summer holiday for him that year. He was part of the Tottenham first-team squad and from that moment would never look back.

Terry Venables has no doubt he made the right decision to leave him in the youth. 'If he had played left wing, it might have been different.' Spurs had a shortage of naturally left-footed players at the time. That was why Andy Turner, another teen-age talent coming through the ranks, was picked from the youth ahead of him.

'I could have played anywhere,' Sol says without a hint of irony.

•   •   •

His days playing for Tottenham youth are good memories. They had a fine team and won the league and League Cup during his time. He was enjoying being part of a winning team. Football was again his escape. His sensibilities off the field had profoundly changed. His time at Lilleshall had been happy, a transformation, a rejuvenation. The delicious smell of green fields and the pastoral echoes of the country wind had now been replaced by the sound of an early morning breeze restless against the ranged brick of a terraced house with a hint of decay and the smell of Newham's dirt-strewn streets. He hadn't noticed it before. Why would he? Newham was all he knew. But now he did and the surge in his senses would never desert him. He had opened his eyes and he was wide awake. He would always be in search of beauty, maybe not always finding it but noticing it when encountered.

His return to Newham coincided with a newfound potency in his game. It was at Lilleshall that he started to believe in his talent; the opportunity to make football his career. Now Tottenham was waiting and he was ready to work harder than anyone to reach the top. Even when he was a regular playing for England, his intensity would rarely flounder. David Dein tells a story of when he travelled with the England squad to Hong Kong. After the England team and officials had checked in, Dein decided to go for a stroll to investigate the hotel. He went from lobby to lounge to restaurant until he reached the gym. There, working on the Stairmaster, was Sol. After a twelve-hour flight, he went straight to the gym to work on his fitness. 'He was the only England player there. I wasn't surprised. It is a part of him. A part of his dedication to his work.' Tottenham paid him £29.50 per week in his first year and the following year £37.50. The money was sent straight into his bank account. He saved every penny, looking weekly in the local paper at house prices, scanning the best price to buy his first property.

To reach White Hart Lane on time, he'd leave home at Stratford at 7.15am. For breakfast, he would drink a cup of instant coffee and eat cereal, usually Special K, never leaving a single flake. He would always wash up afterwards and put his clean bowl and mug on the sideboard. He'd then increase his pace. It wasn't worth being late, otherwise he'd miss the bus that took the trainees to Mill Hill; then he would have to get a taxi, which was expensive and a waste of money.

He'd make his way to Plaistow station, a ten-minute walk, and catch the train to Mile End, then on to Liverpool Street; the carriage was always crowded with commuters reading their morning papers from back to front. Sol would stand, telling himself he shouldn't grumble. He had a job everyone dreamed of.

At Liverpool Street, he changed to the overground train to White Hart Lane. 'I caught the train just past eight at Liverpool Street or sometimes eight-fifteen. It took about thirty minutes to get to White Hart Lane and from there it was a short walk to the ground,' Sol recalls.

The minibus would be waiting for the trainees inside White Hart Lane to take them to Mill Hill. It would leave at 9am on the dot. There would be no argument. Whoever said punctuality was the thief of time probably had been a football trainee once. If you were a minute late, you would be just in time to see the minibus disappearing from view. The long-serving kit man, Johnny Wallis, a bald cantankerous figure behind the wheel, would ring a bell above his head, slam the doors shut, clench his fist and bang on the steering wheel. 'It's fucking nine o'clock and WE ARE OFF!', followed by something indistinguishable uttered with a howl of laughter lost in the growl of the engine. He would nod his head in the mirror as confirmation of what he had just said and off they went, hooting at every junction, the banging of windows in irritation a cacophonous noise both in and out of the minibus. 'He was a fantastic character,' Sol remembers, 'and despite his pissed off attitude, we all liked him.'

• • •

The coaching staff at Tottenham saw a marked change in him. Sol, as he was now known, was poised, more self-aware, and more confident. 'The experience at Lilleshall gave him that extra self-assurance,' Keith Waldon remembers. He was naturally taller and even more of a physical presence than before. 'When I played football, I was physically a very hard player. No-one liked playing against me and I was never frightened by anybody,' Keith says, 'but once I saw Sol charging at me at a hundred miles an hour – and I've never seen someone so daunting, so huge – I literally jumped out of the way. That had *never* happened to me before. Never!'

His physicality wasn't always a help to him. Mondays, for example, were never Sol's favourite day. It meant a run, a long run, twice round the Mill Hill fields and twice through the woods at the top. The youth would join in with the reserves and first team. He found those runs testing, especially at the start of pre-season. It always took time for him to build up his stamina. Some players could run for hours and not be bothered while others would do anything to avoid it. 'It was not the best ground for training; when it rained, it became a bog,' Sol says.

This particular Monday for Sol hasn't started well. He nearly misses the bus. Wallis is about to close the doors before Sol literally slides in before he can get to the handle. 'You're lucky,' Wallis sneers. At the training ground it is pouring down. The group of players trudge across the field to the start. No-one is particularly looking forward to the run, and the rain doesn't make it much better. The teams are staggered by seniority. They wait patiently before being given the off, squad by squad, the first team followed by reserves and then the youth. Sol ignores the whisperings of the other players' chat about Saturday's game. Instead, he focuses on what is about to happen. 'On your marks, get set, go!' The space between the players begins to widen as soon as they set off. The keenest, or probably the naturally fittest, burst out in front; Sol is somewhere in the middle. As he runs, questions may have entwined him but by the time the training has finished they will have been discarded. Instead he concentrates on his breathing and keeping up with the pack.

Sol is running next to Doug Livermore, one of the first-team coaches, when he sees a player in front of him duck into the bushes. 'Keep running, Sol!' Livermore orders, looking the other way and acting as if he has seen nothing. Who was that? Look, quick. He's gone. It was Gary Lineker, England international and most famous man at the club. Lineker's plan was to see out the first circuit and join the group when they ran by the next time. Sol chuckles to himself. *I don't think I'd do that even if I could.* If, with one insolent sweep of the hand he could finish without the work, he wouldn't take the option. He knows that hard work is the one and only means by which he'll get anywhere in life. That lesson is hard-wired in him.

• • •

'What's happening?' asks Sol.

'Terry wants us to play against the first team.'

The first team are making their way over. It's going to be a twenty-minute game. First team versus youth. Not a long game but long enough. It hasn't happened before. This will be a test, Sol thinks. His eyes set firmly on the pitch, he checks his boots and straightens out the tongues. He undoes a lace, only to do it up again. He is determined to give the management a show. The youth are a very good team. He knows it and is now going to show the first team, with all their swagger, exactly how good they are. He has watched the first-team players closely: how professional they are, how they conduct themselves. He didn't like what he saw. Not all but most. Some of them are more interested in how much they will get for their tickets on the side than improving and working on their skill. It jars with Sol. The lads mentality, with its cheap jokes and caustic banter, the smirks like overpaid traffic wardens. All right for some, but Sol doesn't like it, never did. Some he has respect for, such as Gary Mabbutt – 'one of the finest professionals I played with' – Erik 'the Viking' Thorstvedt and Gordon Durie, but others give the impression of having those half-smiling, self-satisfied faces. He keeps his antipathy to himself. He knows it is wiser to keep his sentiments close. No-one will ever know; better to pass by on the other side of the street. It doesn't really matter, as he doesn't have too much direct contact with them. It just seems like he takes his job more seriously, that his journey to improve will continue with ruthless efficiency and will not stop even if he becomes highly paid and heralded as a football star. In fact, he didn't feel a brotherhood, a common bond on how to conduct oneself as a professional footballer, until years later when he joined Arsenal.

The game ends in victory for the youth. 'We didn't just beat them one-nil. It was the *way* we did it. We totally outplayed them, ran them off the field and played with intelligence. It could have been luck, it could have been that the first team was having an off day, but I saw and felt I was not that far away from them. I was catching up fast.'

•   •   •

Sol remembers one of the Spurs senior players with deep affection: Paul Gascoigne. After his serious cruciate ligament injury in the 1991 FA Cup final against Nottingham Forest, his multi-million pound transfer to the Rome club Lazio was put on hold. It looked as if the door had been firmly slammed. Lazio, though, gave Gazza time, to see if he could regain his fitness before completely pulling out of the deal. His struggle for fitness became the daily diet of the sports pages; watching him go from despair to optimism, from walking with crutches to sprinting round an empty running track. Football supporters cheered him on; we always loved and had empathy for Gazza. We still do.

Spurs had arranged their youth team to play with Gazza in two matches for the Lazio officials who were visiting London to check on his fitness and make a final decision on whether to go ahead with the transfer; the first game on Friday, the next on the Saturday. It was a success. Gazza played exquisitely, dribbling past defenders and leaving them with the feeling that something had suddenly brushed against them in a ghost train at a funfair. He came through both games without a problem. The transfer was back on. After the Saturday game, Sol and the other youth players were changing when Gazza walked in. He went round and handed each youth player £50 (more than their weekly wage) as a thank you for helping him out. After the game, before doing anything else, he'd got straight into his car and gone to his local bank. It was big-hearted and thoughtful and has never been forgotten by Sol. His life may now be gloomy but in the glorious days of the past, Gazza had the innate ability to connect with others, not just through his generosity but also through his humour and sublime skill on the football pitch.

•   •   •

Keith Waldon asked Sol at seventeen to be captain of the youth team. At first he avoided giving him a straight answer, instead asking: 'Can I think about it?' He would give the same reaction to Gerry Francis when he was asked to be captain of the first team a few years later.

Sol was mature beyond his years and a natural leader; the staff could see how other players responded to him. He was not too vocal on the field but his presence and growing influence affected his team-mates. His type of authority was something coaches looked for in a potential captain. But in the end, Sol turned the offer down because he felt more comfortable under the radar.

'I never understood why. He never explained. That wasn't something he did,' Waldon says. Looking back now, Sol says, 'I just wanted to play football. Also, I was still quite shy and didn't want to show too much too early. I needed to build up slow, step by step.' Waldon was still working on his best position. 'Sol was quite clearly going to be a very physical presence wherever he played. He was only sixteen or seventeen, but still unsure on how the game should be played at any particular time.' Waldon thought he was probably going to play at full-back or at centre-half but he had worked out a plan to train Sol to become one of the best in one of those positions in the country. He knew if you played in defence, it was much easier as everything was going on ahead of you. So he devised for Sol to play up front or in midfield, so that he could appreciate the field all around him rather than have the tunnel vision he had for the ball as a defender; basically, to train him to understand how the whole pitch worked rather than just one-third.

When Sol played up front, he got better in controlling the ball with a finer instinct and also to head the ball with better timing and accuracy. 'For a future England centre-half his heading was woeful,' remembers Waldon. 'We call it in football: "having the accuracy of a fifty-pence piece." The ball can end up anywhere! His timing of the jump was not very good, so he had some technical deficiencies that still needed some work.'

As his second year in the youth was closing, Sol was growing more and more frustrated. He was going through that phase of a young man's life where he didn't think he was being properly recognised. Waldon, though, was still unsure about how far Sol was going to reach, still uncertain about his technical ability. But Sol was unaware of what others thought; in his mind, players who weren't as talented were getting their chance in the first team and he wasn't. 'I may have had doubts about how far he was going to get, but I had no doubt he was a special talent that still needed to be nurtured. My job with Sol was not finished,' says Waldon. And yet Sol felt forgotten. He had scored on his Spurs first-team debut in December 1992 but hadn't played again that season. After only three years at the club, he was already thinking about leaving Tottenham and dreamed about joining Brian Clough's Nottingham Forest. *Now they're the type of team I'd like to play for.* It may have been a fleeting thought but he remembers it still, and when he returned after playing for England Under-18s against Spain, to make matters worse he found that a couple of his youth team-mates had been picked for the first team ahead of him. His insecurity over his worth in the eyes of his coaches was escalating. *What more do I have to do? I'm the only Spurs player in the England Under-18s. I scored on my Spurs debut and now what? Where am I? What's going on?* He felt a millstone around his neck and thought he was being dragged down.

He moaned to fellow trainee Jeff Minton. It was the first time he'd opened up about how unhappy he was becoming. It was unlike Sol to confide in anyone. Jeff listened to Sol and reassured him that everything would be all right. Perhaps we all feel this way, Jeff suggested.

'I was livid,' he says. 'I had just played for England in Spain and no-one had come out to see me. Whenever I went off to play for England, I felt alone, not supported by the club. It was a shame because I'd enjoyed my time with the youth. We had a great side and I had the upmost respect for Keith Waldon and Pat Holland, the youth team managers.'

Holland says, 'Very rarely do I speak to a manager telling him this or that boy will one day make the first team but I told Terry Venables that about Sol. I saw it with two boys, him and Ledley King.' With nearly fifteen years in top flight football as a player and coach, Holland was well aware of the pitfalls facing youth players trying to break into the first team. 'It's a big bridge to cross, to be calm and face the challenge. Sol had that ability. You never knew what he was thinking but you knew he would never let you down...Whenever we travelled away and there was a spare single room on offer, Sol was the first to put up his hand. He always wanted it when most boys liked to share, wanted the company.'

'I was lucky to have Pat Holland at that stage in my career,' says Sol. 'I respected him. As an ex-player, he was understanding of what we were going through.'

•　　•　　•

'Every young player thinks he should be playing in the first team. He was no different to how I felt at his age.' Manager Terry Venables had been a Tottenham player in the late Sixties, making 115 league appearances and scoring 19 goals. He returned to White Hart Lane in November 1987 as manager, and led the club to FA Cup success in 1991, a year after finishing third in the league. In June of that year he was appointed chief executive by Alan Sugar. Over the following seasons, the Spurs team was managed by Peter Shreeves and then jointly by Ray Clemence and Doug Livermore. Venables would eventually fall foul of the club as his relationship deteriorated rapidly with Sugar, to the extent that he was dismissed in May 1993 in acrimonious circumstances. Sol confesses to knowing little about what was happening behind the scenes during this time, but his memory of Venables is of a good man-manager who retained a strong influence with the first team. 'He loved characters in his team and of course players with ability, but the type of players who combined both were his favourite,' says Sol. Players liked him. He was one of them. He understood them.

Sol is still aggrieved. He goes out for drinks with his friends but doesn't feel particularly sociable so leaves early, to get back to East London. He travels on the District line from Barking to Plaistow. As the tube train pulls out of the station, he shuffles with relief that he is back on his own turf. The carriage is empty. During the week, it would be so crowded that he wouldn't find a seat. He's tempted to stretch out his legs and take it easy when he feels something close, like the flap of a blind in a cool breeze. He looks round, a little startled, but there is nothing; only his imagination. He sits up straight as the train is coming to the next station, spluttering over the rails.

Nobody gets on or off the carriage, or so he thinks. As the train leaves the station and darts into the dark, he hears a sound. Like a moan, a grumble. The lights in the carriage suddenly flash on and off and back on again. Sitting opposite Sol is an old man with the greenest eyes and the greyest of beards, looking straight at him. Should he laugh, smile or pretend to ignore? He chooses to ignore him. But this doesn't help. The old man stands up, sways and then staggers over to where Sol is sitting.

Sol is not sure if he is drunk. He doesn't smell of drink but he looks as if he hasn't had a good night's rest for a long time. He leans over Sol. 'You should have faith. You are going to surprise everyone.' And then the old man looks at Sol once again and straightens up as the train reels into another station. He doesn't look back and, in what seems like one movement, walks out of the carriage. As the train moves away from the platform,

Sol gets up and cranes his neck to see if he can still see the old man. But there is nothing. The platform is empty. It is still. And he notices a large clock hanging over the exit, which has stopped, and he wonders if in fact the clock had ever worked at all.

•   •   •

The following week, the club offered Sol a two-year contract. The PFA negotiated the terms and he signed rather grudgingly. He still felt unwanted, as if there was an underlying lack of faith in his true talent, but those involved in the club have no memory of having any doubt that his future was full of promise.

That summer of 1993, England were hosting the UEFA European Under-18 Championship and Sol joined up with his international colleagues. In the squad with Sol were names such as Nicky Butt, Robbie Fowler, Gary Neville and Paul Scholes. The team went on to win the tournament with a 1-0 win over Turkey in the final at the City Ground. Sol would end the tournament with two man of the match awards. The *Guardian* described him as being 'as solid as an Ottoman'. It was in this tournament that the manager, the softly spoken Ted Powell, perceptively moved him from the midfield into the back four.

During the summer, Tottenham employed Ossie Ardiles as their new manager and Steve Perryman as his assistant. Employing two Spurs legends was not a bad idea. Alan Sugar and Terry Venables were fighting it out in court to get control of the club, and Spurs had leapt from back to front-page news. Ardiles and Perryman had both seen Sol in the Under-18 tournament and liked what they saw. Perryman had kept in contact with Spurs since first leaving, and had heard about Sol a number of times. John Moncur and Keith Waldon had not held back their praise, so it was no surprise to them that his performances were getting recognition. They had been advised Sol could play in a number of positions. He was six feet two inches tall and was incredibly nimble, with fast feet, which is rare to find in an athlete of his size. 'People forget how fast I was,' Sol says. The news from the coaches and what they had recently witnessed made the management excited by the prospect. They were short of players in a number of key positions, especially in central defence and up front. They thought Sol could be their answer for either position. It is a management's dream to have a true talent among its ranks. 'We saw him as a back at first, but when we saw him up close, we noticed what other coaches were saying: he had the ability to play up front. It's asking a lot of a young player to play in different positions but we didn't doubt that if we asked him, he would be able to do it,' says Perryman.

It was a couple of days after England had won the tournament that Sol got a call. He would have to go without this year's summer holiday and report back to Tottenham for the start of pre-season training. That was going to be just a week after the tournament. He didn't care; it was the call he'd been waiting for.

Ardiles and Perryman were impressed with Sol. Perryman remembers that time: 'Sol was like a shining light with regards to all those problems Ossie and I had to deal with at the club at that time. He was a young player, but he wasn't typical of any of the other young players we had come across. We were confident; we knew he was someone who was going to hold his own. He wasn't flash, he was modest and he didn't get above himself. He was also very considerate and respectful to both Ossie and me. From the very beginning he was a joy to work with.'

Sol was not chosen to play up front when he played the opening games of the 1993-94 season. He was first used at left-back in place of the injured Justin Edinburgh and then took over at right-back from Dean Austin. Spurs won three out of their first four league matches, and Sol played for twenty consecutive games for the first team from the start of the season. After that run, Perryman had no doubt that Sol was going to reach the top. 'It's a difficult science to determine how far you can go in your career. When you see a boy at eighteen as Sol was, it becomes a little easier. Sol's physical power and strength were overwhelming but the one thing that I saw more in Sol than virtually anyone I've ever worked with was his self-belief. Ossie and I used to study his hard work, and whatever he learned, and we trained him to do, he would act on it. He learned very quickly and was keen to be educated.'

There were times after training that Ardiles and Perryman would stop off at a local Italian and find Sol sitting alone, eating his lunch. They would go over to say hello and then leave him in peace. They would notice how he conducted himself. Relaxed in his own company, eating quickly but careful in what he ordered. Eyebrows raised, a weary smile. Always sipping water between bites and after the meal taking a bottle of water away with him. They thought he'd been educated on what to eat. Ardiles indicated with a slightly cupped right hand and fingers pinched together moving in a clockwise circle over his stomach: Sol knows how to eat. It was true, he certainly liked his food and ate a lot to fill his frame, but he had always eaten healthily. This was not a time in football when clubs advised on a player's diet. It was rare to see someone look after himself in the way Sol did. It was not something the young players in those days really knew about or understood how important diet was. 'They would usually restore their lost energy from a hard training session with something less healthy than pasta and vegetables,' says Perryman.

Eat carefully first, a wise man said, and then have fun. 'I was always careful what I ate. It was natural for me. I had a European sensibility when it came to food,' Sol says.

•　　•　　•

White Hart Lane, which had suddenly become the embodiment of everything good in Sol's life (how things will change), stood in silence for one of their fallen heroes, Danny Blanchflower, the former captain of the Spurs double-winning side who played for the club 337 times. It was 18 December 1993. Danny had died nine days before.

Sol stands appropriately to attention as if playing a game of statues. A minute's silence as a sign of respect, he thinks, is beautiful. He looks at the stands. Not a sound. No noise. The supporters pay homage to one of their former greats. How they loved him. How they respect their former captains, especially those who have captained a cup-winning side. They stay in supporters' hearts forever, unless of course... Sol looks down to the ground. He shows tremendous cool for someone so young. He will be a substitute today. His streak of twenty games in the first team since the beginning of the season has come to an end. He's been told they need more experience in defence. But it changes nothing. He is part of the team now. The dispute over the club's ownership does not bother him. He reads the papers but afterwards puts them down, not giving them another thought. Today's opponents are Liverpool. They will fight out a 3-3 draw.

The silence continues. Some grass cuttings from the pitch have flown into Ossie's eye in the middle of the minute's silence. It seems as if he is weeping for an instant. He discreetly rubs his eye with his index finger. The tears would not go amiss. One legend to another. Blanchflower was a great player, a supreme tactician, a fine gentleman. He was also very guarded about his private life. When Eamonn Andrews said the immortal words, 'This is your life,' he quickly replied, 'No, it's not' and walked out. He was the first person to turn it down.

Sol thinks of Blanchflower. They met on a number of occasions. He was still part of the club right up to his last year, before he became so sick that he had to go into a nursing home. How they had spoken. How he'd come to watch the youth. How he had encouraged. He had only become aware of his true greatness in recent months. Before, he knew he was the former captain of the finest Spurs team but now he had learned he was so much more. Sol would try to repeat his success. For Tottenham Hotspur. 'I will always give my best to this club,' he vows, 'in every game I play.'

When the minute's silence is over, there is a general outflowing of breath, immediately followed by cheers and applause.

•   •   •

At the end of the 1993-94 season, which ended with Spurs finishing a lowly fifteenth and unsuccessful in both domestic cup competitions, Sol received a phone call from manager Ossie Ardiles. In broken English and rather formally, like he was announcing the winners at a school prizewinning ceremony, Ardiles said: 'Sol, the club would like to offer you a new four-year contract.' It was what he was hoping for, maybe even expected, but more importantly he had a manager who believed in him. 'You are the future of this club,' he was told. This hackneyed phrase for young players seemed genuine coming from Ardiles. There was no doubting his words were sincere. He was sincere. He was a good man.

Sol asked Sky Andrew to negotiate on his behalf. He had first met Sky while at Lilleshall and the two had hit it off well. Even though they weren't officially working together yet as sports manager and client, Sol trusted Sky. That was already a positive. He didn't trust many. 'He was the most intense person I have ever met when it comes to trust,' says Sky. The deal went smoothly. Sol would receive nearly four times as much as the £200 a week he was currently earning.

Sky Andrew speaks of Ossie Ardiles with the upmost respect for how he conducted the business. 'It was straightforward. None of this backwards and forwards. He repeated to me what he had said to Sol, that he believed he was the club's future.'

'The reason the deal went so smoothly was that Ossie played a lot of table tennis and Sky was a professional player,' Sol jokes. Sky merely shrugs his shoulders at Sol's quip. 'In the end, I helped him out as a friend. I received no commission.'

Sol was now earning enough money to buy his first house in Dale Gardens, Woodford Green in Essex. Sky would also help negotiate the property deal. It was something Sol had dreamed of ever since he was a boy: having his very own space. He could now live with a degree of unregimented freedom. He was leaving behind the noise and claustrophobia of his family home. It was as if he could finally release the fingers out from his ears.

During the summer, Tottenham bought the ex-German captain Jurgen Klinsmann from Monaco for £2 million. How the fans love an exciting signing. Players are no different. They respected what Klinsmann had achieved in the game. He was a World Cup winner, after all. And, although he arrived in the country with a reputation for being a diver, he dispelled it in one of the great PR moves of modern time with a self-deprecating celebratory dive after his debut goal against Sheffield Wednesday on the opening day of the season.

Klinsmann's acknowledgement meant a lot to his teammates. When he said Sol was 'one of the best young backs in world football,' his words encouraged Sol's growing confidence. 'He was a great player and a huge presence around the club. He had a temper though, if we lost. He wouldn't sit down and listen to any prolonged post-mortem. Instead, he'd grab his towel and storm off to the shower muttering a mixture of English and German that we should have done better. He certainly wasn't a good loser.'

The 1994-95 season began at Spurs, as with every club around the globe, with high optimism. With the marquee signing of Klinsmann, alongside those of Romanians Ilie Dumitrescu and Gheorghe Popescu, there was an air of excitement at White Hart Lane; a belief that the team had those three essential ingredients – talent, self-belief and luck – nicely mixed. And even if the first couple of games were lost, as long as the play was exciting, the board and fans wouldn't totally give up on hope. They still had many games left to rescue their season. Didn't they?

At least Sol was now a regular in the first team and would remain so for the rest of his time at Tottenham. He wore the number 23 shirt. 'I like numbers. I feel connected to some. And twenty-three was given to me by chance when they handed out the squad numbers at the beginning of the season. We were still at the time when high numbers were not the norm for first-team regulars, so it felt different. It felt good every time I looked at it.' He would wear number 23 for the next five seasons until George Graham wanted his first team to wear the classic one to eleven. 'Yes, that really pissed me off,' remembers Sol.

Steve Perryman worked with the players in training and also individually. 'He took his time to stay behind when the squad had finished the training session to train with me one-to-one,' says Sol. 'We would go back to White Hart Lane and work on the astroturf above the car park. Ossie would watch from the sidelines.' They were still searching for Sol's best position but it didn't bother him, he just wanted to play, even though at the beginning of the season he would be cruelly exposed by the tactics.

Attacking football was in abundance, but defensively the team was exposed and terrible. The attitude of you score five and we score six seemed never to have been so true. 'The tactics were wrong because no-one was experienced enough to hold the back line and play that type of football. It just came too early for me. When I played for Arsenal, it was not far from what Tottenham were trying to achieve, but of course we had the players.'

Clubs don't like losing, however entertaining they are. After a dire run of results, Ardiles and Perryman were fired unceremoniously. The dismissal still rancors with Perryman: 'In my day, Bill Nicholson ran the club. Yes, there were directors but I never met them. In fact, I had to ask a team-mate who those old men in suits were.'

'Well, they direct the club.'

'What does that mean?' Perryman queried.

'Well, if Bill Nicholson wants something, he gives the green light.'

Perryman believes that interference from the boardroom restricted his and Ossie's ability to manage. 'Sol being a young player didn't have the attention he should have had,' says Perryman. 'I was deeply disappointed that my work with Sol

had been cut short. I do remember Sol looking on as a specta-
tor and wishing that we weren't going. He didn't say anything,
he was always quiet, but I could read his face. I wanted to tell
him more. I wanted to tell him what was going on behind the
scenes. But I know he must have seen how disrespectful the
club was. As a serious young man, I am sure he was affected by
the club's behaviour.'

The insinuation is clear: that watching the club treating
two of their most respected figures, legends to all the fans, so
dismissively may have affected the team. Sol was indeed disappointed in the way the club treated Ardiles and Perryman.
'Steve Perryman guided me through my first season and I will
be forever grateful. His experience and knowledge had an influence. It was important to have someone like him so close at the
beginning of my first-team career. So yes, I was sad to see them
go. And of course these are the men that brought me into the
first team. Did I judge the club? I used to think about things
but judge them at that time? No.'

Steve Perryman is asked one question more than any other
from Tottenham supporters: Were you disappointed that Sol
left Spurs for Arsenal? The question is asked probably because
Perryman is Tottenham's more loyal player, making 653 appearances. His answer is so: 'At first I didn't like that he went to
Arsenal. But having said that, everyone is told that when you
decide to leave your first club, it's the biggest wrench in your
career. Normally, when it takes such a long time to make the
first move, second and third moves are very quick. The fact that
he decided to leave Tottenham and stayed with Arsenal and
won all those trophies makes me think that maybe he did, after
all, make the right move.'

•　　•　　•

It's November 1994 and Gerry Francis has become the new
Spurs manager. His first game in charge is a 4-3 home defeat
against Aston Villa.

Training became more intense. Sol would never experience such intense routines again, in his entire career. Francis was popular with the players but he was an authoritarian; if there was one thing Gerry Francis believed in, it was hard work. Every Tuesday, he had this strict running session. He ordered his players to run from box to box; from one penalty box to the other. Back and forwards. To the halfway line and back. An assortment of short and longer sprints. The players were all noise, the air full of curses. Sol cursed a lot. Again and again, until it was over and the squad were all smiles, simply because they had nailed it and survived yet another Tuesday session.

By Christmas, the season had picked up and was full of promise. 'We had a good team. One of the best teams I played in for Spurs,' Sol says. 'Klinsmann, Sheringham, Barmby, Anderton, Popescu.'

The FA Cup run was a highlight, Spurs winning away against Liverpool (a Klinsmann winner) and reaching the semi-final. It was played at Elland Road against Everton. Tottenham were expected to reach the final but it turned out to be a big disappointment for the club. Everton dominated the game in the early minutes and never let go. Tottenham lost 4-1. Sol missed the game due to injury. He'd had a hamstring injury and was down to play but that morning failed a fitness test. 'I watched the game from the tunnel. When I was injured it was the place I liked watching from.' Gary Mabbutt thinks if Sol had played that day, Spurs would have gone through to the final. 'I was very disappointed to hear Sol would not be playing. I think if Sol had been fit, we would have won the game; that's how important he was to our team.'

Klinsmann took up his option to leave the club after just one season, much to the disappointment of fans and the anger of his chairman. He had scored twenty league goals and was voted the Football Writers' Association Footballer of the Year in 1995. Spurs finished a respectable seventh, two places off a UEFA Cup place. Like so many seasons for Tottenham, it was nearly there, that is, forever nearly ready to challenge for the top four...But the race for the top in the coming seasons would constantly change, moving further and further away from Spurs.

•   •   •

The following seasons, Tottenham struggled in mid-table mediocrity. They finished eighth in 1995-96 and tenth the following season. Sol was becoming frustrated. Just when there was a chance to move things forward, he felt there was a resistance to do so.

He was still enjoying his football. He had won his first senior England cap against Hungary in May 1996 and had been a member of Terry Venables' Euro '96 squad. He was thriving in his role as Tottenham captain and proud to be playing for them, but there was just something that stopped the club from making that leap to join the leading teams. It was beginning to nag. 'They see quality and they try to nick it, for less money, trying to get away with it, even though what is in front of you is a masterpiece,' says Sol.

Sol in the meantime had signed a new contact for three years. Gerry Francis met with Sky Andrew. It wasn't to be the calmest of meetings; the opposite to his first contract negotiation with Ossie Ardiles. Firstly, Gerry Francis did not like table tennis as Ossie had; and secondly, he did not seem to like Sky Andrew very much. When Sky made demands for his client, he faced a barrage of abuse. 'He [Francis] called me many names and threatened to run me out of the business. He wasn't the easiest man to deal with,' Sky says through gritted teeth, 'but we got there in the end.'

•   •   •

It was at White Hart Lane, after training, that manager Gerry Francis approached Sol.

'Sol, I want you to be our captain.'

He was playing more than the current captain David Howells, and Francis had decided to make a change. As when Keith Waldon put the question to him about captaining the youth team, Sol asked Francis whether he had time to think about it.

'Yes. You have the weekend, no longer,' Francis replied.

Sol didn't show his manager any emotion. It was as if he didn't care and walked away from the brief meeting with the nonchalance of a man who knew he was wanted. He went out at the weekend with friends. The team had won and he was in a good mood. Ah, victory can so help the mood. He relaxed. He didn't tell any of his friends what he was considering, what had been offered. He would, like with most things, make the decision alone. He felt a sense of relief that his manager had recognised him. It is the best feeling when the manager believes in you. He hadn't even thought about becoming captain until the morning he was approached, but now the question had been asked, he knew it would be difficult to turn down. 'I thought about saying, "Look, when David Howells is unfit I'll stand in." I know sometimes choosing a new captain can cause trouble. I was sensitive to that. But, by the end of the weekend, I decided to go for it, and do the best job I possibly could.'

On the Monday he spoke to Francis and accepted the captaincy. He was proud to do so, even though no-one would be able to tell from the outside. His name would join other legends from the club. He thought of Danny Blanchflower, Dave Mackay, Steve Perryman and 'Mabbsy' (Gary Mabbutt). *These are good people. Wonderful players who lead by example. I plan to be like that.* There weren't any big perks that came with the job. No big fanfare, no special car parking space, maybe some free tickets, but that didn't bother him either way. The news leaked out and it was accepted without complaint from anyone.

Sol never told his father about the honour. 'It wasn't discussed,' he says. 'There was no point.' His father only heard of it in the pub when one of Sewell's friends mentioned it.

'I didn't know your son was captain of Tottenham.'

'Nor did I,' Sewell replied and went up and ordered another drink.

•　　•　　•

In July 1997, Tottenham bought David Ginola from Newcastle, with Les Ferdinand following soon afterwards, for a combined transfer fee of £8.5 million. 'David was so strong and very skilful,' says Sol. 'Yes, there's a feeling he could have done more with his talent but I had little to complain about. The team used to moan that he didn't run back to defend, but as his captain I used to encourage him to get back. It was no point just shouting the words. You had to coerce him. He had to be man-managed. He certainly had the stamina to get back. He used to run forward the whole length of the pitch at least three times in a game, and sometimes even more.'

Sol recalls a match in Ginola's early days at White Hart Lane. It's half-time and Sol is dying for a leak. There is no 'Excuse me sir, I have to go.' He just shuffles away uneasily as manager Gerry Francis is turning up for his team talk. As he enters the lavatory, Sol thinks it's deserted, until he hears movement coming from inside one of the cubicles. He then notices a plume of smoke rising to the ceiling. Is someone smoking in there? At half-time? Surely not. He looks down and sees a recently stubbed out cigarette on the floor. Whoever's in there is already onto his second. He sees the football boots. He recognises them. He smiles. Who else could it be?

The lavatory bursts into a flush and then abruptly stops. The door opens smartly and out steps the culprit... None other than David Ginola. They don't exchange a word; instead, Ginola strides back and joins the rest of the players as the team talk continues. By the time Sol returns, Ginola is sipping a shot of espresso. He drinks it down in one. 'Aaaahh,' he sighs. The half-time break comes to a close and Ginola stands up ready to play the second half. Sol chuckles to himself. A shot of espresso and a cigarette for half-time: the new diet for the professional footballer. As Sol walks back onto the pitch, Ginola take a deep breath and sprints past his captain with renewed energy. Sol shakes his head. *Whatever it takes...If he keeps playing like he has this season, who cares how he spends his half-time?*

Les Ferdinand had mentioned to Sol the season before that he was thinking about joining Tottenham. They were in a nightclub when he asked Sol about it. What Sol actually said surprised him. 'You're doing so well here, Les. Why would you want to move?' It was true; Ferdinand had gained the respect of the Geordies by scoring fifty goals in eighty-four games and helping them challenge for the Premier League title. *Why can't Spurs be challenging?* Sol questioned himself for the thousandth time. *I need to be in a team that has the chance to win the league.* Frustration had resurfaced. 'I would never try to persuade him not to join. Never! I was a Tottenham player and had been since I was fourteen, but I honestly couldn't understand why Les was considering leaving a team that was challenging for the league title.'

Ferdinand had already made up his mind. He had supported Tottenham since he was a kid, and always dreamed of wearing the white shirt, playing his football at White Hart Lane. When he joined, injuries stalled his first months but, by the end of the season, his goals helped save Spurs from relegation. Ferdinand eventually played in two League Cup finals for the club (winning the first and losing the second) and scored the 10,000th goal in Premier League history for Spurs in December 2001.

After a very poor start to the season, Gerry Francis's reign had come to an end in November. He resigned with Spurs struggling. 'When the papers start saying the manager has three games to save his job, you know it is only matter of time,' says Sol. And indeed it was. Chris Hughton took over as caretaker boss for one week, which included one game, a 1-0 home defeat to Crystal Palace on 24 November. 'I would have liked Chris to take over. I've always had great belief in him.' But the idea was never discussed. 'I always knew it was a temporary role,' says Hughton.

The job was given instead to Christian Gross, a Swiss who had success in his native country with Grasshoppers Zurich, winning two league championships and the domestic Swiss Cup. Perhaps he was Spurs' answer to Arsene Wenger. Gross needed little persuading. Looking like he could be cast as a sergeant major in *Dad's Army*, he was known to be good at organising people. He arrived believing he could save a once-great club and get them back to those halcyon days, but feared he might have a shortage of good players to make the dream possible.

Gross was unknown when he first arrived in the UK, but not for long. When he was late from Heathrow for his first press conference and brandished his underground ticket with the words, 'I want this to become my ticket to the dreams,' it was going to be a long road. The press had found their joke and weren't about to let it go.

The team didn't get the bounce everyone hoped for with the new manager. He experienced a 6-1 home defeat against Chelsea and a 4-0 away loss to Coventry, and other than wins against Fulham and West Ham and a draw with Arsenal, the club's Premier League status was slowly disappearing.

Gross met Sol early on to discuss his style of captaincy. It was in the lobby of the team hotel. He sat down as sedately as possible, took a deep breath, and leant forward as if he was about to tell Sol the facts of life. The manager and captain were meeting together alone for the first time. Sol's immediate thought was: *Let's hope this speech isn't too long.* It wasn't normal for Sol to feel irritated but Gross seemed to bring it out in him. Gross moulded each syllable with care, waiting for it to connect with Sol before continuing. He needed Sol's help to achieve the dream. He wanted him to be more connected with his team-mates; be the first at the training ground and greet everyone with a firm handshake, encourage him or her for the day ahead. Sol thought he was having a laugh. 'Surely it's how I am on the pitch that's important. What I might say at half-time. But this meet and greet style is not for me.' It was not like Sol to be so sharp in his opinion of others. But the team was flatlining and there was no room for concession in any of his relationships. He hated losing and it was becoming more prevalent.

'Christian Gross was robotic, stressed and seemed to have no life in him. I knew as soon as he joined that he wouldn't last long in the job,' Sol says. Ramon Vega, Sol's Swiss team-mate, said he didn't recognise the man he knew from back home. He was not wrong. When Sol was on England duty and the team played away against Switzerland, Gross was there. 'He was laughing, trying on a hat and making a fool of himself. And I thought if he'd been able to be more self-deprecating and a little less earnest, he would have been okay at Tottenham. The players would have taken to him,' says Sol.

With the team sliding towards relegation, chairman Alan Sugar re-signed Jurgen Klinsmann on loan for the second half of the season. It proved to be a masterstroke. 'He most definitely helped,' says Sol. 'He was a leader, inspired at times. He lifted the side.' It was a side that couldn't win. A side that had become stale, even bored, not only with the actual situation but also with the lack of further promise and potential to win trophies. 'It was a difficult time. When you keep losing, you tend to go through the motions. That doesn't mean you don't give a hundred per cent but you say to yourself, I thought I was here to win?'

Alan Sugar got involved after the team's poor form. He gathered the first-team squad at White Hart Lane and handed each one a black baseball bat. He clenched the handle of his bat and swung it in the air. 'I want you to bat all your problems away and get us out of this crap,' he snarled. 'I still have the bat!' says Sol.

Tottenham survived relegation by drawing and winning two of their last five games. They eventually finished fourteenth. Christian Gross survived getting the sack and lived for another day, or rather the start of a new season. Sol's memory of Gross fades in importance like the sun behind the clouds. 'It's neither good nor bad. He never did something that surprised me and his dour management style probably reflected on the team.'

•   •   •

Christian Gross didn't last long at Spurs the following season, 1998-99. He was sacked after ten months and only three games into the new campaign. His face, even after winning his last game away to Everton 1-0, was of a man due to be hanged later that day.

Chairman Alan Sugar didn't waste time; he signed George Graham as his new manager. He asked David Pleat, Spurs' director of football who'd stepped in as caretaker manager, if he had any problem with the appointment. Pleat said no. He respected Graham. He admitted it was a slight disappointment though; he had always hoped to get back his job as full-time manager, having been Tottenham boss for one season only back in 1986-87.

As an ex-Arsenal favourite, both as manager and as a player, George Graham was never going to be the most popular of appointments. To many at White Hart Lane, he wasn't just Mr Arsenal, he represented their whole ideology. He would need to win, and win big, if he was going to appease the Tottenham fans.

For his first game, he watched from the stands. It would be left to David Pleat to give the team talk. Before Pleat began, Graham walked into the dressing room with Alan Sugar to introduce himself to the players. He stood up straight in front of them, and authoritatively held up his finger. He then acted with speed and clarity. 'I'm going to work hard and I expect everyone below me to work hard.' With that, he left the room smiling to himself that his first words were delivered with a little more spirit, even venom, than usual. His intent was clear. It was certainly heard by the players and his new chairman. But the words did not go down well with Sol: 'From that very first moment, he lost me. I work hard anyway. If players don't work hard in training or in the game, then deal with it individually and privately. But giving threats to the whole squad on your first meeting, and just before we were going out to play, wasn't a good idea.'

Sol would find it difficult to recover from their first meeting. It gnawed away at him. To him, Graham's self-righteous ultimatum was irritating, and his relationship with the Scot was never going to be straightforward from that point on. 'He should have talked to the players individually,' admits David Pleat, 'but George had a style. He had a big reputation. He was probably just showing his authority. When he first arrived at the club, he wanted to cut the squad. Those he didn't want could train elsewhere. I advised him against it. That sort of thing can cause unrest.'

Sol and Graham did not connect. Sol wasn't keen on him and guessed Graham wasn't particularly wild about him, either. It was quite a knee-jerk reaction from Sol. He needed to get over it as quickly as possible; George Graham was not going anywhere in the foreseeable future and Sol was, after all, his captain.

•　　•　　•

Leicester City 0 Tottenham 1, Worthington Cup Final, Wembley, 21 March 1999

LEICESTER CITY: Keller; Ullathorne, Taggart, Elliott, Walsh; Savage (Zagorakis 90), Izzett, Lennon, Guppy; Cottee, Heskey (Marshall 74). Unused subs: Arphexad; Campbell, Kaamark.

TOTTENHAM HOTSPUR: Walker; Carr, Campbell, Vega, Edinburgh; Anderton, Freund, Nielsen, Ginola (Sinton 90); Ferdinand, Iversen. Unused subs: Baardsen, Young, Dominguez, Armstrong. Goals: Nielsen (90). Sent off: Edinburgh (60).

Att: 77,892. Ref: Terry Heilbron.

In a largely forgettable final, Tottenham go down to ten men with the harsh sending off of Justin Edinburgh after a tangle with Robbie Savage on the hour, but snatch a last-minute winner from the head of Dane Allan Nielsen. It's rejoicing all round for Spurs fans as captain Sol Campbell lifts the trophy.

Eight months after taking charge, Graham lead Spurs to victory over Leicester City in the 1999 League Cup final. It was one of Sol's finest days. He became the first black captain to lift a major trophy at Wembley. He wasn't aware of the honour at the time, but reminisces with pride now. His brothers and mother were there to see the game. It would be the first and last time Wilhelmina would see him play professionally. 'I felt so happy. I was so proud. He is the greatest to me. I didn't have to go and see him again. I knew he would be all right,' she says.

The day is a sea of memories: thousands upon thousands of Spurs fans with smiling faces and blue and white scarves tied to their necks and banners held aloft. Sol hugging the League Cup in his arms on the sacred Wembley turf. What music. What excitement. The Spurs choir singing their hymn 'Glory, Glory, Tottenham Hotspur' followed by a brief snatch of the Chas and Dave song 'Ossie's going to Wembley'. Ossie Ardiles, the man who brought Sol into the first team. *Thank you, Ossie.* Sol joins his team-mates on their lap of honour. *I've worked for this.* His voice, so rarely heard by the fans, is yelling out to them in excitement, 'We've WON! Here's the cup!' Here are some of the faces that will one day fling scorn at Sol, but on this special day there is no hint of malice, just adoring celebration. No baying, no bitching, no hatred. Just love. Hug your neighbour, we've won the cup!

'If the game had gone into extra-time we would have been in trouble. I think we would have lost. We were dead on our feet,' says Sol. But the Norwegian Steffen Iversen, using his pace, broke free on the right in stoppage time, his shot rebounded off Leicester keeper Kasey Keller and Allan Nielsen followed up with a diving header to score and send Tottenham fans into bliss.

The dressing room was also celebrating, except for Graham. 'He didn't seem that overjoyed,' says Sol. But then again, we all have different ways of showing our happy side. Sol sits for a moment before taking off his kit to shower. The dressing room throbs to the sound of laughter. What a great day it has been. They say winning a football match in a final at Wembley is the best of feelings. It is. Enjoy. Enjoy what is beautiful. He remembered just for a moment the street he was born and brought up in. The street he worked to get out from, to be in the here and now. He is truly happy. He's now established in the England team, had the taste of international captaincy and played in his first World Cup in France '98. He is captain of Tottenham Hotspur and has just lifted their first trophy for eight years. This is part of his and the club's history. *All I want to do is continue to play well and win trophies; nothing is better.* But without anyone realising, least of all Sol, winning the League Cup and relishing the day brings his departure from Tottenham a little closer.

The League Cup winning party was held at Sopwell House near St Albans. Sol left the party early to spend time with his then-girlfriend Michelle (who used to date his team-mate Justin Edinburgh's brother) While his team-mates had their partners with them, Sol's had remained at home. He felt he needed to keep the relationship secret from the gossipmongers – maybe if the press had found out it would have saved him from all the remarks about his sexuality.

The following season, Tottenham's European adventure ends prematurely in November. 'It was one of those nights you just want to rub from your memory,' says Sol. Tottenham had lost 2-0 in the UEFA Cup second round second leg to FC Kaiserslautern. The disappointment was palpable from the Spurs fans. George Graham's defensive strategy nearly paid off but two last-minute goals, one an own goal, saw the Germans through 2-1 on aggregate. It was another example for Sol of Tottenham not being ready to join the elite of Europe, or become one of the top teams in the Premier League. He had, after the Worthington Cup triumph, a faint optimism that the club shared the same ambition. He knew they needed to spend to re-live the joy that everyone connected to the club experienced that day at Wembley. It had been the perfect day.

Well, near perfect. There was something that had been shadowing him during those blissful hours of victory. Sol Campbell had been called up on a charge of assault.

•   •   •

Back on 3 October 1998, Tottenham had beaten Derby County 1-0 at Pride Park. David Pleat was still acting as caretaker manager; it would be his last game in the role before George Graham took over. 'I was happy. We got three points and I scored the winner,' Sol says.

After the game, Sol walked off the pitch towards the dressing room when Colin Calderwood dashed past him and confronted a Derby player, Francesco Baiano. A fight between a group of players broke out. Sol stood back. *What's happening? Is this serious?* Difficult to judge the dividing line between playing and fighting, but this was serious all right. Spurs' captain shouted: 'Everyone stop fighting and get back to your dressing rooms!' That was it. One big testosterone tussle, ending before it began. Sol wouldn't have given it another thought until David Pleat, now back to being director of football, approached him after a training session two weeks later. He remembers lying on a bank of grass looking up at the sky and seeing clouds wrapped around the sun pulling tighter and tighter. It would be a sign of things to come.

Pleat paused and said to Sol, 'We've received a letter from Derby County saying that when we played them, a scuffle started and you broke a steward's arm.' Sol wasn't sure what Pleat had just said. He asked him to repeat himself. He did. Sol dismissed it. 'Pay no attention,' he said. 'It's a load of rubbish.' And, because of the stony expression on Sol's face, Pleat said, 'Okay Sol, let's leave it.'

Sol was irritated for a moment and then lost interest. It was nonsense, a wild accusation. But the story wouldn't go away. Pleat approached Sol again a couple of weeks later. He was relaxing after a heavy training session and there he was, Pleat again. 'Sol, about this incident at Derby. The police want to take a statement.'

'Why?' Sol asks. 'There's no truth in it.'

'He never gave anything away with his facial expression. I never had an indication as to what was going on in his mind,' recalls David Pleat. But inside, Sol was in turmoil. It was beginning to sink in that this wasn't going to disappear.

Sol is accompanied to Tottenham police station, a mile up the road from White Hart Lane, by the club's company secretary, John Ireland. He feels wronged and he begins to feel a little threatened. At the station he makes his statement. He speaks slowly and in detail about exactly what happened: about the scuffle, shouting at everyone to cool down. It is all pretty straightforward, which I imagine it is if you are telling the truth. When he is facing the officer, snippets of his childhood come back to him. It surprises him. How he felt imprisoned in his family home. Maybe there was a connection in how unsettled he felt.

Afterwards, Sol is paraded round the station. Some of the policemen are brought in from the back to shake hands with the great man, to pose for a photograph. Faces brighten. It wasn't often you got the Tottenham skipper visiting the local constabulary.

The days pass and the whole episode is beginning to shadow Sol. Just going to the station made him feel uneasy. When you are accused of something that you are totally innocent of, it is like being trapped on a bolting carousel that one day will crash. This is how Sol is beginning to feel. The case escalates with Sol now asked to report to Derby police station. He thinks he will have to go through the same routine: a statement followed by a couple of posed photographs for the local constabulary. He's nearly right. He hides in the back seat of the car as it pulls up in front of the station, so as to avoid the press pack who have heard the Tottenham skipper may be reporting there. He is now beginning to feel like a villain. He gives his fingerprints, has his police mugshot – 'turn left, turn right, look straight ahead' – taken. And then he is officially charged with assault, released on bail to appear before Derby City magistrates on 1 March.

This is getting out of control.

He's had that thought many times over the last months. He's getting angry. And confused. Maybe he knocked into the steward without knowing.

Am I already beginning to confuse fact and fiction, becoming the sort of person who tells a story with such realism that he believes it is true? How ironic.

He's accused of being in a fight, which he wasn't in, and now he's embarking on his own fight over right and wrong. His football has not been affected. He is still playing well. These have been good days, great days. Football once again is his escape. But now the days are soiled. No-one can tell he's in pain. Once again it is buried. He is becoming even more insular.

What will my mother say? What will she think of me? I have to act. NOW. Get my own people involved? Preferably put a line through it, even DELETE! It's time for it to stop. Think! Think!

Dialogue continues in his head for weeks. And still no-one can tell him what is going on. Or they know and are keeping it to themselves. Paranoia sets in. To the outside world stands a strong man, but inside his mind is in turmoil.

Meanwhile, the club asks him to support them over a libel hearing with the *Daily Mail*. Chairman Alan Sugar is taking the paper to court over accusations that he is 'miserly' in his stewardship of Spurs. Their former striker, Teddy Sheringham, has accused Sugar and the club of lacking ambition. 'I'm not mean!' Sugar said to Sol, showing him bank statements. 'Call that mean?' Sol doesn't want anything to do with it. Sugar had told Sol that for his new contract he would be the highest paid player at Tottenham, but when the club were requested to disclose their players' salaries to the court in support of their libel case, it turned out David Ginola was earning more. 'Typical Sugar!' says Sol. *Leave me alone. Don't you understand I have my own problems?*

'The last thing I wanted to do was get involved in another court case,' Sol says. Spurs feel let down by his attitude. Even George Graham comments he's heard from the top that Sol isn't being supportive of the club. *It's strange, every time he speaks to me, I have this image of him showing me his pips on his uniform. Ridiculous, really. He doesn't understand what I have been going through. You're my manager, you should support your player first, your captain.* Sol felt, ever since Graham signed Tim Sherwood, the Blackburn Rovers captain, in February 1999 for a reported fee of £3 million, that he wanted Sherwood as his Spurs captain. Nothing was said directly. But Sol knew and wasn't just going to give it up. He's in a quandary. *It's about time I have it out with Graham. Isn't part of my trouble that I avoid confrontation?* If they were going to take the captaincy away from him, they would have to rip the armband off his sleeve. He had a glow of pride at the efficiency with which he'd taken to his role as captain. He had doubts at first, but now it was different. He was beginning to think he should have always been a captain: at Lilleshall, for Tottenham Youth when Keith Waldon asked him, for England...

Tim Sherwood was stirring. When Sol wasn't playing, he took over the captaincy. After he scored once at White Hart Lane, he pointed at the captain's armband. Not directly to Sol but at the crowd. He knew what he was doing. Sol didn't react but a few weeks later when he was in the players' tunnel before a match against Newcastle he overheard Alan Shearer, an old mate at Blackburn, saying to Sherwood, 'Have you taken it off him yet?' and the two chuckled like naughty schoolboys. Sol says: 'I'll never forget that time with Shearer. It gave me even more energy and desire to beat him when I came across him as an opposition player and manager.' As for Sherwood, he couldn't believe how the captaincy was getting to his head. *Why are you getting Alan Shearer to fight your corner? Who the hell are you? You've only been at the club for five minutes. You have your swagger because you think you have George Graham behind you.* 'With Tim Sherwood, aside from the football, I couldn't have any respect for him and his lack of character,' says Sol.

Sol paused, and with a look of disgust, he walked on. *Don't let it bother you. You have other demons to deal with. Don't let anyone live rent-free in your head.*

•　　•　　•

John Ireland approaches Sol at lunch and shows him a newspaper cutting of a Lord being bound over.

'What's this?' Sol asks.

'This is what happened in that case,' Ireland explains. 'If in your case you agree to be bound over and pay a small amount of compensation, the whole thing will vanish. There will be no record. You will never have to appear in court.'

'Bound over. What does that mean?' (In layman's terms, a magistrate of the court can agree to release the accused to be bound over to be of good behaviour or to keep the peace; such an order meaning no conviction is recorded because it is a civil matter.) Sol is bewildered. He stifles a grimace of total disbelief and then says, 'When is this going to stop?' And then he speaks with such conviction that no-one can doubt what he means. 'I will live and die by my own words. I had nothing to do with this. Tell them to go away.'

Then Sol receives an official letter from the club, dated 18 June 1999, from John Ireland, with reference to the assault charge, stating: 'I am instructed by Mr Sugar to inform you that I am unable to continue to act for you in this matter...You should make alternative arrangements.' So Tottenham, his own club, were washing their hands of the case. 'When I needed people the most, they weren't there. I was looking for every excuse to stay at Tottenham but, after receiving this letter, it gave me a reason to consider leaving. It started a long thought process of what the alternatives might be,' says Sol.

He decides to get his own solicitor involved. Bon Battu, Sky Andrew's lawyer, is sent the court files from the club. Battu

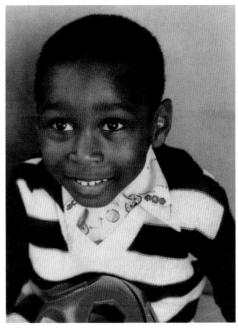

Sol, aged two, in the garden.

As a four-year-old, with his red and blue football toy after the visit of Lady Diana Spencer to his nursery.

The FA School of Excellence, year 1989 intake. *Back row (left to right):*
S Cousin, C Dean, D Hill, N Rust, Sol Campbell, D McDougald, A Turner.
Middle row: K Sharp, A Gray, Stuart Campbell, S Binke, S Daly, L Cotterell,
J Forrester. *Front row:* I Blythe, D Jones, A Pickering, G Pickering, G Toogood,
D Phillips, C Simmons, J Cartwright.

Don Howe presents a sixteen-year-old Sol Campbell with his cap at the graduation ceremony for the FA School of Excellence at Lilleshall.

The England Under-18s squad that won the European Championship trophy in 1993, beating Turkey 1-0 in the final. *Back row, left to right:* Andrew Dent (team doctor), Dave Galley (head physio), Kevin Gallen, Kevin Sharp, Chris Day, Andy Marshall, Sol Campbell, Rob Bowman, Nicky Butt, Ted Powell (manager). *Front row:* Julian Joachim, Paul Scholes, Noel Whelan, Jamie Forrester, Chris Casper, Darren Caskey (capt), Robbie Fowler, Mark Tinkler, Gary Neville.

First senior England cap. Sol comes on during the England v Hungary friendly, Wembley, May 1996 as a 65th minute substitute for Paul Ince.

Sol battles with Gianfranco Zola, who scored the only goal in Italy's 1-0 defeat of England in the 1998 World Cup qualifier at Wembley.

Paul Gascoigne and Sol during an England training session. Sol thought the world of Gazza; the warm-hearted Geordie was an inspiration to the young players at Tottenham.

England squad photocall ahead of the 1998 World Cup. Under Glenn Hoddle, and with proven internationals like Shearer, Adams, Ince and Sheringham alongside the precocious talents of Beckham and Owen, Sol believes England should have got to the final.

A ticket from the Tunisia match on 15 June 1998. It's an important memento for Sol – his first World Cup game for England.

England v Tunisia, France 98, with Sol in action during his country's 2-0 opening group game victory.

Sky Andrew, the football agent who Sol first met at Lilleshall, represented Great Britain in table tennis at the 1998 Seoul Olympics.

Referee Kim Milton Nielsen waves away the appealing Gary Neville after Sol's header into the net against Argentina at France 98 is disallowed. 'It *was* a goal,' insists Sol.

Derby v Tottenham, Pride Park, October 1998 where Sol scores in a 1-1 draw. He is later charged with assaulting a steward at the game, only for the case against him to be dropped the following year.

Sol acknowledges the White Hart Lane faithful after his equaliser for Tottenham against Manchester United in the 2-2 draw in December 1998.

Manager George Graham and captain Sol Campbell lead Tottenham out before the 1999 Worthington Cup final at Wembley.

The sweet taste of victory. A jubilant Sol with the Worthington Cup trophy alongside team-mates Steffen Iversen, Ian Walker and Les Ferdinand.

An intimate dressing room moment for Sol, clutching his first major trophy for Spurs.

Arsenal vice-chairman David Dein and Arsene Wenger announce the signing of the Tottenham captain in front of a stunned press at Highbury in July 2001. Sol: 'I just hope everyone respects my decision.'

Arsene Wenger and Sol shake hands on the deal to bring the Spurs captain to Highbury.

'It was a special moment for me.' Sol makes his debut for Arsenal, coming on as a substitute during their pre-season friendly in Austria against AS Roma in the summer of 2001.

Sol with mother Wilhelmina and father Sewell.

Sol with friends at one of his birthday parties.

is confident that the case against Sol is weak. It is mistaken identity, as basic as that. 'You don't have to worry,' he tells Sol over lunch. 'We are gathering key witnesses. We are compiling our version of events, which varies greatly to what has been said.' Sol tries to listen but he is so concerned that, every time his lawyer opens his mouth, he doesn't catch what is being said. He doesn't show Battu how worried he is. How worried he has been. They first met in 1991 and Battu readily admits he still finds it difficult to see what Sol is thinking today. This lunch would be no different.

Then, three weeks before Sol is due to appear in court on 8 July, Battu receives a fax and is informed that the case has been dropped. He rings Sol and his agent Sky Andrew to let them know the news. 'It's over,' he says. Sol, who is having coffee in a local cafe simply replies, 'Thank you Bon, for letting me know,' and switches off his phone. The impact of the news is powerful. He is relieved. Takes it easy. One breath after another. The pall of concern, which had been hanging over him but was virtually impossible to detect from the outside, was suddenly erased. He pulled himself together and returned to his coffee.

'Through all this time, over nine months, I'd been living the life of a pariah. I couldn't go out to my local shop without whispers that I was some sort of thug who would bully and beat up on an elderly steward.

'Why did this go on for so long, on such flimsy evidence? I was an innocent man, but no-one seemed to be listening. It was obvious that I had nothing to do with the steward's injury – according to the hospital admissions report, he was admitted an hour and a half *before* kick-off, and more than three hours *before* the trouble in the tunnel when the game ended. What's more, my name as the alleged assailant on the report was not the original name written down. It had been written in afterwards. Yet this evidence had not materialised when Spurs were representing my case.

'I asked myself: *Were Spurs trying to get some leverage over me, in order to force me to sign a new contract? Did they really want to go that far?* This was the beginning of the end for me at Spurs. I was sick to my stomach of it.'

You sense Sol changed after the Derby incident; for him, it was the lifting of a veil to see that few can be trusted. This chapter in his life took place when he was earning money, owned a house, was playing for England, and captaining his club side. He thought he was safe from the outside, but he now realised he was as vulnerable as anyone else; maybe even more so, now he was in the public eye. How insignificant everything becomes after the car crash of one event. It is one of those episodes in life that wounds; he suffered.

David Pleat congratulated Sol on hearing the news and said he knew things would work out. *Really?* Sol thinks. *I was beginning to have doubts.*

•   •   •

The disappointment of England in Euro 2000 affected Sol. He was now the defensive lynchpin for his country, but not progressing out of the group stage was deeply disappointing. It would be the least successful tournament he played in for England and afterwards he felt he needed a long break. 'I was mentally exhausted,' Sol says. But George Graham wanted him back for Tottenham's pre-season tour of Norway and Denmark. He had no choice and reluctantly returned to the club, flying back from the Caribbean and, on the same day, travelling on to Norway. 'I went because I was asked, but knew I was still tired and needed more time off.'

On 19 September 2000, Tottenham played Brentford at Griffin Park in a second round, first leg tie of the Worthington Cup. A first-half injury to Sol and a red card for Tottenham goalkeeper Neil Sullivan were the main talking points in a goalless draw. It was a bad injury for Sol, a dislocated shoulder caused by a mid-air collision. He fell to the ground and lay motionless. The trainer tried to lift him up from the injured shoulder. He yelled in terror. 'Leave it fucking alone!' He was in agony. His shoulder went numb through shock, until he felt a shudder pass down from the top of his spine to his ankles. Even now, when he thinks of it, he remembers the crowd being deathly quiet as he struggled off the pitch. He refused a stretcher. They stood in silence. The silence when a crowd knows something is wrong. No chants. Faces looking on open-mouthed, shuffling in their seats, witnessing the pain etched on his face; it was as if they were watching someone walking to the guillotine.

He was tired. He knew he was off his game. He knew he had been hurried back. He believed his lack of mobility had caused the damage. If he had been heard and left to regain his full fitness, he was convinced it may not have happened. He would have been sharper and instinctively capable of dealing with the challenge. 'I knew I needed a break, physically and mentally. A lot of players are rushed back too quickly. I understand they are needed for the team but it is short-term thinking. Careers can end early because of unwise decisions. In the end, I was out for three months. I missed the beginning of the season and the start of England's World Cup qualifying campaign for South Korea and Japan.'

Sol is an advocate of the winter break. 'I know Europe is right to take time off. They have it sussed. It's not only for physical reasons but also mental. It's good to get away. It only helps our national team, maybe not immediately but after a few years we will see the benefit.'

Following keyhole surgery, Sol spent his time watching the Sydney Olympics, sitting still on his sofa, no sudden movements, unravelling in slow motion so as not to irritate his shoulder. His nights were disturbed because he had to sleep with a pillow between his arm and torso, and in a different position than he was used to. By day, his arm was in a sling and he had daily changes of dressings.

After a month, he began his slow recuperation on an exercise bike. 'I was conscious that I had to take it slowly.' He went to watch games and tried to occupy his mind which was preparing itself for the gathering storm over his contract. He didn't react to any questions. He was a Tottenham player for now and that was all-important. The season hadn't begun for him. His training was like starting pre-season all over again. 'I don't want to know what you're hearing,' he told Sky Andrew. I have no interest. Sky kept to his word. He let Sol concentrate on getting fit again.

Within two months, Sol was back in the first team playing against Leicester on 25 November in a 3-0 home win. But the shoulder injury triggered other problems. It had a knock-on effect on his ankle, which had never caused trouble before. He started to use strapping. He didn't like it. He felt it was a crutch that weakened his focus. *The sooner I get rid of these the better.* When he was walking around his house in the New Year, he felt a pull in his leg. He hesitated. *What's wrong now?* It was nothing. He was just being oversensitive with his body. He felt physically vulnerable. He had never felt this way before. Yes, he was rushed back from the Euros but he was beginning to realise it wasn't just that. The constant attention surrounding his contract was starting to take its toll. Will he sign? Won't he? It wasn't just affecting his everyday thoughts; it was affecting his physical fitness.

The Tottenham fans were agitated. They demonstrated outside the ground for a change in manager. They had a new owner coming, which placated a few, but the sense around the club was that of being restless. There was uncertainty everywhere. With all this happening, Sol was looking for a fundamental answer to the questions: 'Can Tottenham change? Will they spend to challenge for the top and win trophies?'

'If the new board doesn't look to change things,' a voice muttered on his shoulder, 'better face the truth and move on.'

●   ●   ●

George Graham, after his strong start, was unable to maintain his team's winning ways. And, because of his Arsenal connection, Spurs fans couldn't wait to see him go. ENIC, the sports and media group that had bought out Alan Sugar to the tune of £22 million, were Tottenham's new owners and decided to sack Graham for breach of contract for publicly disclosing what the club deemed to be private information from in-house meetings between the manager and his new bosses. Spurs legend Glenn Hoddle was installed in Graham's place in April 2001.

Graham seemed to represent those inconsequentialities, which Sol hoped would evaporate from his life. 'I'm sure he knew I was a top-notch player, but I never felt he rooted for me,' Sol says. Tottenham Hotspur Football Club was clouding all his available thoughts. His search for the right club remained central to what he believed could make him happy both personally and professionally. Was it still Tottenham? He was still asking that same question eight, seven, six, five weeks before the end of the season. Whether he knew it or not, the question was gaining a sense of ominous pre-destiny.

Sol had one meeting at the Royal Lancaster Hotel with Tottenham chairman Daniel Levy but nothing was resolved. Then ENIC arranged a meeting in offices at Conduit Street with David Pleat, non-executive vice chairman David Buchler and Sol's agent, Sky Andrew. 'It wasn't a very good meeting,' David Pleat recalls. 'Sky Andrew was late and when he finally arrived, he was a little aggressive in his approach. David [Buchler] said he could possibly reach £60k a week and Sky said make Sol a written offer and he would take it to Sol. The atmosphere was tense. After the meeting I felt we had hit an impasse. I knew we were losing him.' Sky says about meeting with Buchler: 'We met once. He was a good guy, straight-talking and was positive to move things forward. We talked about meeting again but it never transpired. I never heard from him.' But whatever the truth, a deal was becoming ever more distant at the time.

Club captain Gary Mabbutt remembers feeling the same. He had a call from new chairman Daniel Levy asking if he had any influence with Sol. Mabbutt did not know but he thought that they had a good friendship and that Sol respected him. 'Try to keep him at the club,' Levy told him.

They arrange to meet at West Lodge Park Hotel in Hadley Wood, a thirty-minute drive from Sol's home. Both are punctual, greeting each other by the front desk. They follow each other into the lobby and sit towards the back. The place is surprisingly quiet, not as silent as a morgue but, for early evening, not particularly crowded. 'Would you like a drink?' Sol asks. Mabbutt shakes his head. They both drink coffee.

They speak for about for half an hour on everything but football, until Sol turns round to order another coffee. He moves his neck slowly, as if he's been under water for some time. He continues to notice the slight stiffening of his body over the months. Mabbutt asks how he sees his future. Before he answers he thinks, *I respect Gary. I like him, he is a true professional, and someone I've always looked up to. I like that he wants to know how I am, if there's anything he can do.* He then answers quickly, as if to make up for lost time.

Looking back on that time, Mabbutt now says, 'Sol said that he wanted to improve his play and was unsure he could do that at Tottenham. He was always very much his own man and knew what he wanted. He never got led away from his ambition, so what he was saying came as no surprise. He had a heavy heart because he said he loved Tottenham. He spoke about his determination to win trophies and wanting to continue playing for England. He gave the sense that staying in London appealed so he could be near friends and family. We didn't talk about money. If we had, and he'd said he hadn't been offered enough by the club, I would have gone back to Daniel [Levy] and told him that. But money was not spoken of.'

The two talk on until it starts to darken outside. They pay the bill and walk out together. They shake hands. As Mabbutt drives away in his blue Range Rover, he asks himself the question the whole country is asking: 'Is Sol Campbell going to leave Spurs?'

He has little doubt. Yes.

SKY ANDREW

'I always watched his back and put him first... I never looked at what I was going to get out of it.'

SKY ANDREW

He slept in a room, eight by eight, until he was sixteen years old. He shared it with his younger brother; two single beds crammed close together. A bucket was under the bed for them to pee in, to avoid having to use the outside toilet with the cold porcelain of the lavatory bowl in the middle of the night. The whiff of stale piss when the door suddenly swung open; sometimes the smell would catch him by surprise and he'd shove the pillow to his mouth to stop him retching.

Sky Andrew, like Sol Campbell, was born in East London; the second of four children, three boys and a girl. His mother Zeta worked in a pie factory; his father Patrick worked for London Transport, pasting advertisements on the sides of buses. Like Sol, his father emigrated first to the UK and then earned enough money for his mother to follow. And, like Sol, his mother means everything to him. She impoverished herself further to make sure her son had the best chance in life. She gave him values, a sense of decency, and it was instilled in him at a very young age.

When he talks about his mother, Sky has an overwhelming sense of being humbled by having such an influence in his life. She used to go and watch him play cricket and bring him his sandwiches to make sure he didn't get too hungry. 'She travelled with us in the minibus to the games,' he recalls.

His conversation now flows easily but it hasn't always been that way. At school in East London he was quiet, tentative, hovering in the background, not usually heard, and when he did talk most of his friends thought he was joking. He was very different to the tough negotiating agent he would become.

He was a born sportsman. He played centre-forward and was an opening batsman for Newham District's football and cricket teams. 'If I had pursued even one of them, there was a good chance I could've turned professional.' Instead, he was drawn to table tennis and as he says, 'Once I got the bug, that was it.' Len Hoffman, one of England's most respected table tennis coaches, encouraged Sky to pursue the sport. 'You have something,' he said. He joined Hoffman's youth club in Forest Gate and would go there directly from school, sometimes not having had time to change from his school's green football kit, mud peeling from his knees. The rest of the players would be kitted out in the latest table tennis outfit: the blue short-sleeved polo shirt, blue shorts, latest gym shoes or trainers. Sky seemed like an urchin compared to the others, who looked at him with diffidence and suspicion. 'I used to play every night. And soon I realised I had a chance to go to the Olympics if I grafted.'

He played the game with varying degrees of zeal and delight. He had a dream: *To hell with education, I have a chance to make it to the world stage.* 'I was told by my English teacher that I wouldn't amount to much if I continued my passion for the game.' At nineteen, he was part of the England set up and started to travel the world. He was ranked sixth in England, but for the European Championships in Moscow he was overlooked for someone ranked lower. It proved to be a turning point in Sky's life. 'I am never going to allow anyone or anything to get the better of me again,' he confided to himself. 'I'm going to work so hard that whatever I do, I'll become indispensable.'

At their first meeting in Lilleshall, Sky remembers seeing Sol line up for food, 'not once but three times!' In his Arsenal days, Arsene Wenger would also notice his appetite. 'He liked a good dinner. We had to watch his weight.' Sol's response is simple. 'For my size I needed feeding.'

Sol thinks he first caught sight of his friend and future agent playing table tennis. Whatever the truth, their friendship marked a fork in the road for both. 'We came from the same area and just started to talk,' Sky says. He was at Lilleshall training with the England table tennis team. He travelled to the West Midlands from London every four weeks. The journey was a trip he always looked forward to. He loved it there as much as Sol did. Common pleasures such as having a shower or a bath every day were a treat. Although, the shower was something Sky never got used to. He always took one with trepidation. There was no shower at home and he always treated it as something different, out of the ordinary. He could only take a bath once a week and never took the indulgence of refilling with hot water once he had started to bathe. There was never enough of it. He never had the treat of twiddling the taps with his toes or experiencing an overdose of bath bubbles. But at Lilleshall he could stay in the bath for as long as he liked. The water was hot. In fact, very hot! It's almost as if they were deliberately trying to scald the boys. Even when it got to a reasonable temperature, there was no guarantee it would stay that way. But he didn't mind. He was being spoiled.

Their upbringing was similar. From the same background, the same streets, the same area. They shared a desire to get out, to better themselves. 'We talked about East London a lot,' Sky says. 'We shared the same mentality, the honour of coming from that part of London.' Sky would, some afternoons, head down to the football pitch and watch the young boys train. He immediately saw Sol was different. His attitude was unlike the rest. He had a focus and a determination. He knew he'd seen something special, not unlike the music manager who goes to a club and hears a sound he hasn't heard before. 'He was taller than the others and had incredible presence, even though he was a shy person,' he says of Sol. 'I watched him train and behave properly. He had a focus at a very young age. He has never lost it throughout his career. He didn't need encouragement on that front; his intrinsic nature for hard work was already formed.'

• • •

Sky has popped out to get something for his mother from the local supermarket. It's a journey he has taken many times. As he crosses the road, he catches sight of this huge figure dwarfing a BMX with long legs spinning round and round, virtually hitting his chest. There goes Sol. There is no-one like him. No-one would cycle in that awkward manner or have a face of such determination. *Where are you heading? What are you escaping from? Slow down!* He neither calls out nor follows him. He feels no compunction to chase after him. It's as if this moment is destined. And nothing is going to change their reconnection. Sol is halfway down the street before he suddenly grinds to a halt. He doubles back and says hello. He doesn't get off his bike. He talks to Sky still sitting, his long legs stretched out. This is the first time the two have met outside the Lilleshall grounds. They talk and decide to meet later that week. As he disappears down the street, Sky thinks to himself: *One day that man will be a top footballer.*

• • •

The friendship between Sol and his future agent grew. They spent more and more time together. They would hang out at weekends, and go out clubbing together. 'He was always more fashionable than me,' says Sky, who generally knew the guy at the door who treated them like VIPs, although Sol was not yet famous. 'He's the next big football star,' Sky would whisper, and say it with such belief that doors would open and sometimes they were invited in without further questions. Maybe that's the definition of success for boys so young. Before booking their Saturday night out, he would wait to see Sol's result. If he'd lost, Sol wouldn't join him, being too miserable to have a good time. It would be something that never changed through-out his career. A losing Sol was never a pretty sight. But when he won, they had a good time: Sol the quiet one, Sky the more vocal with sweeping gesticulations. His own sporting dreams were drawing to a close. His new job was to guide his protégé, teach him about how to look after himself. It was never dis-cussed openly, it just happened naturally. 'He loved watching me talk to people, make deals. He knew I had an acumen for it,' says Sky proudly.

He seems to mourn the memory of forging their friendship, working together in their mutual passion for striking the right deal, to better themselves. He even helped Sol buy his first house in Woodford. 'I bought it for approximately £185,000.' (Sol would later correct him: '£159,950'.) You could almost hear Sky's pleasure travel around the room. When Sol wanted a con-servatory for his new home, he asked Sky to find someone to help. Within a day, Sky was leading someone up to his front door. 'Come this way!' He had brought along a local man. 'A chirpy type,' Sky recalls. The two had decided that Sol would wait in the kitchen while Sky negotiated. Sol already knew that, with him being a recognised footballer, the price would go up. He listened from the kitchen as the conservatory salesman talked up his deal. He could hear their voices distinctly.

'How about twenty grand to do the whole job,' the salesman says.

Silence.

'You're having a laugh?' Sky says, not even looking at him. The salesman's now out with his tape measure, measuring and re-measuring. 'Fifteen?' the salesman's chin held up slightly, giving that look of self-assurance. 'You have a good deal.' But Sky is having none of it. Sol is still in the kitchen. 'Twelve grand.' Again Sky shakes his head. 'Is that a no?' Yes, no. And it goes on and on … The chirpy salesman is there for twelve hours. Yes, twelve hours! Sol is too nervous to come in. Finally, they agree. 'We shook hands at three thousand, nine hundred and eighty-five,' Sky remembers.

As the man slinks away, Sol comes into the room. Sky strides towards him with hands in the air as if playing the tambourine. The two men laugh and keep laughing. Slaps on the back. Sol had been upstairs for what seemed like an eternity while his erstwhile friend did his negotiation. And what a negotiation. When the salesman returned to check on the conservatory three weeks later, he explained that he was 'camping out' until a price was agreed. 'I was told by my boss not to leave until we shook.'

When Sol bought his second home, a floor fitter came to the house. Same routine. Sol upstairs, Sky downstairs haggling the price. But this time when the negotiation starts, Sol comes downstairs, shakes the wood fitter's hand, turns to Sky and says, 'I'll take over from here.'

'It was the first time he did that,' Sky remembers, like an older sibling. 'He was becoming more confident.'

•   •   •

A financial advisor kept telling Sky that it was about time he formalised his relationship with Sol. 'She thought it was time to make it official. Earn from it.' He was still earning from his table tennis: he was doing some coaching in Germany and was part of the international setup. There were other jobs too. 'I was writing scripts for *Spitting Image*, thinking of a career in television,' says Sky. It was enough for him to get by. 'I'd approached Sol saying I wanted to be rewarded for the work I had done. It was taking up a large part of my time. I said to him, "Give me what you think is fair." He did. He gave me a grand.

'Guys were approaching him all the time but he didn't trust them,' recalls Sky. But going forward, Sky needed to make things more official. *This is not easy. I don't know how to approach him.* He thought about it, not for days but weeks. This usually confident man was for once unsure. *Why should I ask for a commission? I'm his mate, aren't I? Isn't that what mates are for, to protect each other? Well, isn't it? No. Yes. Of course...Yes.*

Would this change things between us? No. Why should it? It could. It might.

It did. After weeks of self-analysis, he became diffident to the situation. And we all become brave when we are diffident. When he finally brought it up ('I think it was over lunch'), Sol did not hesitate. 'Do my next deal with Tottenham, then,' Sol said. It was the Gerry Francis deal, which wasn't, as we know, the easiest negotiation. He secured Sol around £13,500 a week. They were now an official agent-player team, and Sol his demanding one-and-only client. 'He expected me to be always available. I could get a call from him at any time of the day,' says Sky. He had two phones and the peace was shattered by both suddenly ringing at once. 'It would be Sol trying both lines. I didn't mind... I suppose if I did, I would have stopped it.' But it was consuming his life. His client was becoming the best defender in the world. The interest in him commercially, press-wise, was growing. The demand opened up both to a new world. Sky loved it, his mind fixed on financial numbers that the majority of us could only dream of.

'I always watched his back and put him first,' Sky says. 'I never looked at what I was going to get out of it. That's what most football agents do. They think of their own pockets. I would never advise or coax him to sign somewhere because my commission would be bigger. Barcelona was the perfect example. It was not how it worked.'

FAREWELL

'I wanted Spurs to show me that they were going to challenge.
Not just win cups but reach the very top.'

SOL

The clock had been tick-tocking away all through the 2000-01 season like an unexploded bomb. Everyone, fans, players and owner, were asking whether Sol would sign a new contract. Will he? Won't he? Even old Spurs favourite Jurgen Klinsmann, who ran into Sol at a game, wanted to know. 'Jurgen, please!' Sol replied, not quite believing he'd be that interested. It was as if Sol had no idea what was developing in the outside world, as if he'd been in solitary confinement. Why would anyone be so interested? The injury at the Brentford game had given him too much time to think about things in the early part of the season. That is what injuries do. You sit around, not being active and sink into your thoughts. Too much spare time. He started to shut down, be even less communicative. Weary of what he said, watchful how he behaved in front of people. Ironically, he went out more to restaurants, to clubs, trying to relax, but he was alone in other people's company.

He remembers being on the treadmill at Tottenham's training ground at Chigwell working to regain his fitness. He found himself wearing dark glasses watching the team outside all training together. Someone walked in and asked why he was wearing dark glasses. He didn't know. He had never done that before. Perhaps he was subconsciously beginning to hide even at his own club. He remembers the music he was listening to in his headphones. It randomly came on the radio: Craig David's 'Walking Away' followed by Anastacia's 'I'm Outta Love.'

When he returned to the team he gave them a hundred per cent assurance that he was not going to change. But it began to be more difficult to turn in the performances. 'I had lost faith in Graham and couldn't see any change in the club's ambition.' He found himself tiptoeing around during those last months.

The plan to have Sol sign a new contract had started a year before. David Pleat made an initial approach to gauge what Sol was thinking. 'He may have said, have you got something I can tell Alan, but I don't remember,' recalls Sky. 'It was Alan Sugar I spoke to mainly, but it was about Sol's ambition and what he wanted from the club.' Halfway through the last months of his contract, there was still no official word. Just silence. The media kept hearing rumours as they sniffed around making enquiries, drawing conclusions, demanding to know more 'in the public interest' and printing 'hot news'. And those who were meant to know, those closest to Sol, were a target for any connection to the story. 'I had a journalist friend,' Sky says, 'who when it was announced that Sol was leaving Spurs, called me and said "I thought we were friends? How could you do this to me? Why didn't you give me the scoop?"'

If Sol didn't sign a new contact by the end of the 2000-01 season, he was free to move under the Bosman ruling. The ruling meant that Tottenham would not profit from his transfer even though the club had helped develop him into the player he was, an England international. 'I wanted Spurs to show me that they were going to challenge. Not just win cups but reach the very top. I've always wanted that from them. I hoped to win a league championship with Tottenham,' Sol says resolutely, with words that seemed to have been boiling up inside of him. 'The fans may have believed in me, but I felt the club didn't, or they would have done more. They didn't ever make me a serious offer to show me otherwise. I was prepared to sign a four-year contract, with a break after the first year if it turned out they didn't go and buy quality players.

That's how it was then and that's how it is now. You have to buy good players to make a challenge for the very top. That's how it works!'

David Pleat says, 'Sol used to come to my office asking what was going on with the team. Who were we signing? I think he came three times. Very few players did that. Maybe David Ginola was the only other. Sol was always courteous, never critical. He was desperate for the team to do better. He was very serious about it. I may have tried to placate him with suggestions or ideas, but I could see he was uneasy. He was also very serious about his fitness. Even if he only had a slight niggle, he wouldn't train or play. He knew that you had to think long-term, and to play when even slightly injured could cause lasting damage.'

So he waited and waited through November, into December. From the beginning of January 2001, he was in a position to listen to offers from foreign clubs and not be in breach of contract. Bayern Munich, Barcelona and Inter Milan wanted him. A representative from Real Madrid had courted Sky for two years but didn't contact him once they were open to foreign offers. 'I heard from them consistently over the previous two seasons but then they went quiet. Why, I don't know.' Bayern made an offer in February but demanded an answer immediately. If they didn't get one, they would go elsewhere. Sky talked with Sol but he could hear his client was hesitant. 'Okay, let's leave it,' Sky said. 'I could tell, or rather hear, that he was still keen to stay at Tottenham. I was not going to push him in any direction. I was listening closely to what he was saying and supporting him. It was not about the money. It was about how ambitious the club were going to be.'

Bayern went away and true to their word never came back. Barcelona told Sky to call them when Sol was ready to make a decision. Even in March, with six weeks before the season's end, the departure of Sol was, as Sky consistently says, '...Still some distance away. He wanted to stay. He was waiting to see if the new owners were prepared to build a squad. Clubs might have approached Tottenham but no British clubs approached me directly; I told any agents that contacted me, we weren't speaking to anyone.' (A British club cannot speak to a player without permission from the club that holds the player's registration.)

Sol concurs but, although he believes what he says, he always follows up by bemoaning the fact that Spurs weren't trying to get him whatever it took. He felt, during those months, like he was running down an endless tunnel, in which long arms grabbed at him. The long arms belonged to every team but his own club.

According to Sky, Spurs had made an offer but it wasn't good enough for someone who many considered to be Tottenham's most important player and probably the best defender in the world. Sol says: 'I was on £13,500 a week, after starting on £10,000 initially. Even then I was the lowest paid player at my level. I had muppets as team-mates who were on treble the money.' But Sky says this wasn't the main point. 'The issues were about what squad the club would assemble for the following season, and making a reasonable offer for someone of his calibre.' Tottenham have continually and consistently refuted this. They wanted to make it work. The club has said that he simply wouldn't listen to them. That Sol had already made up his mind. The club's frustration remains clear for everyone to hear: they wanted him to stay.

Fans were reading and hearing that Sol was staying. He said it himself on television; there was a snippet on YouTube. Sky says this: 'Let's be clear, once and for all. I will say it again. He did want to stay. He had no intention of leaving. He wanted to remain at Tottenham – but *only* if they went out and bought some new star players and we could negotiate the contract. Whatever anyone says about Sol, he is an honourable man. He didn't, like other players, demand a transfer. He was contracted for a certain amount of time and then hoped to renew his contract.' Sky was in full flight, and frustrated. 'If a deal can't be made, because neither side can meet in the middle and there's inflexibility, then there is a stand-off and there's little you can do. We were continually waiting for a serious offer.' The reality is, communication between club and player had broken down some time before. Nothing of any sense could be heard from either side; there was an underlying mistrust that had been building for years.

Alan Sugar had left the club in February without having secured Sol's signature to a new contract. 'He blames George Graham, and me,' says David Pleat. 'He says that we should have dropped Sol and kept him in the reserves until he had agreed to sign. We didn't. He was too important for the team.'

•　•　•

Glenn Hoddle's first game as manager of Spurs was a big one: the FA Cup semi-final against Arsenal at Old Trafford on 8 April 2001. Sol and Glenn of course knew each other from his time with England. They had a mutual respect. Their first conversation after Glenn was made manager was about Sol's fitness. Would he be ready for the FA Cup semi-final?

Sol was of course desperate to play. He had been injured for the club's last cup semi-final against Everton at Elland Road in 1995 when Spurs lost 4-1. He had watched that match in despair. He was desperate to get on the pitch this time. It was a game Spurs were expected to win. Sol was having trouble with his right ankle. He was in pain, and was no more than fifty per cent fit. But they both knew a half-fit Sol was better on the pitch than in the stands. It was a risk they were both ready to take. Sol, although fiercely against playing when injured, was determined not to miss out. Injections and adrenalin would help. Hoddle decided Sol would play.

•　•　•

Arsenal 2 Tottenham 1, FA Cup semi-final, Old Trafford, 8 April 2001

ARSENAL: Seaman, Silvinho, Adams, Keown, Dixon, Vieira, Parlour, Lauren, Pires, Wiltord, Henry. Subs: Ljungberg, Manninger, Luzhny, Kanu, Cole. Goals: Vieira 33, Pires 74.

TOTTENHAM: Sullivan, Young, Campbell, Perry, Carr, Sherwood, Clemence, Doherty, Ferdinand, Iversen, Rebrov. Subs: Walker, Korsten, Leonhardsen, King, Thelwell. Goals: Docherty 14.

Att: 63,451. Ref: Graham Poll.

Spurs score the opening goal through Doherty but that only seems to force Arsenal into action. On 33 minutes, Vieira equalises after Campbell fouls Parlour – in doing so, the Tottenham skipper gets a yellow card and limps off the field with an ankle injury, for the last time wearing a Spurs shirt. For the Arsenal winner, a fine cross by Wiltord presents Pires with an easy tap-in. Arsene Wenger's team reaches yet another FA Cup final.

The gamble involving Sol hadn't worked. 'I wasn't fit but thought, or rather hoped, I could still influence the game. In the end, the ankle injury I sustained put me out for months. But I still wanted to give a hundred per cent for my team, for my club, for Tottenham. On that front, nothing had changed,' says Sol.

Ledley King came on as sub for Sol. The King is dead. Long live the King. The Spurs fans would be moved to applaud their skipper as he walked dejectedly from the field. It would be the last time they would cheer him. The last time they would see him as their hero. Some of the Spurs fans clapped hesitantly, like they were unsure what was going to happen next. The camera followed his exit as if it knew something no-one else did. The fans still had no idea what was going on. No news is good news, they convinced themselves. But of course, they were in search of forlorn hope. They were all asking what would be the next act of this extraordinary drama.

As Sol took those slow steps, he knew that unless there was some sort of miracle, it was the end. This was going to be his final game for Spurs. All around him, situations and events had stirred in readiness for change and challenges ... and victories and defeats.

A couple of weeks after the game, Sol went to visit Glenn Hoddle at his home in the evening. In secrecy. Away from everyone and everything. It was time to hear Hoddle's take on the future. All started well. Polite.

'Good evening. Everything all right?'

'Fine, just fine,' Sol said, perhaps too quickly.

The meeting turned out to be awkward. Two individuals that like to avoid confrontation. Sol believes Hoddle didn't try hard enough to assure him things would be any different now he was in charge. Hoddle leaned forward, not meeting Sol's eye. 'He didn't give me any reassurance and did nothing to try and keep me at Spurs. His body language was as if he couldn't be bothered. They used to call him "chocolate" – he loved himself so much.' It was as if Hoddle already knew it was too late, that Sol had already left the club. He wasn't wrong. A new beginning, maybe, would be best for him and for Tottenham. They shook hands. Time to go. A slightly awkward handshake. Still with much left unsaid. Sol walked out to his Porsche and turned the ignition. Nothing. The car wouldn't start. Typical! He had to go back and call the AA. Nothing more embarrassing than graciously leaving and then having to go back to the person you've just said goodbye to. He went inside and asked if he could use the phone. 'My car!' he said. He was there for an extra hour in half-silence, drinking cups of coffee. Sol didn't see it as a subliminal sign: *Don't be in such a hurry to leave, stay with Tottenham.* No, he didn't think of it for a moment.

For the rest of the season, Sol watched from the sidelines. The days moved slowly. He hardly noticed anymore the way most observers scrupulously examined the expression on his face. How they reacted to his movement. No-one knew what he was thinking, or what he was planning, right up to his last hours at the club.

The last meeting between all parties took place at the training ground. 'Those present were Daniel Levy, David Pleat, Hoddle, Sky and Sol himself. 'It was amiable. There was no shouting,' Sol says. 'I said the least while Sky represented my feelings. They talked about numbers. If we win this, you will get this bonus; if we finish here, you will get this. I thought, how are we going to reach these goals if we aren't buying any new players? How can we? I do remember as the meeting drew to a close, I said, "I hope this conversation stays within these four walls." We all agreed. Unfortunately, it was repeated in the press that same night, and at that point I definitely knew it was over.'

Lifelong Tottenham fan and soon-to-be FA chairman Lord Triesman says: 'I thought he was a tremendous player and losing him was always going to be distressing. And him going to Arsenal was particularly distressing. But I don't carry any grudge. He was our captain and dominant on the field. I saw the players around him get better. So, when he left, we didn't lose just one player, we lost a few...'

There was no fanfare as Sol pulled out in his Porsche, away from White Hart Lane. He left Tottenham on that last day feeling maudlin, like sitting in a plane, not having to say goodbye, but having no-one to say goodbye to, either.

ARSENAL

'Winning means you're willing to go longer, work harder
and give more than anyone else.'

VINCE LOMBARDI

The weather was surprisingly warm for so early in the morning. Sol woke and immediately sat up. He liked, as he always had, the sense of some real peace and solitude. Today was more important than ever. He wanted to be ready. It was going to be the day he would announce to the football world his transfer; and, the day his family and friends would find out. It was part of his personality to have kept it to himself. Not the odd remark here or there, pandering to the million or so questions he was constantly asked during this time. The only person who knew was his mother and she hadn't taken in the magnitude of his forthcoming move. As long as Sol was happy, she would be. 'Whatever he did was fine with me. He is a good boy,' she says.

Sky arrived at Sol's 1970's Hertfordshire house very early. He was in good time. He hadn't slept well the night before. He had the sort of sleep, when you've been dreaming that you've been dreaming, which comes near to waking. He asked Sol if he was ready. Sol nodded to his agent; he was fine. They didn't hang around. There was no casual morning walk in the large garden, which ran down to a brook. No time to clear one's head. It was all a little tense. 'Come on, let's get going,' said Sky. He would drive Sol to the training ground, where the announcement would take place. He had collected a stack of morning papers.

There were no rumours; nothing had been written. Almost unbelievable in this day and age.

•   •   •

It comes as a surprise. A short journey down the A41 and you're
in Totteridge; an idyllic country backwater a few miles from
Central London. The large family house is welcoming as soon
as you drive onto the gravel. At the back, from the terrace, you
look out on to a large finely cut lawn shaded by oaks, weeping
willows and silver birch. The place has a sense of tranquility,
a calm. On the rare midsummer evenings when all is still,
you can hear the cries of birds and other creatures hidden in
the undergrowth.

Leading up to his transfer, Sol, along with Sky Andrew, met
David Dein and Arsene Wenger at Dein's house twice. He met
Dein on his own a further three times. Because of Sol's longing
for secrecy, they always met very late at night. The first meet-
ing with all four took place at the end of May. 'It was after
Spurs made the announcement that Sol was leaving,' Sky says.

Wenger had noticed Sol's play and stature as soon as he set
eyes on him. 'I had Thierry Henry who used to pass people for
fun. But with Sol, there was a wall. It was as if he was inde-
structible, such a power spread from him. There was something
special there. I wanted him in my side and told David Dein that.'
Dein said that he would try to recruit Sol.

Dein called Sky Andrew and asked if Sol was going to renew
his contract at Tottenham. Just asking; nothing more. He knew
the rules. Sky said he was still undecided. There was still a
chance but Sol would not entertain anything else until he got to
the point where he was moving on. Fine. Dein had the sagacity
to see that it was unlikely he would re-sign. He would leave it
for now but call Sky again once the 2000-01 season was over
and Sol was out of contract. He did. Dein immediately asked
directly what the possibility was of Sol joining Arsenal. 'I don't
know to be honest,' Sky answered. He promised that he would

put the question to Sol. Dein trusted Sky. 'Sky Andrew has the highest quality. One of the real good guys in football. Punctual, discreet and efficient,' Dein says.

Sky put down the phone and rang Sol. He was interested.

Dein and Wenger made a powerful pair. Both as sleek as cats. The perfect blend of a man who knew how to pitch his club as the best in the country and a manager, tactically astute, who spoke the same philosophical language as Sol, with a mentality he installed and reinforced in a player's psyche. 'David Dein made me feel protected. He was going to help and promised to be there for me,' Sol recalls. 'Come to us, he said, and you will be part of our family. We will protect you.' He couldn't have said anything better.

It was a positive first meeting. Dein and Wenger had impressed. They encouraged confidence. They were ambitious for their club and wanted the best. 'I recognised at our first meeting that he was a complex man who didn't show his cards,' Wenger remembers. 'I also met a very deep person. I saw some-one who liked reality, nothing superficial. He wanted to hear the truth. Not compliments. He didn't want to hear from a syco-phant.' They all shook hands firmly. 'I liked him,' says Wenger, 'because from that first meeting and beyond, when he gave his word, I knew he was committed. I have seen so much talent but respect is more linked at the end of the day not with the talent, but with the vision you have of the man. When he says he is committed to go to war for you, I know he will fight for his team until the very end.'

Dein concurs: 'I liked him immediately. He is a deep thinker and I immediately felt fatherly towards him.

'Yes this sounds and feels good,' Sol thinks and is his usual calm self. He isn't going to rush into anything. Never has. They wouldn't be expecting an immediate decision anyway. Dein had told him to take his time. 'Call me if you'd like to meet again to discuss things further. I will be here.' Sol felt their interest was unshakeable; they wanted him. He could see it clearly. He was tempted. Very tempted, even more so when he thought of the most important factor – the quality of Arsenal's players. It is said that if a group of people hang around each other for long enough, the quality they possess will somehow brush off on each individual. In this case, the quality was obvious; yes, what a squad he could be part of. He didn't think for one moment that he was being disloyal to Spurs and their fans. He had given them good and loyal service right up to the end of his contract. They had never tried to sit him down, like Dein and Wenger just did. Told him he was wanted. That he was their future. It was the truth. He's looked back at that time again and again, especially after all the things he's gone through, and says, with hand on heart, that Spurs never said he was truly wanted. Yes, they made him an offer but they never said, 'We love you and want to build a team around you.'

'Whether you believe me or not, they never took that extra yard to keep hold of me.

•   •   •

'Well. What do you think?' Sky asked, as the car drove away from Dein's home after their first meeting.

'Yes, it was good. Very good,' Sol replied.

But first, he had other business to attend to. He was being courted by two of Europe's most famous clubs: Inter Milan and Barcelona were still pursuing him.

•   •   •

He did not fly direct to Milan. He had spoken to a friend, ex-Crystal Palace footballer Dean Gordon, who was going to Monaco to attend an event. 'Come with me to the South of France,' Dean said. Sol agreed. He could see Monaco for the first time and then go on to Milan, a three-hour drive away.

In Monaco, Sol attended the Laureus World Sports Awards at the Grimaldi Forum hosted by Heidi Klum and Gregory Hines. Tiger Woods and Cathy Freeman won the top awards and anyone who was anyone in the city was invited to an event full of bright summer dresses, with sportsmen looking their best. Before he reached the party, he was in a boat in the harbour when a tender passed by and this massive man shouted out across the water: 'Hey, Sol!' 'I thought, who the hell is this guy?' says Sol. Later on he bumped into the same man at the Laureus party. He looked at Sol with intense interest and Sol wasn't sure if he was very interested to introduce himself, very myopic or both. He finally announced he was Paul Kemsley, a new director at Tottenham; just one of life's coincidences. Kemsley had established a property and securities company, Rock Joint Ventures, with the help of ENIC and Spurs chairman Daniel Levy. Rock was an investor and developer of commercial and residential property. Kemsley told Sol to relax, not to worry about 'all this transfer stuff'. He would sort it. *Too late. Far too late*, Sol thought. He felt very calm. He was going somewhere else, to another team, maybe even Inter. Whoever signed him would get one of the best defenders in the world. He had never felt so confident of his talent. Never.

The drive to Milan is uneventful. The weather has remained fine, the roads easy. Finding the Inter corporate offices proves a little more difficult. The GPS at first leads them to the wrong street. Milan is light on traffic; it's the middle of summer and the Milanese have headed to the seaside, but it doesn't seem to help Sol navigate a maze of streets. He stops to ask someone the way. He swears he hears the man laugh. Perhaps he's an AC Milan supporter sending him to the rival offices? They aren't too far away now. But the traffic lights are red on each block. When you're in a hurry, they're always red; when you're not, they're green all the way. A policeman holds up his hand and stands poised in the air, like a yogi. *It's all right for him to look so pleased with himself; he's not in a hurry. Come on*, thinks Sol. *I don't want to be late.* It is the only time he gets flustered, if he thinks he's going to be late. Eventually they get there. Dean leaves Sol and drives away. He might have said, 'Good luck.' Sol doesn't remember.

He takes a deep breath and enters the building. He is immediately asked upstairs. There is no waiting. He is meeting Inter's sporting director, Giuliano Terraneo, and owner, Massimo Morrati, the son of Angelo Morrati who led the famous club through their golden age. Since Massimo took over, he has dreamt of emulating his father's success. In 2001, he had yet to succeed.

Tall, grey haired, bespectacled and in a dark blue suit, Massimo Morrati is charming, a man who makes an impression without even trying. He welcomes Sol. He offers coffee; the best Sol has tasted in any meeting. He then drinks mineral water, which is poured by the owner himself. 'We shall arrange everything,' he says; the royal 'we', as if anything is possible. He speaks of the history of the club, the scudettos they've won, outlining their plans for the future, what action is going to be taken to make his club, *our club*, great again. He encourages confidence. Sol is tempted. He strokes his chin; he hasn't shaved. 'And now you will be taken to our stadium and the training ground.' He makes for the door but not before Morrati has said, 'I hope we meet again.' He acts as if he has just hosted a fine dinner party. *Nice man*, thinks Sol.

It was the duty of Giuliano Terraneo to take Sol to the San Siro. He leads Sol out into a waiting Mercedes, driver at the ready. The ground is not far. Well, it certainly doesn't seem far. This time the lights are green all the way. As the car motors through the city to the stadium, Sol gives a passing thought to East Road, to Tottenham, how he has begun to feel wanted by those he has recently met. *It's not a tough science for owners and managers to understand what their top players need; it's often no more than a little bit of love. Sometimes it's staring them straight in the face.*

'He asked many questions. He wanted to know everything,' remembers Terraneo. Sol is guided round the San Siro like a tourist. After visiting the dressing rooms, media room, and executive boxes, he walks onto the pitch. There isn't a soul in the stadium. No-one marking the pitch, no-one in the stands. A white sun illuminates an utter stillness. He feels totally alone and thinks of the legends who graced this field: the great Italian defender Facchetti, the backbone of La Grande Inter Burgnich, Picci, and Milan's Baresi and Maldini. The imagination fills what the ears cannot hear. Eighty thousand fans chanting for their heroes, a chorus of cat calls for the opposition. He looks up to the very top tier where surely the fans can hardly see anything going on but just live with the chants of fellow supporters. The vast overhang on one side of the stadium shadows half the pitch. Sol walks away from the shadow and is met by the burning sunlight. He's suddenly lost in the moment. And then the sprinklers turn on and he wakes from his daydream.

Inter's training ground is named after Angelo Moratti and is 40km outside the city, in Como. Built in 1961, at the time it represented a new age of football. But now, as Sol concludes his tour of his new suitors at their training facilities, it is beginning to look a little tired. The pool is small, the dressing rooms dilapidated. It gives the impression of an Italian stately home that has been in the family for years and nobody wants to spend to bring it up to date. 'I got the impression as he left that day, it was a straight choice between living and staying in London or moving to Italy and playing for Inter. We were certainly offering more money,' says Terraneo. 'When he made his final decision, he called up directly and thanked me for the time and interest we had showed. I appreciated that.'

•   •   •

Sol flew back to London the following morning. Arsenal had called Sky asking if everything was fine. A follow-up call, nothing more. No talk of money. Too early for that. 'Is there anything more we can do?' Dein wanted to know. Sol said he would go and see Dein that night, this time on his own. He asked Sky to call him. 'Tell him, I'll be over just past midnight.'

'David Dein was the best in the football business: the way he spoke, his understanding of players and how they would work within the club,' Sky says.

Barcelona were still in the hunt. They had been since the beginning of January. They had flown in to London to meet with Sky. They wanted a face-to-face meeting. 'Barcelona made a huge offer. We didn't jump.' Barcelona didn't stop there. They are a club you don't just walk away from; they come back until they get what they want.

Sky's phone rang. He was still at home. It was an agent who was trying to help make the deal. 'Sky,' he said, 'I am here with the owners of Barcelona. Here in the same room.'

'Hola Sky...' The executive's words blurred as if a blanket had been pulled over their heads. 'We want to make the deal for Sol not today, but this morning.' There was still time for that. The call had been made very early. 'We are prepared to increase our offer by fifty per cent. Fifty per cent, Sky! We will even set up an office for you in Barcelona to look after your client; every-thing included, phones, faxes, paper...Your own secretary. But today Sky. It has to be done today.' They hung up. Sky looked at his watch. This was a life-changing deal. These were numbers he hadn't heard before. *This can secure us financially.* He called Sol immediately – forget the time! – and told him what was on the table. 'You must do what you think is right,' Sky said, biting his tongue. He meant it. He wasn't going to try to persuade him to play for Barcelona. Their long friendship allowed Sky to forget his own pocket. He thought of his client first. 'I did. It is sometimes difficult to think of the wealth that deal would have brought me. And I'm not sure even if I had advised him to sign that he would have listened. I will never know. Some agents think of themselves before their clients, but I never did.'

Sol was tempted by the offer but not for long. Perhaps an hour. Call it what you like but fundamentally it was instinctive. Barcelona had consistently been mentioned. The team had shadowed his name. He remembers watching on Sky TV Barcelona beat Valencia 3-2 on the last day of the 2000-01 La Liga season. 'Rivaldo scored this extraordinary hat-trick, his third goal the most incredible overhead kick I have seen, and Gerry Armstrong, one of the commentators that night said:

"Sol Campbell is in the ground and about to sign for Barcelona. He must have been impressed by what he saw." I just laughed at the invention of it all.' Despite that performance, they were not yet the Barcelona of Pep Guardiola; they were a side treading water. Maybe, above all, Sol didn't want to move abroad? New Language. Unknown streets. He denies this. 'Moving to Europe held no threat,' he says and takes a pause, before making what sounds like a formal statement: 'My decision was essentially about the Arsenal team, the squad of players. What trophies they would win. Whatever happens in your career, no-one can take trophies away from your record.'

He turned Barcelona down. What about Inter Milan? There were rumours that the Brazilian Ronaldo was going to leave (he departed a year later for Real Madrid); the club had finished fifth in Serie A and had been knocked out of the qualifying rounds of the Champions League. What was expected to be a short siesta for the Italian giants had turned into a lengthy doze. He didn't see them waking up for a while. He turned the Italians down.

But even then there wasn't that rush of blood to quickly sign for a new club. He knew his standing. He carried no fear; his talent was his stock. He knew someone somewhere would want him. But all the while he couldn't get the Arsenal team, their squad of players, out of his mind; he kept returning to their football skill, what it had been like playing against them. They were good and would only get better. He knew it deep inside.

Sol met David Dein alone. Dein knew that for Sol to want to meet again meant the transfer was not far off from becoming a reality. He didn't know who was competing for his signature. He didn't ask and it wasn't brought up in their conversation. This time the two men walked around Dein's garden into the early hours of the morning. 'We hardly sat still. We generally got up and walked around for hours talking about everything, from football to his upbringing,' says Dein. The day had begun windy but, by the early hours of the morning, the wind had abated, although there was still a slight rustle in the surrounding foliage. The moon cast a spotlight that seemed to follow the two figures as they moved from one end of the garden to the other. It was their only light other than the faint glow from the kitchen. If you had been standing only metres behind, the conversation would have been indistinct. Like musical instruments heard from outside the concert hall, the two seemed to have a resonance more evolved than just language. Sol felt he was being understood probably for the first time in his life.

• • •

The following day he returns to Newham. When in doubt, he always went back to his roots. He walks his neighbourhood. He visits West Ham Park with his mum. It feels good and safe to be by her side. He talks and his mother listens. Measuring things up; this is good, this is bad. He looks at the strip of grass he used to play on; the tennis courts he went straight to after school in search of those lost tennis balls. He chuckles to himself. On the wall he used to practise against for hour upon hour, he notices a loose brick and thinks for a moment someone may have had a secret hidden inside. He notices a fly land on his hand. It annoys him. He wants to slap at it, yet doesn't want it to die. In the same way at times he wanted to sleep, yet didn't want to be unawake; to think, yet not want his brain to work. He looks at a group of kids sitting on the grass in a circle sharing a laugh and intermittently at the fly, which isn't moving, stationary as if it has nowhere to go...then suddenly, it flies off into the blue sky. *It's time to step off the ride.* To somehow let go of all that pressure that has built up in the previous months.

They walk out of the park towards his childhood home. As he carefully leads his mum into East Road, he thinks of his last days at Tottenham. He is no longer happy. He had some good times, some of the best of times, but things have changed, or perhaps have never changed. That's it. *They have remained the same.* Their ambition may never match his. His face is a discord of disappointment, fatigue, and resignation with perhaps a tinge of sorrow. *What will the fans think?* But as he asks the question, his sense of sadness fades. *It's been done before, hasn't it?* Pat Jennings made the move. He didn't know of much fuss with that. In fact, Jennings was still a hero. He had seen him at White Hart Lane. He was admired. Still loved. *It won't be different for me.* He is sure some of the fans will not be happy, but eventually they will understand. *Won't they?* Yes! *Hey stop giving yourself such a hard time. It has been done before. You have an extraordinary opportunity. Lighten up! The world is yours. This is the best, most exciting time of your professional life. You will be joining one of the best clubs in the world with some of the best players.*

His mind is made up. He starts to dial a number on his mobile. He gets straight through. 'Sky, make the deal. I've decided. It's Arsenal.'

•　　•　　•

The final meeting with Dein and Wenger was again held at a late hour. The atmosphere was relaxed and, of course, welcoming. These were his new bosses. They had got their man. But Sol still needed another face-to-face to confirm everything. He could still pull out, couldn't he? *'We must be willing to pay a price for freedom.'* What he didn't know on that day, at that time, was how big a price he was going to have to pay.

They sat once again in the living room on a sunken sofa. Dein spoke of the players they had signed and the ones they were still pursuing. Van Bronckhorst and Inamoto would sign before the start of the new season. But they wanted to sign more Englishmen. A month before they had signed Francis Jeffers from Everton for £8 million. 'Francis Jeffers...' and Sol was about to say, 'I'm not sure about him,' but he kept it to himself. There was no point; the signing had already been made. 'Perhaps they saw it in my face but I felt it wasn't the time to start to advise on new signings.' He can tell the quality of a striker, though. It's his trade to assess the strikers he is going to face. 'Jeffers was a good player but he lacked something. I didn't find him that dangerous. I intrinsically knew he wasn't going to maintain his ability at the top. Rooney for instance, is strong, works hard, and has the imagination to change things. You're never too sure what he's going to do next. I have to be on my top game to deal with him. You could tell he was going the whole way. Shearer was the same. He had a fantastic work ethic, strength and movement, shot. He had this habit of nudging the defender as the ball was coming towards him; a slight push, a twist to give him space. And with that space, he was lethal.'

The manager spoke of how he saw Sol's role in the side. Wenger was methodical and thoughtful. Each time they spoke, Sol was more impressed by his knowledge, his philosophy. He found reassurance in his tactical knowhow and felt the Frenchman's authority in his life would have a positive effect on his game.

By now it is three o'clock in the morning. Dein's son Gavin walks in after a Saturday night out. Dein asks Sol if he is hungry. He is. He always is. Gavin prepares French toast. How appropriate. Every member of Dein's family has made him feel welcome. As the offering is placed in front of him, he feels a tremendous warmth. Like the blossoming flower on spring's arrival, or the encouraging word, the helping hand, given at the perfect moment; it is worth more than anything that has gone before. A simple act, which resonates profoundly. *This feels like home already.*

•   •   •

Only two people knew about Sol's pending move: his mother and his agent. He spent three days before the announcement away with close friends on a stag party in Portugal, but nothing was said. Nothing was given away by words or nervous gestures.

He behaved like a spy without secrets. There was no clue anything out of the ordinary was about to happen. He was in a good mood and spoke excitedly about the future. Even during late night gossip with a little drink inside, nothing was divulged. 'It's amazing that he didn't tell a friend, even the day before. Saying something like "Be prepared, tomorrow there will be a bomb!"' remarks Wenger.

Sol simply says, 'That's what makes me different.' Beneath a surface of normality there often lurks a far more intriguing world. Imagine the thrill of the double secret: your secret from your world at the forthcoming signing; their secret from their world that you are about to sign. All being done, what's more, under an assumed secrecy.

Wilhelmina was told hours before. He hadn't told her that day in West Ham Park. He waited. It was a simple phone call just before Sky arrived. Her reaction was calm, not fully understanding the magnitude of the decision, or of what was she was being told: 'If that's best, Sulzeer. I have faith in you that whatever decision you make will be the right one.'

'I need to be appreciated,' he told his friend Edwin, a couple of days after the announcement. Edwin listened and after the one conversation, he understood why Sol had made the decision. He was supportive and would be in the future. 'It was difficult, and yes, I was taunted about being his friend and a Spurs fan. And when I tried to rationalise the decision, many didn't want to listen, but he was proved right. Sol has always been someone who surprises people and I learned early on never to underestimate or second-guess him.'

•　　•　　•

Sol is in a car destined for the Arsenal training ground at London Colney. As he heads round the M25, his mind is facing a host of last-minute questions. All questions that have been asked before, but as the announcement of his transfer is nearing, the doubts magnify and all he is trying to do is put a simple tick of the affirmative in the appropriate box.

He looks down at his feet: polished black shoes, tightly laced. He sees his reflection in the window. His reflection gazes back

at him. *Have I done the right thing?* He lifts his head and looks
out to his left. He notices a van in the lane alongside. He looks
at its logo. It has the words SOL CROWN printed on its side. He
smiles inside, and has a rare feeling in his bones that it is all
going to go well. 'I like symbols. They have guided me all my
life. I recognise them. By seeing those words at that time, it
gave me the reassurance I was on the right path.' It was a collision of thoughts with a chance external event. His shoulders
begin to feel more relaxed. They are now minutes from their
destination. He gently clenches his fist. *Come on! Let's do this!*

They pull in at the training ground. Sean O'Connor, the manager of the training facility, is waiting at the gate. He has been
told that a new signing is arriving with his agent. 'The boss
[Arsene] didn't tell me who it was going to be,' he looks back
now. 'And then I saw this Range Rover draw up and recognised
Sky Andrew. I ordered the gate to open and let the car pass
through. Then I saw who was sitting beside him. It was extraordinary. It was the Tottenham captain. I think I just said, "Hello
Sol" as if we had known each other for years. It was the biggest
surprise. Yes, the biggest shock! I don't think it could ever be
repeated.' Sean gets into the back of the car and directs it to the
side near to the manager's office. The agent and player are led
through without anyone seeing them. The secret has remained
secret; some would say impossible in the modern world.

Wenger is waiting for his prize capture. There is little better
than getting hold of a player you admire. The manager knows
he has a powerful man with great pace, one of the best defenders in the world. 'I knew we had someone very special who had
a fantastic ability to win the challenge.'

The atmosphere is light. Conversation spasmodic. An early
morning feel. Sol begins to relax. He has coffee and biscuits. He
takes in where he is sitting. Looking out of the open window, he
senses the fresh air over the manicured football pitches.

'Come, 'tis not too late to see a newer world.'

'This was the real thing. Years ahead of Tottenham. Better
than Inter Milan. It's a beautiful place. It's how football should

be at the top level,' Sol says enthusiastically. 'I was still a little nervous but after the drive I felt better, excited to get on with it. I'm never too comfortable facing the press. I just like to get on and play top football.'

The announcement is planned for midday. Time passes. Time waits for no-one but as he's on his third coffee he believes that cliché might not be true. It is like someone has tampered with his watch. Time itself has started to act strangely. And when the announcement is made, it will go berserk. David Dein joins them and is going to make the introduction to the press. He was looking forward to this. He knew what he was going to do.

Sean returns to the office and says, 'They are ready.' He leads Sol, Sky, Dein and Wenger through to the press room. Dein is adjusting his tie, Wenger straightening his jacket while Sol, who has remained calm, rubs his thumb and little finger in slow motion. How Sean had wanted to tell the waiting journalists what they were about to witness. He knew the tranquil mood with stifled yawns was about to be blown apart by instant pandemonium. There is a smallish turnout. The journalists presume they are there to see the introduction of the Ipswich Town goalkeeper Richard Wright. Nothing to set the pulse racing there.

They pass no-one as they walk into the press room. Sky nods at his client. He will watch the action from the wings. Out to the front walk Wenger and Dein; Sol will come out when called. The drama continues. There is a touch of showbiz about the whole scene. *Touch of showbiz? This IS showbiz.* Dein speaks first, making the introduction. 'Thank you, gentleman.' Pause. 'I would like to introduce our latest signing.' Wenger and Dein look left...

Out walks Sol Campbell. From the slow beating of the drums to cymbals crashing all around. The gathered jump out of their skins. They say the reaction in the room could be heard in St Albans. More likely, throughout the country. 'Before a question was asked, I saw every journalist in the room pick up his mobile to call his news desk. There was disbelief. I have never seen anything like it before...or since,' Sean O'Connor says.

Sol Campbell, the Spurs skipper, has joined Arsenal. It is a huge shock. It takes a moment for the journalists to gather themselves. 'I could feel their surprise, the shuffling in their seats,' Sol says. Questions are finally asked. Sol answers diplomatically and remains, not for the first time in his life, the calmest man in the room. 'I was very keen to stay in the Premiership; it was important to me. Sven-Goran Eriksson, the England coach, is here and the majority of games he sees are here in England,' he says, scanning the few members of the press. *If I were abroad I might have been forgotten*, he thinks to himself while answering the question. But why Arsenal? 'There were a number of factors I had to go through, but in the end it was overwhelming for Arsenal. I've made my decision and I'm happy. I just hope everyone respects that decision.' The word 'hope' is not emphasised, the question isn't properly answered; just the thoughts of someone eager to step into a new chapter of his life.

Wenger sums up his joy in capturing one of the world's finest defenders: 'For me, he is the best. I felt we could not compete on a financial basis with the top clubs but we could give him a football challenge.'

Sky is watching everything out of sight. 'I just remember no-one really knowing what to do when Sol walked out. There was mayhem for two minutes. Phone calls, cameramen trying to work out where to point the camera. It was an amazing scene.'

'But why Arsenal?' Sol is asked again.

This time he is more clear. 'They are a fantastic club and have a great manager and the setup is geared to win. I want to be here and I'm here now.' Dein and Wenger instinctively smile.

'How have you managed the pressure of the last months when it seems many around you were being affected by it?'

He replies without pause. 'I have kept my head when other people around me were losing theirs.'

When the news conference ends, the gathered break out into an almost apologetic applause; no-one is quite sure how to react.

•   •   •

The manager and his new signing walked out into the sunlight and posed for photographs. Sol was in dark suit and white shirt; Wenger in a grey blue suit with the widest of shoulders and polka dot tie, his hair parted to the right, matted, thick. They shook hands. Posing like two good friends, Sol and Wenger gave their best Colgate smiles.

As he walked with Sky back to the car, Sol felt relief and had a glow of pride. His heart was set on a team that would win things. He knew he'd found it.

'You all right?' Sky asked his client.

'Yes,' Sol replied. Then he took a long pause and Sky held his breath, unsure what the next part of his response was going to be. He felt responsible. He had stood by his friend, his client, but, even with the million words they had shared over this decision, he was still unsure of Sol's innermost feelings. Finally Sol, with a knowing look in his eyes, said to Sky, 'This is the right decision.'

As the car drove away from the training ground, he felt like he was floating on an ocean of calm. He glimpsed back over his shoulder. *Today, professionally, I've been reborn.*

• • •

'When I first played against Sol, I thought, who the hell is this? He's strong, fast and has instinct. Thank God he's now on my side,' says Thierry Henry.

Sol felt immediately at home. He was happy. He had a minor injury so it was arranged that he would take the next four days off in Sardinia to get into shape before all the Arsenal players reported back for pre-season. So, while one half of North London buzzed and the other half was fuming, Sol was out of the country.

On his return, the training was intense but relaxed. He enjoyed it. 'It [Arsenal] was all about positioning, timing, getting fit and about getting the best out of everyone. Basically, don't waste a second on the pitch. We played eight-a-sides –

tighter, less time on the ball, think quick, don't be lazy, move it quicker. The idea was to solve problems before they got to you, and then when you do have space in a competitive game the time on the ball seems longer, a gift.

'At training we played more across the pitch, more side-to-side. If we did play up and down, which was rare, it was more of a passing game. If you were playing forward you could have a third touch. The emphasis was on controlled passing moving forward.'

It was a good time in his life. He was testing his skills all the time. 'It was my dream to play on the same side with some of the best players in the world. Training with them every day naturally raised my game. They tested me every day and because of it I got better. There was hardly a session when something extraordinary didn't happen, where I'd watch in awe at a certain skill. I had to up my level. They would stretch you. There was no point going into training and feeling you could take it easy. There was no hiding place. That decision was taken from you. You would have to give a hundred per cent. Maybe you wouldn't go into a full tackle but you always had to be switched on to deal with the likes of Dennis Bergkamp, who was very strong and so gifted. People don't think that Dennis had such strength but believe me he was one of the strongest I played with or against. Kanu was also strong and inventive. He could do something out of the ordinary. It was a privilege to play with such players.'

Sol's first game for his new club came in a pre-season friendly in Austria, when he took to the pitch for the last twenty minutes against Roma. 'It was a special moment for me,' he recalls. He'd felt unfulfilled at Tottenham, and it was only now, in this new setup, that he realised how unhappy he had been. 'I knew I was talented and I was always thinking about the game and wanting to improve,' says Sol. 'I wanted to be in a club whose ethos was about training and bettering oneself. They had that and it was the perfect environment for me.' Wenger had promised that on their very first meeting, and Sol felt vindicated. 'He showed me things I knew I had inside me but I didn't have the platform on which to show it.' He was at last beginning to fit into his skin.

•   •   •

Sol made his Arsenal Premier League debut on 18 August 2001 away against Middlesborough. The Arsenal side that day was: Seaman, Cole, Adams, Campbell, Vieira, Pires, Ljungberg, Lauren, Parlour, Wiltord, and Henry. It was an easy 4-0 win for the Gunners, despite Ray Parlour's sending off in the second half. Parlour said afterwards, 'A few lads knew Sol from England. That helped him to settle without any problems. There was a lot made of him coming from Tottenham but that didn't phase him one bit. He slotted straight in and was confident about what he wanted to do at Arsenal. I remember him doing very well in that first game. Shame I couldn't have stayed with Sol on the pitch until the end. But it was great to see him become one of Arsenal's all-time greats.'

The players were welcoming. 'He was quiet at first but it wasn't long before he opened up,' says Patrick Vieira. 'We could see very quickly he was focused, calm and concentrated. He gave off a sense of knowing what he wanted.'

Sol was glad the Arsenal fans got behind him. 'I felt they had the attitude of let's see what he can do, what he's made of. And when I put on the shorts for the first time, it felt good. It felt really good. I understand that must be hard for Spurs supporters to hear, but I was in a good place and felt comfortable with everything that went with it. The club seemed to do things properly; they were fair. They never tried to pull the wool over my eyes. If they wanted to make it work, they would find a way of making it work. They had really good people who cared about football.'

It seemed he had finally realised he was simply a happier footballer, who had left behind the problems of playing for Tottenham. He was sounding optimistic, something his new team-mates soon came to appreciate.

'I thought he was crazy when he first arrived,' says Thierry Henry. 'Here's the Tottenham club captain, joining Arsenal! But if there was person who could make it work, it was Sol. We now had in our team one of the best centre-backs in the world!'

The team was gelling and his connection with the manager was growing by the day. He speaks of Wenger with the utmost respect. 'Wenger had a German mentality, more like a bookworm. Sometimes you need that intelligence, but you need the balance of a warm side. He has his own way of talking and approaching people, slightly reserved. I knew I could learn from him.'

•   •   •

Sol liked Highbury; he liked its sense of history. The team bus drawing up to the main doors of the East Stand; the players stepping out onto the pavement. The fans waiting, all on display in red and white scarves staring, in awe of their idols, autograph books in hand. 'Sign here! Sol, sign here!' Sol gives an unconfident nod at the recognition; his shyness has never left him, even though he now has to deal with it daily. 'I've never felt that comfortable being famous; I'd prefer to be invisible, unnoticed. I always have.'

Then, into the marble entrance on the way to the dressing rooms, past the bronze statue of Herbert Chapman, a moderniser of the game who brought in a new form of training as well as championing floodlighting and numbered shirts. He was Arsenal's manager from 1925 to 1934 who, in his time, brought the previously trophy-less club an FA Cup and two First Division titles. He died at the age of 55 from pneumonia but left, as a legacy, a club that would be the dominant force in English football in the 1930s, winning five league titles in the decade. 'I loved the tradition,' Sol says.

The Highbury pitch was one of the smallest in the league. He remembers the first time he walked into the stadium as an Arsenal player. The smell of cut grass, the sprinklers on like at the San Siro a few weeks before. He walked from the North Bank to the Clock End and back again, taking in his new home. He liked to do that, to check out the space. *I want to play here.* It seemed so different to when he came here with Tottenham; much more stately now. Two workmen were putting up advertising hoardings. Someone once said, 'You can understand the ideals of a club by its advertisements.' Maybe that quote comes from another decade. Nowadays, it's all about the big brands, not the local butcher or neighbourhood Greek restaurant.

Sol believes the tightness of the pitch didn't really suit Arsenal's style. 'I think if we had been playing at the Emirates with that team, we would have won even more matches. At Highbury, the opposition could almost cover their mistakes. We loved playing away because we had more room, a bigger space. There was a freedom, with another four or five yards on either side. If you were really good at retaining the ball and good at the counter-attack, you could kill off teams. Our players were suited to that.'

The atmosphere and tradition at Highbury would motivate any Arsenal player. The bars, even when cleaned, smelt like the morning after the night before. Cigarette ash littered the floor like confetti; there was a lingering odour of spilt beer. Thousands upon thousands of people would shout from every corner of the ground, the noise converging on the pitch. Despite his reservations about Highbury suiting the Arsenal way, Sol knew he could feed off the crowd in that cauldron. 'If the atmosphere was going, you could feed off the energy. In big games, you could feel the intense pressure from the crowd, which I loved, as it was all about the game. The tightness of Highbury, where I could literally see the faces and almost catch the half-conversations, made it feel for me like a theatre. I was there to perform.'

By mid-November, Arsenal had lost twice in the Premier League, both games at home. Their Champions League campaign had been stuttering. 'I don't remember much of it,' Sol stiffens, as if to wipe the stain from the memory. But his new club and his rediscovered self-belief were about to face their biggest test yet, just four months after his headline-making transfer.

• • •

Tottenham 1 Arsenal 1, White Hart Lane, Saturday 17 November 2001

TOTTENHAM: Sullivan, Perry, King, Richards, Taricco, Freund (Davies 85), Anderton, Poyet, Ziege, Ferdinand (Rebrov 70), Sheringham. Subs not used: Thatcher, Beasant, Bunjevcevic. Goals: Poyet 90.

ARSENAL: Wright, Lauren, Campbell, Keown , Cole, Parlour, Vieira, Grimandi, Pires, Bergkamp (Kanu 70), Wiltord. Subs not used: Tavlaridis, Ljungberg, Van Bronckhorst, Taylor. Goals: Pires 81.

Att: 36,049. Ref: Jeff Winter.

In typical frantic and fevered North London derby, the home side dominate but can't finish off their chances. On his first game back at White Hart Lane since his transfer to Arsenal, Sol Campbell is prominent as he and his fellow defenders face an onslaught in the first half. Late in the second period, an Arsenal counter-attack sees Pires' first-time curler from 25 yards beat goalkeeper Sullivan, only for man of the match Gus Poyet's final-minute volley to slip through Wright's hands and gain a deserved point for Tottenham.

Arsene Wenger made up his mind early in the week that Sol would play on the Saturday. 'When you are manager you think, do I play this player or not, and you come to a conclusion. If you don't do it now, next time it will be the same. Then you give credit to the idea that he did something wrong, and then, as well, you punish your own team for not playing one of the strong players. I thought it was an important hurdle for him to overcome, and I thought the sooner the better.'

Sol had spent the night before the game in the team hotel. The atmosphere was convivial, with Dennis Bergkamp and Patrick Vieira making jokes at Sol's expense about his return to

White Hart Lane. 'It helped,' Sol recalls. That may have lightened the mood, but no-one knew exactly what was waiting for him, not even the swarms of tabloid press hacks looking at every angle for a story.

He had spent the week meticulously planning how he was going to deal with the game. 'I felt I was going to war. I knew I had to put my armour on, not only because of the team in front of me but the thousands watching and shouting. I knew I had to protect myself.' He took solace in the experiences from his early life. All the time he had spent alone was now going to help. He was never bored or at a loss being by himself; it had given him the discipline to remove himself mentally from the chaotic noise shadowing his everyday life.

The Saturday was overcast. Sol woke easily. He shaved, washed, dressed almost mechanically. For breakfast he had cereal and a cup of black coffee with one sugar. At first he sat alone, but was soon joined by team-mates Henry, Bergkamp and Vieira. They read the papers and talked about nothing much, nothing that Sol can remember now. He'd had a good night's sleep and managed not to think too much about the day ahead. 'I knew what was coming; it was my emotions that had to be sorted. If they get out of control, your game goes and then you have nothing.'

Arsene Wenger didn't say anything to him that morning. He didn't feel he needed to make a fuss. But the vitriol that was waiting on Tottenham High Road and in the stadium took even the manager by surprise. 'For some players, supporters feel they are a part of them,' says Wenger. 'It is more difficult when a player comes from out of your ranks; you give him a chance and then he goes.'

When Arsenal's coach pulled up within a block from the ground, the crowd started to build. Six, seven, ten deep. A mob was baying at the Arsenal bus, a Dickensian mass waiting at the gallows. The dark coach windows shielded the players' faces from the staring, cursing fans of their North London neighbours. 'When I saw them carrying signs with Judas written on them,

I thought, oh hell, this will be a real test for Sol, but I tried to treat it as normal,' says Wenger.

The Arsenal players remained calm. Many had played at Tottenham before, but this was different. 'I remember arriving at the game, bricks and bottles being thrown at me, but the first thing was the roar and when we reached the clock it was like a sea of people. They wanted blood,' recalls Sol.

As the coach moved towards the front of the stadium, the police pushed back the crowd, packed together so close they could sniff the dirt on each other's necks; now ten, twenty deep. Faces were grotesque with fury. 'There were banners directed at me. I heard the shouting, the insults. It took a lot of energy, it took a lot of guts and heart to get through those moments and what was about to happen.' He continued: 'I couldn't fuck up, I had no choice. I had to hit the bullseye,' and then he recited the words his father used to say to him. 'You have one chance. Grab it!'

He was prepared, mentally strong. He was ready to take on the world.

•　　•　　•

Sol had been sitting towards the back of the coach. His face was plain with no expression. He was alone in his thoughts. As the coach pulled up outside the ground, he was the last off. No-one spoke to him. His team-mates knew instinctively that he had to deal with this in his own way. The Turkish doorman welcomed him back with a warm smile. 'Welcome back, Sol.' 'It was Muzzy Izzet's cousin,' recalls Sol, from his earlier days at White Hart Lane.

The team walked down the corridor to their dressing room. Sol was at the back, the groom at a shotgun wedding, looking at, half-smiling at, dozens of faces he recognised so well and yet none of which were now familiar. When he reached the dressing rooms, he stopped for an instant. It was always going to happen, wasn't it? Sol went to open the Spurs door. A steward pointed to the visitor's dressing room. 'I think you are meant to be going into that one, sir.'

Sol realised he was sitting in the away dressing room for the very first time. He laid out his kit meticulously; not his team shirt, though. He would put that on just moments before leaving for kick-off. For now, he put on a blue sweatshirt and looked to the exit. He was going out for a twenty-minute warm-up.

'I had planned how I was going to do this. It took all my experiences from my life before, how I had been brought up, what had happened to me. Going onto my old pitch I felt... Nervous. Nerves had already been there, but I'd had to control them. There's a fine line between nerves and being too relaxed. You needed nerves but I didn't allow them to overtake me completely. You almost feel heavy, with jelly-like legs. The whole crowd was probably looking at me. I felt that. This was what I agreed with myself that I was going to do: I was going to cover the pitch and run a full rectangle. Get every single bit out there, don't warm-up away from it, go to it, take it all in and absorb every single ounce of it. I wanted to feel it, for it to hit me big time. I remember seeing black faces, white faces, Asian faces, and people almost frothing at the mouth, grown men with their little kids. I wanted to feel every single bit. I didn't want to wait until kick-off when I was on the pitch and then get the full barrage. I wanted to absorb it, get above it, and adjust to it. That was a conscious decision by me.'

'I remember the day like it was yesterday. I remember his eyes. They were so motivated,' says Patrick Vieira. 'We wanted to win the game for Sol.'

The team had a final debrief from Wenger. 'I spoke about how important it was to win this game and to get the focus just on that, and basically to be professional and focus on what was important.' Wenger did not show a flicker of emotion to what was happening out there. 'It was a football game that we wanted to win and I wanted Sol to be a part of that. Sometimes, when you say to a guy don't make a special occasion of it, you make it special,' says Wenger.

The two teams walked on to the pitch together. Sol looked quickly from left to right, striding boldly forward to take the afternoon into his own hands. Within the first minutes, he made his presence felt. He swooped, swooshed and smacked the ball away from Spurs' Les Ferdinand. It was an extraordinary tackle. 'I had some apprehension but after five minutes, when he played his first ball, I thought okay, he will be alright,' says Wenger. 'I knew that, on the day, it created such adrenalin in his body and I trusted in him, because somehow this guy is extremely proud and he will not fall on a day when everyone looks at him.'

One action summed up Sol Campbell, his game, his character. At half-time, a team-mate of Les Ferdinand said, 'Hey Les, he was trying to get you.'

Ferdinand shook his head. 'No, he wasn't. That was just Sol. Making sure that everyone knew he meant business.'

As the second half got underway, Sol felt he could take on anything and everything. Nothing was going to stand in his way. Then a moment that would haunt him forever. 'I went up for a corner late in the second half,' he recalls. 'I was looking at the faces in the Spurs end. Then I caught sight of him. A knife to my heart. Behind the goal, I knew that face. My older brother. Tony. A Spurs fan, in among the slurry of bile violating my name.' Sol pauses, almost choking, his voice neutered. *Who are you? What are you doing?* 'I couldn't believe he was there.' The two have rarely spoken since. Sol could not understand why his brother continued to go to the games when he was surrounded by so much HATE. 'I heard he had been going all season. I was...' He struggles now to find the words. 'I mean, we are brothers. We are blood.'

The game ended 1-1. As the final whistle was blown, Sol walked away from the Park Lane End towards the tunnel. The Spurs players shook his hand, Steffen Freund gave him a hug and Glenn Hoddle appeared in his line of vision. The Spurs manager acknowledged the ex-captain; he recognised what Campbell had been through, and admired his performance and the dignity that went with it.

Wenger said, 'At the end of the day, you cannot assist him with every ball he plays. He has to do his own job, inside of himself. On that day I saw him change; he became different.'

He didn't give any post-match interviews. His performance had spoken a million words. As the Arsenal team prepared to leave the ground, Sol left the dressing room and took a step outside into the empty stadium. All was peace again. He looked at the empty rows. There was an urge to cry out to anyone, to anything. He opened his mouth but there was no sound.

'Come on Sol. It's time to get going,' one of the Arsenal staff called.

Sol looked at White Hart Lane once more and turned away to leave the ground. *Thank God that's over.*

•   •   •

Arsenal 2 Chelsea 0, FA Cup Final, Millennium Stadium Cardiff, 4 May 2002

ARSENAL: Seaman, Lauren, Campbell, Adams, Cole, Wiltord (Keown 90), Parlour, Vieira, Ljungberg, Bergkamp (Edu 72), Henry (Kanu 81).Subs Not Used: Dixon, Wright. Goals: Parlour (70), Ljungberg (80).

CHELSEA: Cudicini, Melchiot (Zenden 76), Gallas, Desailly, Babayaro (Terry 45), Gronkjaer, Lampard, Petit, Le Saux, Gudjohnsen, Hasselbaink (Zola 68). Subs Not Used: De Goey, Jokanovic.

Att: 73,963. Ref: Mike Riley.

After a dire first half in which the two London heavyweights trade blows to little effect, two stunning goals by Ray Parlour and Freddie Ljungberg seal the game for the Gunners. Parlour's curling right foot effort from 25 yards into the top corner, and Ljungberg's surging run and finish from the halfway line ten minutes later, mean Arsenal complete part one of their bid to be 2002 League and Cup Double champions.

The fourth of May to the eighth of May 2002: four days that would prove to be the most satisfying and successful of Sol Campbell's football career.

Sol has fond memories of his team's FA Cup final victory over London rivals Chelsea. 'I played centre-back alongside Tony Adams that afternoon which was really good because with England I always played with him in a three at the back. Mind you, it was a bit harsh on Martin Keown who had played in most of the FA Cup games that season. But Tony was one of the best defenders England has ever produced. I respected him. He was not the most naturally gifted player but he overcame his weaknesses. His passing was not the best but he was dogged and his positional sense was exceptional. His nickname of Captain Courageous was spot-on. He had a great presence and desperately wanted to win. He wasn't the fastest of players but he saw things before anyone else, and made up for a lack of speed by thinking two paces ahead of the opposition. He was a good talker with everyone. He was Mr Arsenal and it was a privilege to win the League and Cup double in the same team and on the same pitch.'

The Millennium Stadium in Cardiff on Cup day was an exultant carnival. 'I hadn't heard noise like it,' says Sol. 'It was a magical day. It was tough opposition; Chelsea were a great side. We were rocking and rolling, the atmosphere was amazing. The stadium was designed acoustically because the Welsh like to sing. The volume the crowd reached was even more than at Wembley, as it had been designed to rebound and amplify. So whenever there was singing, you couldn't hear anything else. It was just an incredible atmosphere. I really liked playing in Cardiff and, of course, to win. Winning the FA Cup is epic. It is very special in the hearts of the English people. To be a part of that history is incredible, it will live on forever.' Sol's voice cracked, as if he might at any moment burst into tears. Patrick Vieira and Tony Adams lifted the cup as the golden evening sun glistened over the stadium. It was a very happy day for all Gunners fans.

• • •

Manchester United 0 Arsenal 1, Old Trafford, 8 May 2002

MANCHESTER UTD: Barthez, Phil Neville, Blanc, Brown, Silvestre, Scholes, Keane, Veron (Van Nistelrooy 58), Giggs, Solskjaer, Forlan (Fortune 68). Subs Not Used: Carroll, O'Shea, Wallwork.

ARSENAL: Seaman, Lauren, Keown, Campbell, Cole, Ljungberg, Parlour, Vieira, Edu, Wiltord, Kanu (Dixon 89). Subs Not Used: Jeffers, Bergkamp, Wright, Stepanovs. Goals: Wiltord (55).

Att: 67,580. Ref: Paul Durkin.

Arsenal survived a ferociously fought first-half in which United battled sometimes illegally to gain a foothold in the match, before a mistake by Silvestre allowed Ljungberg a shot which Barthez saved magnificently, only for Wiltord to steer the ball home. The Gunners' resilience proved enough to seal the league title and add another Double to their previous triumphs in 1971 and 1998.

On Wednesday 8 May, Arsenal went up to Manchester and Old Trafford needing a point from their last two games to clinch the league title: 'It was a sensational time for me, one of the great nights of my career. Because of the pressure I was under, I could not fail. I felt I had been tracked from the day I signed. I was part of a fantastic team and I just loved it. To win the Premiership, and in Manchester, was sensational. You know you're the best team in the land.'

Sylvain Wiltord was the hero of the hour. Sol says, 'He was a great striker, a fox in the box; quiet for a lot of the game, and then suddenly popping up from nowhere to be in the right place at the right time to score. He did it that day. Those type of strikers are difficult to defend against.' When the final whistle went, Sol strode forward and hugged his team-mates, his head held high as if this moment was always meant to be. Could life get any better than this? The Old Trafford crowd clapped graciously. 'The Manchester United fans behaved with real class.'

The Premier League trophy was presented at Highbury on Saturday 11 May, the last day of the season. It was the final game for Arsenal stalwarts Tony Adams and Lee Dixon. Dixon says of Sol: 'He was quiet in the dressing room. I didn't get to know him and I don't think anyone really did.'

Two goals by Thierry Henry help Arsenal secure a 4-3 victory over Everton and the title celebrations begin in earnest. As the Premier League trophy is presented to him, club captain Tony Adams holds it aloft in a way that he has done before. He passes it along the line. Sol gently places both hands on the silver trophy, picks it up and then abandons a cautious approach, shaking it with pure joy. 'Adulation, fulfillment, recognition and redemption. I felt all those on that day. I also felt a little sad that I had to go through extreme pressure to get to this point. But ultimately, I was happy that my instinct to join Arsenal had been proved right,' Sol says.

The Highbury crowd gathers in a crescendo of cheers and applause. Sol is witnessing one of the great scenes of his life. The team goes on its lap of honour. Martin Keown passes Sol the trophy. 'Go on, Sol,' he says, pointing to the press box, 'Show them! Show them what you did!' Sol smiles and lifts the trophy again.

The next day, a Sunday, Arsenal celebrated their double triumph in an open-top bus parade through the streets of north London. The victory celebrations reached a climax at Islington town hall, where the excited thousands heard Sol and his teammates thank their supporters. 'It was an unbelievable scene,' says Sol. 'I will never forget to my dying moments the joy of our fans that day. It's what makes being a footballer so special.'

He felt exhausted. The pressure of his first season for Arsenal had been ever present. 'I was so pleased. I'm a team player, not every footballer is, but I am and it gave me a pure joy that my team were champions. It was almost like I'd found another family.' And he means it. His words are passionate and moving.

'When I got home that night I broke down. I thought of everyone who helped me get through. People like Pat Rice and those behind the scenes who were an important part of my journey, and who had put their heart and soul on the line. I thanked them out loud.'

Arsenal lost just three matches in the Premier League in the 2001-02 season, all at home. Their league record was: Played 38, Won 26, Drew 9, Lost 3. 'To be a part of that history is incredible,' says Sol. 'It will live on forever. I felt peace and redemption. I knew then for certain, I'd made the right choice.' His voice was soft and yet his pride resonated with such energy that his words might have been heard all over the neighbourhood.

•   •   •

The following season, 2002-03, saw Sol maintain his form and Arsenal as title challengers again. After a ten-game unbeaten start in the Premier League, the Gunners struggled in Europe where they failed to progress beyond the Champions League group stage, but a fine run to the FA Cup final, during which they knocked out both Manchester United and Chelsea, saw them approach the crucial spring period in fine form and looking to repeat their Double exploits of the previous season.

For Sol though, a red card at Highbury in April against Manchester United would mean a premature end to his season. 'It was a dreadful decision; the worst of my career. The baby-faced assassin went down like a sack of potatoes. He wasn't given that title for no reason.' Sol pauses and says, 'I was devastated and pissed off.'

After referee Mark Halsey had discussed the incident with his linesman – who confirmed that he had seen the Arsenal defender 'deliberately elbow Ole Gunnar Solskjaer in the face' – he marched straight over to Sol and showed him the red card. Sol turned and walked as quickly as he could towards the tunnel, his stomach churning with indignation. By the time his head had disappeared from view, he had already started to calculate how long he was going to be suspended. When he was alone in the dressing room, which felt more like a mortuary, he'd already worked out he'd probably miss the FA Cup final. 'I felt like fucking shit!'

Those were still the days when, if a player was sent off in the League, the suspension would include cup games. Arsenal immediately launched an appeal but it didn't help. The last thing Manchester United were going to do was support Sol's case, with rivals Arsenal challenging them for the title. The decision stood. He was told by the FA that he would be banned for four matches, including the FA Cup final.

The announcement of his suspension is heard again later that night on the television. He remembers clearly the newscaster saying 'Sol Campbell will miss the FA Cup final,' as if he was saying it a dozen times over. He called his former Spurs team-mate Gary Mabbutt, who was now a member of the FA disciplinary committee, to see if he could help, but his efforts were in vain. Arsene Wenger was furious at the perceived injustice of it all. 'Every week there are examples of people who have done ten times more than he did and they are not punished. The team will support Sol and fight to win the League and FA Cup for him.'

For the first match of Sol's suspension, Arsenal fell to a 3-2 home defeat to Leeds, which virtually spelt the end of their chase to retain their title. Despite wins in their final two games, they finished the season in second place, five points behind Manchester United.

In the Cup final, against underdogs Southampton, Sol sat uncomfortably in his suit just behind the Arsenal bench. He yearned to play and found the game difficult to watch. Arsenal retained the cup by beating Southampton 1-0, Robert Pires scoring late on in the first-half. 'It was difficult not being involved. Of course, you want your team to win but it nags that you're not out there helping. It fact, I was heartbroken.' As the final whistle went, Sol hugged his manager and went onto the pitch to celebrate with his team-mates. For Arsene Wenger it had been a year to enjoy. 'Overall, we had a good twelve months;

we won the FA Cup twice on the trot and we were very close to a double Double.'

•   •   •

The Invincibles

'He knew what he wanted and he went to get it. The only comparable player in my whole career was Marcel Desailly,' says Patrick Vieira. He talks about Sol, as he does about his other Arsenal colleagues, without giving way to interruption, making it clear who is the boss.

Sol also talks about his Arsenal team-mates proudly as they approached a defining 2003-04 season. 'Naturally there were clashes, clashes of egos, but we got on with it. Our attitude was to get onto the next game; to win trophies. We had good men, proud men, each team member had talent and no-one liked playing below their best.

'Robert Pires had the special knack of anticipating where to be, he could smell a chance where others couldn't. Thierry Henry was fantastic, a natural gambler, he could create space out of nothing. He could shift the ball against his opponent's body weight, so as a defender you were always off balance. Dennis Bergkamp was one of the best players I've had the privilege to share a pitch with; his vision was incredible. He stretched me physically and mentally in training – he filled my memory bank ("Give me more, give me more!") and I gained the tools to play against any type of player.' Sol becomes a little tentative when picking out individual players. As if one voice is speaking about those we all want to hear about, while his other voice is babbling about the other members of this extraordinary team. 'Don't forget [Ashley] Cole, Touré, Lauren…Their strength of mind. After a while you get to know the team's mentality, you understand them and their approach in sustaining it. I loved all that; I hated slackers, and those thinking they were good when they weren't that special. There was a lot of that at Tottenham, a lot of people trying to talk their way onto the pitch instead of working for it. Pure froth; it used to irritate. I didn't have any time for that. [At Arsenal] I was surrounded by talented players in every part of the field.' He sighs at the memory of those halcyon days and says, 'Arsene knew I would never let him down.'

Thierry Henry doesn't disagree. 'Sol always gave a hundred per cent. He gave his heart and soul. He understood the game and was at his best when his back was against the wall.' And like Vieira, he compares Sol with Desailly: 'On pure defensive ability, I compare him with Marcel Desailly, and also Lilian Thuram. All three were unbeatable in their prime.'

Arsene Wenger adds: 'Sol had become one of our main players, and we now had an absolute physical presence and stability at the back. He is monstrous and, with his full power and also his ability to score a goal, you have an outstanding player. With Jens Lehmann, Ashley Cole, Lauren, Touré, they were all winners. With a defence like that, of course it made my job much easier. For a long time, people had it in their minds that the old Arsenal defence was irreplaceable – Dixon, Bould, Adams, Winterburn – but we changed four or five and we had a fantastic defence.'

Those who played for the Invincibles, as the Arsenal team of 2003-04 were later to be known, reached the height of their powers at the same time. 'It didn't matter what age you were; everyone was firing on all cylinders. Our time had come. Fortune chooses you. You do not choose it,' Sol says. Wenger is more pragmatic in his assessment: 'It was a balanced team, made up of mature players with top quality as well.'

●   ●   ●

On 21 September 2003, Arsenal played Manchester United at Old Trafford. Sol was absent that Sunday; he was due to bury his father that week and had been given leave. He needed space. He felt he'd been watched all day of the funeral. All eyes were on him, the famous son. People whispering loudly as he stood close to the coffin. He was the only one of the family to give a eulogy. 'I was glad to be able to mourn at the funeral. Speaking to relatives helped me get close to my dad, in another way.' He could hear all the mutterings, not directly of course, but close enough to wherever he stood. He dreaded walking out of the church after the funeral service. Dreaded to see the world the same as when he walked in. Relieved to see the world was just the same as before he went in. He needed to escape, yes, to be on his own *again*, this time to deal with his grief. He kissed his mother goodbye and left the rest of the mourners; yet another escape from his street, from his family. Not an escape outside to play football, like when he was young, but to get to his house, and watch on the television a recording of his club, Arsenal, play Manchester United; the former champions playing the reigning champions.

The outside of his home is quiet. As he approaches the front door, he hears the rustle of the trees and instantly remembers the times in West Ham Park when he used to play football and used the trees as his team-mates. He thinks of his father. Could he have joined me in the park? Could he have played with me? And then he quickly dismisses it as a wasted thought. He scolds himself, tells himself not to be so damn stupid. *This is how it is. Stop even trying to create the perfect scene.*

He goes into his living room and switches on the television. He makes himself a coffee and hears the commentary, but not clearly, more like some echo from the distant past. He watches the game. He watches it unmoved, as if it's on constant replay. It is one of those games that can go by without anyone noticing anything, until, that is, the last minute. Martin Keown pulls down Ruud van Nistelrooy. A penalty is given. Van Nistelrooy is going to take it. If he scores, that's the game. Sol watches Van Nistelrooy pick up the ball to put on the penalty spot and, quite naturally, his mind switches to how he plays him. How, the first time they had met on the pitch, Sol had dived in too quickly and the Dutchman had taken advantage and scored. *Don't sell yourself and tackle; let him beat you.* It's now logged in his memory. Van Nistelrooy is clinical, which makes him one of the best. With him you must lock his first movement, and then you're on the way to being okay. Be close enough so he can't get his shot in.

Van Nistelrooy hits the bar with his penalty. Keown leaps up, arms in the air, in front of Van Nistelrooy, as if he has just tasted his blood. It's an iconic photograph. The game ends in a 0-0 draw. The consequence? Only at the end of the season will that be known.

Sol thought again about other key games that season. The match at Stamford Bridge in February when Arsenal came from behind to beat their title rivals Chelsea 2-1; facing Liverpool at Highbury in April soon after their exit from the Champions League and FA Cup, down 2-1 at half-time before storming back to win 4-2; then, just two weeks later, a crucial match at White Hart Lane, of all places, and the chance to crown a remarkable campaign. 'The Liverpool game was one of the best performances that I remember being part of with Arsenal, coming on the back of a couple of cup defeats. At half-time, when we were losing, we got together and agreed we couldn't let this happen to us. We had to change it in the second half. Arsene was calm. "Keep true to your game," he said. "Find the line, play forward, keep the ball." And Thierry's performance in the second half was truly beautiful. We all played our part but Thierry sprinkled his magic dust over Highbury. It was football as art.'

As the season was drawing to its close, the team remained unbeaten; God's luck, God's choice. 'We always thought our run could end at anytime. We never took any game for granted. We had to concentrate every moment. We all knew any team could have their day. It can just happen, without you even noticing it. You lose and you've forgotten how that happened. So there was no let-off. Whether you were playing the top teams, or those at the bottom.' Sol reflected back for a moment to Old Trafford, and how the match had been a distraction, when all his senses were heightened by his father's death. And how he watched the game on his own, feeling hopeless as his team faced defeat.

What if the penalty from Van Nistelrooy had gone in? He connected with God's will of how life can change quite suddenly, whether in sport or your everyday existence.

Sol looks up to the sky like the subject in a religious painting. 'I hadn't really thought about the record. We just didn't think about losing that season. Then the papers started to write about the possibility of us going through the entire season unbeaten.

'Once you start talking about records, your chances diminish,' he says. 'So, by the time the last few games came round, I thought we had less chance of achieving it because now everyone was talking about it. Once everyone starts talking about things, I always feel uneasy. As if it curses you.'

Then, to the match at White Hart Lane. 'We won the title at Tottenham.' He pauses. The roots of coincidence. 'It was all too much really, going back to Tottenham to win the League. I knew we'd get a point there. I just knew.' It was never easy for Sol going back to Spurs. Never. The story was burning as strongly as when he first left, and the abuse had not receded. 'I was so pumped up for this game. I change when I'm on the field. Not in a bad way but I'm different. Just different,' he says, gauging and processing the metamorphic change in personality. What does it mean? Who is this other character that lives inside?

He steps back in time. He is leaving the away dressing room on that 25 April day. He has initially zoned out. He doesn't hear the crowd. That day they seem very separate, as if they are there but not really. He is looking at the players as if they are in a video game. Not a virtual game, but more like a matrix. His feelings are surreal. So different to his last visit.

His fitness is good. He feels strong, he's fully prepared. He has everything mapped out. He knows what the team is going to do before they even do it. He has intuition and that day he is in the zone. When he was in the zone, he felt free; more liberated than in any second, any minute, of his life. Flying through the air, anticipating, tackling and passing. No-one can get through him or stop him. 'I just loved it. I felt a natural high. It was like a drug for me.'

• • •

Tottenham 2 Arsenal 2, White Hart Lane, 25 April 2004

TOTTENHAM: Keller, Kelly (Poyet 79), Gardner, King, Taricco (Bunjevcevic 90), Davies, Brown, Redknapp, Jackson (Defoe 45), Kanoute, Keane. Subs Not Used: Ricketts, Hirschfeld. Goals: Redknapp (62), Keane (pen 90).

ARSENAL: Lehmann, Lauren, Campbell, Toure, Cole, Parlour (Edu 67), Vieira, Silva, Pires, Henry, Bergkamp (Reyes 80). Subs Not Used: Keown, Clichy, Stack. Goals: Vieira (3), Pires (35).

Att: 36,097. Ref: Mark Halsey.

Needing only a draw to clinch the title, Arsenal began swiftly with goals from Vieira, after a lightning counter-attack, and Pires, following good work by Bergkamp and Vieira again. Spurs turn things round in the second half. Redknapp's low shot arrows past Lehmann and in a tense finish, Pires hits the crossbar before Lehmann fouls Keane who slots the resulting penalty home to rescue a valuable point for Spurs. But Arsenal are record-breaking league champions.

Arsenal were majestic at the start. Vieira's goal was scored with an ease characteristic of their unbeaten season. Sol recalls the steps by which Arsene Wenger developed his team's fluency: 'He wanted the ball to be on the ground; he wanted the ball passed through the lines, always looking forward, always looking for the opening. Speed and accuracy, the right angles and timing were all-important. Even for me when defending. Of course, sometimes you have to put it in Row Z but even if you were under pressure, you still had to look for the next man to pass it on to, even with your head. Using that half a second, I've seen the player on the right side or the one in midfield. You have that instant to ignite something; to control the opposition, not the other way round.'

Robbie Keane had a chance, which Sol headed clear, again summarising the quality of his and the Arsenal team's season from the back line to the front. 'I always try to head away to the sidelines when clearing. First, it is safer and second, there may be one of our players ready to start an attack. We had quick thinking guys who consistently found themselves in the right position. It made life on the field easier. With the speed and intelligence of Henry, Bergkamp, Ljungberg, Pires and Patrick [Vieira], marauding, ready to break forward and also cover the back, we could do unbelievable things. It was a privilege to be on the same field.'

Bergkamp was the architect of the second goal, scored by Pires. 'Dennis flourished under Arsene. It was the first time Dennis was managed by someone with real intelligence, and his play just got better and better. It was incredible to watch.'

Despite a second-half comeback from the home team, the final whistle sees Arsenal as champions and still unbeaten. The players run towards their fans in celebration. They are screaming their heads off, not only because they are champions again but also because they have won the title at their rival's ground. All the team is there except Sol, who quietly walks away, back to the visitors' dressing room. 'I thought it best. I didn't want to be disrespectful in front of the Spurs fans.' When all the players return, Sol is waiting. He has spent the moments alone, not in celebration but in frustration. He turns on his goalkeeper.

'I was really fucked off that we gave away that last-minute goal. I so wanted to win the game. I want to win every game. It's the beginning and the end for me. I always gave a hundred per cent if I could, for whoever I was playing for. To see Jens throw it away like that really pissed me off. So there's everyone enjoying themselves, and I'm having a right go at Jens.'

The argument fades. They are in heaven. The title is theirs. The players return to the pitch to celebrate again with their fans, and this time Sol joins them. He thinks of all the hard work he's put in to get to this place: the early mornings, the care over what he put in his body, the training sessions, his unfailing determination to improve every time he went onto the field, on the road in those crappy hotels. Fleeting thoughts when he steps on the White Hart Lane soil, but there nevertheless.

The stadium is now empty except for the deluge of noise coming from the far corner of the Park Lane End. A banner has been displayed. 'Why did Sol leave the Lane? Arsenal Champions! 43 Years and you're still waiting!' Sol looks up and sees it. He finds comfort in the word 'Champions' but nothing else.

Patrick Vieira slaps Sol on the back. His captain; they had become friends. 'He was very much our captain, a good captain but he loved me to shout at him. "Sol!" he would yell, "I like it when you shout at me! It gets me going."'

'I liked him shouting at me because there were times I could fade out of the game. He always kept me focused,' says Vieira.

'He was an intelligent man,' Sol says. 'So were many of that team. It helps…'

When you look back at the history of successful sides over the years, they always had players that were intelligent on and off the field. It seemed Arsenal were overflowing with them. 'It's true,' says Sol. 'Henry, Vieira, Bergkamp, Ljungberg, Seaman, Kanu …and me, of course.'

• • •

Arsenal remained unbeaten for the rest of the season, finishing with a 2-1 home win over Leicester City in the last game. Their league record that season was 26 wins, 12 draws and 0 losses, over 38 games in total. 'As a team, we loved and cared for each other. Sometimes, we didn't have to talk and we knew how the other felt. It reflected on the way we played our football,' says Thierry Henry.

There wasn't much time for Sol to celebrate his team's remarkable achievement, as England were off to the European Championships in Portugal. Some people are said to find an excess of success as difficult, if not more difficult to handle than failure. But not Sol. He knew his success, and that of the team, was justified. His body stature, which was always naturally positive, became even more so. He walked through everyday life with an air of hyper-confidence. He may not have noticed the change but his friends did.

Sol spent these days in silent communion, feeling justified in leaving Spurs for Arsenal, taking comfort in joining up with the England squad as a champion, and basking in the respect he got from friends and Arsenal fans. He didn't go overboard in congratulating himself – 'Once you start believing the plaudits, you have to believe in everything else' – but these days were good for Sol. Sadly, the winning feeling would not last long.

•   •   •

Sol came back from Euro 2004 a disappointed man. It is painful to return to your country when your international team has been knocked out of a tournament, made even worse at that time because Sol truly believed England could have won.

He tries to avoid switching on the television. Each time he does, there's something going on about the Euros. Leave it, he tells himself, and takes out the plug from the wall socket. All it creates is frustration, a feeling that the team should still be out there, playing.

He keeps to himself, not venturing out from his house, not even once. No restaurant, no shopping. It is difficult to face anyone. This is not simply about losing; it is far more. It's dealing with the hopes and disappointment of a nation.

He needs to get out of the country, away from the news, the constant murmur of disappointment from...Everyone. He feels fatigued. Mentally exhausted. He arranges a ten-day break in Italy on the Amalfi coast. He rents a boat and spends his days finding a peace. He wakes up early and goes up on deck. He spends the early hours looking out at the blueness, the sea and sky appearing to converge into one. It's the first time he has the space in his mind to reflect on the death of his father the previous summer. He had been too busy concentrating on the present, not the past; winning the Premiership and then playing for England in the Euros. Now he feels completely alone. He paces the deck, wondering what on earth he's doing there. It's as if he's received permission from God to avoid thoughts about certain things. But what about his father's death? He tried to understand his character. Looking at his life as a whole, not just parts. Not to struggle with it, but to surrender. 'Although he never recognised how hard I worked to get to the top and also to stay there, I tried during that period to see it his way. His upbringing, his family, how nothing was given to him. So to succeed, you would naturally have to work hard. So why should he notice me? It was something he expected.' Although Sol tries to live for the present, he was looking to come to terms with what was behind him.

•　　•　　•

Sol missed the opening games of the 2004-05 season. He had a knee injury and was still tired. 'It isn't surprising that I was susceptible to injury. On reflection, I was exhausted. I learned when I went to Lilleshall, how to look after my body. I had to work hard to maintain my fitness. I saw that. I knew then I had to get the best out of my body to compete at the very highest level. I remember having a physical. It was a series of tests: 3,000 metre runs, sprints, jumps, circuits. The first time the results were announced, I was fourth from bottom. I even think the goalkeeper beat me. I promised myself this would not happen again. Never. So the next time we were tested, I finished fourth from top. From then, I've always maintained my fitness as best as I could. Fourteen years old is a very good age for a footballer to address that side of his game. It then becomes natural. Part of your everyday routine.'

Arsenal won the Community Shield 3-1 against Manchester United and continued their unbeaten run in the Premier League. They equalled the unbeaten League record by beating Middlesbrough 5-3 at Highbury, after coming back from two goals down at the start of the second half, which is described by many Gunners fans as the most intense twenty minutes of football they ever witnessed. Three days later, they surpassed the previous record of 42 games held by Nottingham Forest, by beating Blackburn 3-0.

●   ●   ●

Manchester United 2 Arsenal 0, Premier League, Old Trafford, 24 October 2004

MANCHESTER UTD: Carroll, Gary Neville, Ferdinand, Silvestre, Heinze, Ronaldo (Smith 85), Phil Neville, Scholes, Giggs, Rooney, Van Nistelrooy (Saha 90). Subs Not Used: Howard, Brown, Miller. Goals: Van Nistelrooy 73 pen, Rooney 90.

ARSENAL: Lehmann, Lauren, Campbell, Toure, Cole, Ljungberg, Vieira, Edu, Reyes (Pires 70), Bergkamp, Henry. Subs Not Used: Van Persie, Taylor, Fabregas, Cygan.

Att: 67,862. Ref: Mike Riley.

Arsenal's 49-game unbeaten run in the Premier League finally comes to an end at title rivals Manchester United. In a match that threatened to boil over in the first half, a controversial penalty decision against Campbell gives Van Nistelrooy the chance to open the scoring in the second period. The visitors fail to make all their late pressure count, and in the final minute Rooney bags United's second from close range to send the Old Trafford faithful home happy.

Sol had returned to action a few games previously. The first and all-important goal featured Sol. 'It was a terrible decision. He dived, as simple as that,' he says about the penalty awarded against him after Rooney went down like a skater on melting ice. 'He knew, I knew, and by the end of the game everyone watching on television also knew.' Rooney then doubled the score late on. 'I refused to shake his hand at the end. He cheated,' Sol says.

Back in the dressing room, Sol was removing his boots when he heard a scuffle going on outside. In the papers the following day, the incident became known as 'Pizzagate'. The dressing room door flew open and Sol saw players and staff from both sides pushing and shoving each other, like trapped cattle in a pen. A slice of pizza, allegedly a margherita, was hurled by an Arsenal player and hit the Manchester United manager Sir Alex Ferguson. Sol recalls the incident as if squinting at a faded photograph. 'The area outside the dressing room is very narrow and tight. Something was bound to happen. I didn't really see the incident with my own eyes. In the end, no-one came forward but it wasn't taken that seriously by the club. It sort of brought the team even closer together. Us against the rest of the world stuff.'

Names were mentioned but the perpetrator never stepped forward. Ashley Cole best sums it up: 'The culprit wasn't English or French, so that should narrow it down.' For a couple of days, the incident submerged the extraordinary 49-game unbeaten run from 2003 to 2004 that had just ended for Arsenal. It was a record to be proud of.

	PLAYED	WON	DRAWN	LOST	FOR	AGAINST	POINTS
HOME	25	20	5	0	63	21	65
AWAY	24	16	8	0	49	14	56
OVERALL	49	36	13	0	112	35	121

'For me, there was a sense of relief that the record was over,' says Sol. 'It started to become incredibly intense, following us everywhere. I was very disappointed we'd lost, and in the manner by which the end came, but I felt as if an albatross had been removed. My overriding feeling was of pride to be part of history and a group of players that became a family.'

Wenger said of his team, 'I felt very privileged to work with these players, not only because they were strong but also because they were respectable. They were dedicated players who came from all over the world and created a unique bit of history in football. It was truly amazing.'

•   •   •

Sol was pissed off. He'd been left out of the team.

As the 2004-05 season progressed, Wenger had begun to pick Kolo Touré and Pascal Cygan, then Philippe Senderos, as his regular central defensive pair, meaning Sol was no longer first choice. Only a year before, he was the number one pick in defence for one of the best teams ever in the Premier League. That defence had let in twenty-six goals all season. Now he was being dropped and was on the bench. 'Things in football can change very quickly,' says Sol. It was time to talk to Wenger about it. Not to tell him he was leaving but to have his say and understand where he stood, what was happening. *Come on, look at my quality. I just need you to back me up and help me to get over the bumps in my form.* He was thinking exactly this as he walked to the manager's office. He didn't often want, or even need, to see Wenger face-to-face. But this time was different. On entering the office, he noticed immediately how tidy it was. Nothing out of place, papers neatly piled, pens in a straight line and the phone positioned close enough to grab for an important call. There was little hanging on the walls apart from a few football photos; they were devoid of personality. This place had a sense of peace. So peaceful, in fact, that he almost felt he needed to whisper. But instead, he put forward his case in a forthright way he'd rehearsed earlier. Even then, Wenger remained unmoved.

'These two are playing well,' Wenger said. 'And I don't want to change it.'

'But Senderos isn't playing well,' replied Sol. 'He's a lucky player. I've been watching him. He keeps making mistakes. His real luck is that none of his mistakes have been taken advantage of. But it won't last...There's nothing personal here, I like these players, but I don't think they're up to the job.'

Wenger shook his head in disagreement. Sol took a deeper look at his manager. He asked Wenger to repeat what he thought he had just heard.

'They are our future,' Wenger said.

Sol couldn't see it. He wanted to argue but he knew it would be a waste of time. He was speechless. The meeting finished calmly. Wenger stood and shook his hand firmly. He made it clear to Sol that he wasn't just part of the club but a very important part.

•   •   •

Arsenal had a successful run in the FA Cup, progressing all the way thanks to a reasonably favourable draw to the final to play Manchester United later that year in May 2005.

The manager didn't immediately tell Sol that he would not be playing but he didn't need to. 'I probably knew three or four days before. You always know because you are playing on the other team, the reserve side, in training.' Senderos had remained the preferred choice. There was little chance Sol would make the first team unless someone got injured.

He asked Wenger a second time what was happening. On this occasion it was following a team meeting, and after everyone had left the room. 'The boss basically said he was happy with the way the team was playing. I left it at that. I had to look at the bigger picture.'

For a defender, just as it is with a goalkeeper, it is more difficult to get back in the first team. A striker can go out and score a last-minute winner and change everything in a second. It doesn't work the same for someone in defence, and Sol was well aware of the fact. But he was patient, held counsel on how much this was hurting, and sat on the bench. 'Life is shit on the bench,' he says, looking back now. 'It feels unnatural, just sitting there watching. Perhaps it's the same for anyone, but for me it was torture.' He watched the entire cup final from the subs' bench, rigid, every second a beating pulse urging him to get on the field. It was as if someone had struck him on the back of the head. This was an emotional strike, which added to a pain that was already growing. 'I remember he was very disappointed to be left out,' Wenger said. 'He took the FA Cup very seriously. He understood its history and importance. I noticed if we were knocked out of the competition, he more than anyone took it the hardest.'

When Patrick Vieira scored the winning penalty in the shootout, Sol ran onto the pitch to celebrate with his teammates. There wasn't a moment's hesitation in supporting his team's success. He was happy for them and ultimately for himself; he'd picked up his second FA Cup winner's medal with Arsenal.

LOST WEEKEND

'He had his boots off and I said come on Sol, put those on and let's get on with the game... he shook his head and said, "I can't." I knew then, something was very wrong.'

THIERRY HENRY

The man opposite woke up coughing and muttering something to himself. Sol was looking out of the window as the train pulled past the backwaters of England. He noticed the parks, the empty football pitches. It reminded him of his childhood back home. He indulged in the memories of those days, of that time. He stretched his legs in a deeper search for a solution. *What's been going wrong? Why am I here now, escaping from everything I have worked for?* But, as the Eurostar train hurried away out of the UK towards his refuge in Brussels, Sol began to take comfort in the fact that he was escaping from a life that had become his entrapment, his prison, and just maybe he could for a short time gain some solace from the ordinary things seen on an ordinary peaceful day, without the pressure that had constantly grown over the last few years.

Less than twenty-four hours earlier, on 1 February 2006, he was driving his Range Rover into Highbury to play for Arsenal against West Ham. He hadn't being playing well of late. He knew it. He was a perfectionist and it was causing concern. He was losing his command of the game.

When the half-time whistle was blown, Arsenal were losing 2-1 and Sol had had a pitiful time. First he mis-kicked the ball to allow Nigel Reo Cocker through to give West Ham the lead, followed by Bobby Zamora easily barging him out of the way to score a second. Looking back at the footage now, you see the pain veiled over his face. 'In truth, I'd played worse over previous weeks. I had an injury and wasn't able to physically pull myself out of the slump. It's always difficult when you're not fit enough to lift your game,' he says. As he walked off the pitch at the break, he heard someone shout abuse and make a gesture. A hand fashioned itself into the shape of a gun, which was pointed in Sol's direction. As his index finger pulled the trigger, the fan's lips made a little explosion, and his mouth stretched itself into a bayonet smile. He did not flinch. He continued to stare. And to sneer. Sol took no notice, at least tried to take no notice but he was beyond the point of caring anyway. He opened the door of the dressing room and as he stepped inside, he knew what he had to do. What was happening now was stripping away the armour he'd built up ever since he was a young man. He felt naked, vulnerable; 'Everything that was happening was hurting, bothering me.'

The accumulation of storms in his life had finally combined and on that evening hit him so hard and unexpectedly that he had only one choice left. Escape. This was not going to be a quiet retreat into his house, not answering calls. No. As a public figure, one of the sacrifices you abandon for the rewards, and the fame that goes with it, is privacy. A million people will be told of your story, laughing, hissing, forming their own opinion of what is wrong. But you're the only one who knows.

The players were busy working out what had gone wrong in the first half. The atmosphere was not particularly amplified because of the scoreline; there was more a sense of disbelief, a low. *How are we losing?* Sol made his way to a side room, the physio's room. He talks as if it was not just a different time, but also a different dimension. It's as if he hasn't really gone back there much. That he is digging up a tomb he had hoped would be left alone. But memories such as these cannot be avoided forever, however much you'd like them to be. His father had died. It had been almost two and a half years. Sol had never found peace with his father. 'We always had a very tough relationship,' Sol lamented. His father had a stroke, in front of his mother Wilhelmina, while she was making herself a cup of tea and asking him if he wanted one. He fell to the ground and she rushed to his side to witness his last moments. Hours later he was unconscious in hospital, his family by his side. Some lives end in the most ordinary manner. Sewell's last days were stripped of the pride he carried throughout his life. Sol had an unfulfilled relationship with him. How he still desired his recognition and how, even today, Sol still finds it hard to admit that is what he most wanted, what he most needed. However successful Sol had become, a sublime talent among millions of dreamers, earning more money in a month, in a week, than his father did in years, he never got a moment when his father acknowledged his success. Never. And the irony of Sol's life is that despite all the fortunes bestowed upon him, what he wanted most was something he would never receive. 'I think, on reflection, my father could have looked after us a little bit more.' There is a long silence and, for an instant, his face freezes like marble. He gives a weary smile and quietly says, 'I wanted to tell him how I felt. I wanted and needed it to be different to the way he had been with me. For my life to be emotionally different to his.'

As his father lay motionless in the hospital bed, Sol stretched out his hand and touched his father's skin. It would be the first time he had ever touched him. He grabbed his hand and squeezed it but he did not respond and never would. The last touch of Sewell's hand was cold and unfeeling. Sol told him, 'I love you. I want you to hear and know that. I refuse to be like you!' His father would pass away two days later, the night before Sol's 29th birthday.

When he buried him, Sol cried for the first time in his memory. He began to mourn his loss profoundly. He didn't talk to anyone about his pain; he masked his grief. But as he wept, he thought of the man who arrived from Jamaica with a strict God fearing upbringing and made a life for himself, his wife and children in England. A man who worked nights, drank beer and smoked rolled-up Old Holborns, which had probably brought him to his early death. The overflowing grey ashtray of cigarette butts by his bed in his room; the ash scattered on the floor. The man who, when friends rang and asked for Sulzeer, would say he wasn't in even though he would be sitting nearby. The force of his belt when Sol had done something wrong. The times he puffed out his chest and said, 'This is my house! You do what I say when you're here!' When his father ignored him, even though they were together in the same room. Those silent moments when Sol noticed his father deep in thought. What was he really thinking? He thought of the missed opportunities to talk to his father, and the missed opportunity for his father to take comfort and pride in his success. Sewell had never held, kissed or hugged his son. His avoidance of any sign of affection was overbearing. It took a mixture of courage and pain for Sol to reach out. And it wasn't until that night by his hospital bed that he recognised how wounded his father was. He found the thought utterly and totally unbearable.

•   •   •

Dennis Bergkamp, Thierry Henry and Freddie Ljungberg were in the physio's room. 'Yes, Dennis was definitely there and I think Thierry came in. Maybe there was someone else? Maybe another player walked in and walked out again,' Sol says vaguely. 'It felt like a forest fire; everything in my life had burnt to a cinder and I felt there was nothing left.'

He felt he was letting his side down. He knew something had come to an end.

'I can't go on,' Sol spoke gently.

Gary Lewin, the Arsenal physio said, 'What?'

'I can't go on.'

Sol remembers Arsene Wenger was in there. The manager heard what Sol had said to Lewin. As Sol recalls the moment, he talks rather unconvincingly, unsure of himself and, for an instant, he changes from a confident man into a young boy grabbing the table with both hands for support. He was clearly in torment remembering those hours a few years on. This would be the first time in his life that he had admitted defeat.

'He had his boots off and I said come on Sol, put those on and let's get on with the game,' recalls Thierry Henry. 'I remember he shook his head and said "'I can't." I knew then something was very wrong. "Can't" isn't something Sol Campbell says.'

Sol had always been number one in everything he did with football. Never second, never number two. A philosopher once published an article arguing that the first natural number is two: never with Sol, it had always been number one. Arsene Wenger tried to persuade him to return for the second half, telling him that he still believed in him. Sol remained motionless. The manager repeated and reinforced what he had said but this time his voice was unconvincing, like that of someone making an offer he knows won't be taken up. 'You'll be okay.' Sol shook his head. Wenger knew then. He called for Sebastian Larsson, an academy graduate, to get ready. A little surprised, Larsson started to limber up in preparation for the second half. It would not turn out to be Larsson's finest hour; he was booked and his mistake would lead to a third goal in West Ham's 3-2 victory. It was Arsenal's third straight defeat. For a team that had recently been so dominant, the decline signalled the word 'crisis' on the back pages of the daily papers.

Sol stayed in the side room as the rest of the players had their team talk. 'The boss told us Sol wouldn't be returning for the second half,' says Henry. Sol then heard the sound of muffled studs leaving the dressing room. Robert Pires looked in before he went back onto the field. A strange expression. Without so many words, he asked if Sol was okay. There was an uncomfortable silence.

When the dressing room was empty and peaceful, Sol went in and took off his boots and put on some Nike trainers. He pulled on some trousers and put on his coat. He was still in his Arsenal red shirt as he drove away from Highbury.

'Isn't that Sol Campbell?' an old man asks, spitting to the ground.

'He should be playing, shouldn't he?' another says.

'Not anymore,' Sol replies in his head. 'Maybe never again.'

The rain had begun to fall hard. Sol didn't know how much it was raining until he saw the light, coming out of a pub, close to the ground. A man was clearing his small stall; t-shirts, scarves and badges being carefully packed away. People don't buy after the game when it pours down, and especially when the home team is losing. A man runs to the underground for cover, jumping over the puddles like he's playing hopscotch. Sol thinks he hears a roar from the crowd but it's just his imagination; he is too far from the ground to hear anything. He's not tempted to switch on the car radio; to hear the score, to hear how Arsenal are doing. It's in the past. There is nothing left for him now.

It was that sort of indecisive hour in a person's mind when you have to decide whether to stay for another drink or head back home. But Sol's mind was clear. He knew what he needed to do. He'd get home, pack and go to see a friend. He needed company, the right sort of company. Someone who could and would listen to him, someone he could talk to. There weren't many to choose from. But he knew he needed to get away. He had a desire to escape those themes that had niggled and disrupted and dominated and SCREWED UP his life. He needed to be out of London, perhaps even out of the country, before the night turned into morning.

He parked his Range Rover outside his home. It was quiet. It was always quiet. But the silence as he sat momentarily in the car was probably the most intense silence he had ever experienced; quieter than any library, or the silence in his childhood home when the family was out. He took in a deep breath. He muttered 'Hurry up' out loud and the wind burst in as he opened the front door. *Keep it going. What now? Who's next? How will it end?* He went straight upstairs to his bedroom. He took a shower. The water was hot; in fact, too hot, as if he was trying to scald himself. He got out and wrapped a white towel round himself. He looked in the mirror, eyes resolute. He rubbed his hands over his cheeks. He packed an overnight bag: three white shirts, t-shirts, three pairs of jeans, socks, trainers, leather shoes and a wash bag. It does not signal that he will be gone for a long time but, as he takes the case downstairs, he has no idea how long he will be gone or what the next few days will bring.

The demons were swaying in his brain. *Is there anyone who has not once felt so alone in his entire life? Does part of me still think I am that special and different?* He felt sick. His sickness was genuine; without a cough, a sigh, or tear of pretence. Where was the pain? Everywhere. *My family are being torn apart, they are being destroyed.* He thinks about the news he heard earlier. His brother John had been jailed for twelve months for attacking an East London University classmate who suggested Sol was gay. He was reported to have kicked his victim senseless. The judge said in sentencing: 'I am told you are frustrated when people taunt you about your brother...'

John Campbell, aged 34, was described by his barrister as 'mild-mannered'. He added, 'He has brought shame on his family and most ironically to his younger brother, whose reputation he fought to protect.' It is one of those times when everyone loses. 'My brother John spent time inside because he got into a fight protecting me when he was training, and he punched someone for calling me a homosexual. He punched him out of anger. He was taken to court and was jailed. I can handle it to a certain level, but for my brothers who are in normal workplaces it isn't easy. There are a lot of ignorant people about. Someone from the family rang to tell me his sentence. I was angry. I was very angry. This whole incident had happened because of innuendoes, because someone had started these rumours about my sexuality. All lies. I saw how my mother was. She felt helpless and it broke my heart. We never as a family discussed what had happened. What was there to say? We were a normal family dealing not only with our own stuff but also these outside forces. I saw it destroying us, and at that time I felt helpless.'

•   •   •

John Campbell is five years older than Sol. He is the sibling closest in age. 'I have a feeling John didn't seize the moment. He was technically a better player than I was,' Sol says.

When Sol was ten years old, the two boys would go over to West Ham Park to kick a ball using a tree as one post and a sweater as the other. They played one-on-one. John would dribble the ball, dipping one way then the other, leaving Sol stranded like a mannequin; laughter from John, a frown from Sol. 'We would play for hours. We would practise penalties and free-kicks. John would teach me how to bend the ball round the tree,' Sol says.

Len Cheesewright's disappointment in John not becoming a professional footballer could well have helped younger brother Sol. 'I think the reason he was so determined to get me, to persuade my parents that I should sign for Tottenham, was because he missed out on John.' Cheesewright had wanted John to sign with Charlton but it didn't work out. 'John told me someone was racist, which of course I believed, as I'd experienced it myself. But he definitely had a chance and didn't grab it,' Sol says. 'I think he was a bit lazy with his talent. Sometimes it is difficult, when you have so much skill, but you still have to turn up every day and work hard to get anywhere.'

What a waste, Sol thinks to himself. If only...If only John had seized his opportunity. How life could have been so different. He could imagine John playing for one of the top teams. Yes, gliding by the opposition with such skill that you're not sure you saw it in the first place. But life isn't like that, is it? Nothing is ever easy.

From very early on, it was part of Sol's subconscious to be different to his brothers. Watching his mother trying in vain to get them up in the morning – 'Get on with it! Get on with it!' –

and seeing their lack of motivation, his inner voice used to scream. *You might be tired but it's time to get up!* He thought they were setting a bad example. So he spent his time alone, observing and listening; his eyes following the acts and scenes in the house, while his father said little and let his sons get on with it without his guidance. All their dreams made in a state of mind that was not going to last.

As Sol's fame and wealth grew, his problems were bound up in his brothers' lives. Fame can have a suffocating effect on friends and family. Sol was distant, became even more distant and always felt disconnected. John suffered the most from his brother's fame. 'I remember when Sol signed for Arsenal there were news people outside the house and following us to the supermarket,' recalls Wilhelmina. And John became angry standing there, face-to-face with journalists, questions and accusations harassing his ears. This was a couple of years before he was sent to prison. He was always fending off the inquisitor or the downright rude. His mother was there this time, to save him from himself. 'John, leave them alone, it's not worth it,' she said.

Sol can't be angry with his siblings. He loves them, despite all that's happened. He has helped them out financially. But then, once again, the relationship changes. There are few people in this world who can give away their own money unconditionally. Even if it is given as a gift – 'Don't worry, I just hope it can help' – the benefactor will, in most circumstances, watch and judge how it is being spent. And the benefactor's mind will start to question whether they're being too generous or not generous enough. *Do they love me as their brother or do they love me because I have money?* No-one gets away with it for free. In fact, generally a door slams shut.

'You can't just give away everything without someone giving something back,' Wilhelmina advised her son. Looking back now she says, 'I am proud of how Sol has looked after his money. He has always been good with it.'

When Sol talks about his siblings, there is a sense of loneliness. It is as if when he finally left home, he left forever, losing contact with everyone except his mother. 'It's with a great sadness when I think of my brothers. Some of them have not had the same opportunity as me. Maybe they were born in the wrong area to utilise their particular talent or find someone to help them out and turn them in the right direction. Perhaps I was born at the right time with the right mentality. I was conscious very early on that their lifestyle was not for me.'

•　　•　　•

'We used to date,' says Sol. He calls Theresa from his house. She is coming over. While he is waiting, he calls Elizabeth who now lives in Brussels. He dials the number. She is a good friend who he hasn't seen for at least a year since she moved abroad. Slightly older, a mother who has a family, two children aged between four and six years old. She answers her phone. He tells her he needs to get away. Can he stay? She says she is busy working in the morning but by lunchtime, she'll be able to pick him up from the station. Before he puts down the phone, she reassures him that everything will be fine.

Like so many people in grief, Sol has been trying to make amends. Somehow, although his father has been dead for nearly three years, he feels guilty. Illogical and painful, but that is how he is feeling among the deluge of other thoughts. He goes outside into his garden. He looks out towards the brook and breathes in everything around, if only to remind himself that things here and now are sprouting and burgeoning and flowering... And also fading, wilting and dying. He thinks he hears a bell. He did, it's the gate. He lets Theresa in. She is concerned and they go into the kitchen. Theresa drinks a glass of white wine, Sol drinks water poured from a bottle. He drinks it in virtually one gulp. He is keen to leave the house like a man on the run, which in many ways he is.

Theresa doesn't realise he was playing football in front of thousands of people only a couple of hours before. He says that he is leaving the country. He's going to take the first Eurostar across the Channel. It is still raining as they get into Theresa's car. Sol is now wearing a coat, the collar pulled up to his ears as a form of protection. As he opens the car door, he glimpses his reflection in the car window. He sees an undertaker late for a funeral. He sighs at the impression. The car speeds around the M25 and south towards Ashford. He feels so much older now. His broad shoulders, which have for so long been his defining feature, are momentarily slumped. His fingers have lost their strength. He notices that they fall onto his knees, the joints drooping.

They book into a hotel on the outskirts of Ashford; one of those Holiday Inn type places off the motorway. Sol doesn't remember the name, probably wouldn't even recognise it, but remembers the tone of the voice of the man who booked him in. Strange, the moments the brain chooses to remember.

'How many nights will you be staying?' asked the roundish gentleman with a booming voice. So much for discretion.

They don't sleep. There was a brief romance but now it was simply a friend being a friend and listening to his woes. They are up into the early hours of the morning. The night encapsulates both ends of his current mood spectrum; one minute near to tears of joy for escaping, the other near to tears of anguish. Whether he can articulate it, or even know it, he is deeply depressed.

There is no sense of the morning after the night before when dawn arrives. He feels anaesthetised, practically numb from his head down to his feet. Theresa drops him outside Ashford station and says her goodbye. She is confident he will be alright. She moves away from the station and watches through her rear window as Sol disappears from view with overnight bag in his right hand, his demeanour grey under the matching morning sky.

•　　•　　•

He sits while trying to be as inconspicuous as possible. He calls his mother just before the train enters the tunnel to nowhere...

To somewhere. He reassures her that whatever she may read or hear, everything is fine. He just needs to get away.

A man opposite recognises him. He doesn't approach Sol. Thinks it best to leave him alone. He would say later that he'd never seen anyone lonelier in his entire life.

The train reaches the outskirts of Brussels around lunchtime. It begins to slow enough for Sol to read the advertisements by the railway track. The language, the colour from the posters, immediately give him a sense of freedom. It seems far enough from where he has escaped. He starts to receive a variety of texts, from team-mates, friends. People he hasn't heard from in years, some he wonders how they got his number. It's reassuring but he is still in that space where nothing really means anything. He needs to work things through. The news of his mysterious half-time disappearance was beginning to flood the news stations. Robert Pires allegedly said, 'He has a big worry on his side,' which sparked a series of 'What did Pires mean?' His manager Arsene Wenger is quoted as having said, 'The only thing we can do at the football club is to support people when they need our help. Every human being has the right to privacy.' His sentiments are good; but his inaction, in personally not reaching out during the week, perhaps less so.

At Brussels station, Sol buys himself a coffee and goes to wait outside. They have arranged to meet in the open-air car park to the left of the main entrance. Elizabeth has warned him that she is going to be late but it doesn't bother him. The simple pleasure of his own company in a foreign city is what he needs at this moment. No-one recognises him; he simply leans against a lamppost and watches the comings and goings of a European city.

Eventually a a black mini pulls up. It's Elizabeth. It is good to see his friend again. The drive to her apartment is quiet. Not much conversation. They will have time for that later. The apartment is large and comfortable. Children's toys are scattered around the living room. There is a sense of family, of warmth. *This is exactly what I need now*. A family atmosphere that sadly he never experienced as a young boy. Back then it was just a white noise of arguments. Here was different. Peace, warmth and loving interest. That evening, he helps with the cooking and sits down with Elizabeth and the two children to a family meal. He remembers it being chicken and also remembers the surprising warmth coming off the street. Brussels that week was expecting beautiful weather.

After dinner, when the children have gone to bed, Sol begins to reveal to his friend what has been happening. As he speaks, he follows the road map of his emotions; taking everything slowly, so as not to miss anything. In truth, over the last twenty-four hours, it is the first time he has really thought deeply about everything or anything that has been going on his life over the years since he became famous. Isn't it strange how we can live with torment and carry it around for such a long time without ever tackling it?

He speaks about Janet. He seems to know little about her, even though they knew each other for two years. It was a typical non-committal relationship, like ships passing in the night. 'I was careless, I was caught off-guard.' Conversations that tended to lead nowhere; never looking each other straight in the eye. But there was a physical attraction. She got pregnant and Janet decided to have the baby. He was confused. He couldn't talk about it to anyone. Even when he and Sky Andrew tried to discuss it, and Sky put forward his point of view, Sol didn't want to hear. His siblings had children out of wedlock. They were good kids and he was fond of them, but he wanted his life to be different. He felt trapped when he heard she was having a baby; the instinct to run towards a cry for help vied with the desire to flee from any hint of trouble. What should he do? Ignore? Pretend it wasn't happening? He dithered and then questioned whether the baby was his. *Is he really mine?* Sol asked himself and then was asked the same question in court, following a paternity suit. It has since been proved that he is the father. Sol and Janet don't talk now except through lawyers. The whole episode rests uneasily with him, as it surely does with her.

Most importantly, through all the contradictions and struggles, a child was born on 12 April 2004. Sol's son is called Joseph.

'Whatever I say will only hurt, not just now but in the future,' Sol says. 'But I do hope to have a relationship with my son.' His tentative words echo a move forward.

•　　•　　•

They spoke until the early hours, Elizabeth asking questions but pacing them, allowing Sol to open up in his own time. There were minutes when he literally didn't speak, as if putting his hand over his mouth in mid-sentence. He had changed. He had changed from the quiet, confident man to someone unsure of himself.

He slept well but not deeply, that first night in Brussels. He remembers waking up early. He remembers driving with Elizabeth to drop off the kids at school and afterwards being left in town while Elizabeth went to work. *What a perfect place Brussels is*, he thought. *Just like Paris but more discreet.* He walked through the city taking in the different architecture, each street changing with the pace of his thoughts. No-one seemed to notice that a missing soccer star was in their midst. He sat for hours outside a café near the Grand Palace. He tried to think of nothing that was going on in his life that first morning. Not his family, not the team, nothing connected to his past or present. Instead, he watched without his conscience muttering a single word. Neighbouring cafés were opening; even an ice cream shop opposite had a small line forming within minutes of the start of business. A waiter apologised as he put a white tablecloth on his table. Sol liked the old-fashioned sense of where he was sitting. It was as if he was stepping back in time, observing a different world take shape in front of his eyes.

His mobile was ringing but he didn't take any calls. No calls, that is, except for David Dein's. Wenger and Dein had met and been on the phone constantly since he left the ground. At first they had no idea where he was. Wenger was worried. When he recalled the moment Sol said he couldn't go on, he saw a different face than the one he usually saw in the dressing room. There was something so vulnerable about Sol that day. He was shocked, to think how deep in crisis Sol was and must have been over the weeks. But when you see a man strong on the outside, it is harder to recognise his weakness on the inside. Wenger now saw the suffering going on inside and the loneliness Sol felt even with his team-mates at training.

'You always underestimate how much people suffer,' Wenger says. 'I realised he was in trouble when he left that night because I knew he wasn't a quitter. I had known him long enough to sense something tough had happened. That, lying below the surface, was perhaps a deep anxiety. I said to David Dein, we have to find him. What had happened was so out of the ordinary. I feared he might do harm to himself. I did not know.' It consumed Wenger. How in the end a team game becomes so individual, like the plight of the superstar comedian who suffers inside and alone, and ends his life in a hotel after the show because he has no-one to bear-hug after the laughter.

Dein called Sky Andrew. He hadn't been working so much with Sol of late and told Dein that he had no idea where Sol had gone. Dein called around but got nowhere until he tried Bon Battu, Sol's lawyer. Battu would call him and make sure Sol got in touch. Dein was relieved and immediately rang Wenger. These were long hours for the Arsenal manager. He had spent much time, and would again for many days ahead, asking himself whether he should have noticed what was going on with one of his star players. What could he have done differently?

'We always forget how much stress these players are under. Always expected to perform well and if they don't, people can be very harsh,' says Wenger. 'I think it's especially hard for international players, the ones who consistently play in tournament football like Sol. Everyone argues that they are overtired and we should have a break in the season, say at Christmas, but what many people don't realise is that it's as much mental fatigue as it is physical. They never get a proper mental rest.

And, over the years, it slowly drains them. We forget that the athlete who goes to the Olympic games in the summer takes two months off afterwards. But, for the footballer, three weeks later he's back and expected to perform at the highest level.'

•   •   •

Dein called and Sol picked up. He asked Sol if he could help; straightforward, honest and keeping his word from when they first met. 'We will protect you,' he had said.

He cancelled his meetings and went straight to Heathrow. He took the next available flight to Brussels. He knew from their very first meeting that Sol was vulnerable and needed to be looked after. He saw a deeper thinker who, in simple terms, needed to be loved. 'The first thing I wanted when we first met was for him to trust me,' Dein says.

They met in a small French bistro later that night, with no more than eight tables of which only half were occupied. Low-lit, with plenty of scope for a private conversation. The food was good, and although it was Sol's first visit there seemed a familiarity. At the table was Dein, Elizabeth and Sol. It was pleasant, easy conversation. Sol liked Dein. He had done since they first met and his visit of support would never be forgotten. 'Dein loves his club and that makes everything he says sound sincere,' Sol reiterates.

They drank white wine and ordered fish from the menu. Sol spoke mainly about his football. He wasn't ready to open up to Dein about every part of his life, of why he had escaped, why he had fled to a foreign city. Sol's tone was surprisingly sanguine. He said he felt he was letting himself down and in return letting the team down with his performances. His fight for full fitness was a continuous struggle. 'So when you are trying to regain your form and you're in pain, it makes the road back complicated and very difficult,' says Sol. 'With everything that was going on, I didn't even have my form to fall back on. Football was my life. It had created all these opportunities, my everyday existence was bound up in it and here I was, losing that too. I can't truly express the pain of having the sense that I was losing my career as a footballer. That, on top of everything else, nearly proved too much...'

Dein of course understood. He had great respect for the player he helped to sign. He, like many at Arsenal, had seen what pressure Sol had been put under since his transfer across North London. But he had no idea that the difficulties would escalate to this degree. He certainly hadn't expected it. Dein assured Sol that he had his manager's backing. That he should take his time and return only when ready. They shook hands on it. 'I appreciated Dein coming out to see me, it meant a lot,' Sol says. Yet there is no resentment that Wenger did not call Sol once during those days. It is only sice then that he's heard how concerned Wenger was. 'It's just not his style. He isn't like Alex Ferguson, who has the reputation of knowing, or rather wanting to know, what's going on in his players' lives. Arsene does not. It's okay. I knew how it was.'

After the dinner, Sol began to believe he was already on the road to recovery. His mere action of escape had helped clear his mind. Although he had only been in Brussels at that point for four days, he felt better, so much better. 'I'll be back before the week is out,' he thought.

The next few days followed the pattern of days before; Elizabeth dropping Sol in town before she went off to work and Sol finding a bar or a café, where he could slink away with his demons, clearing them slowly from his mind. He spent evenings in with Elizabeth and the children. He had started to reply to his messages. He called his mum every day. *My poor mum*, he thought. The family had been ripped apart by his fame, his success. His brother's prison sentence, the gossip and lies about his sexuality. *I'm quiet. That's all. I'm just reserved. People are suspicious of that. God help me! Why don't people understand I'm just different to most professional footballers? I keep myself to myself and because of this everyone thinks I'm odd.* He leaves the café, which has become his second home, and walks into the Grand Place and looks around at the locals and tourists as they take in its beauty. He feels part of them, not separate as he had when he first arrived. Yes, it's time to go home. He may not be cured but he is certainly strong enough to return to England. He is determined to pick up his career again and see through his contract with Arsenal.

The following morning, he was driven to the station. He said goodbye to the children and thanked Elizabeth for her true friendship. He will be forever grateful. The Eurostar home was without incident. He slept most of the way. When he arrived in London, he hailed a black cab. As the cab moved away from the station, the driver looked into his rear mirror and recognised his passenger. He said nothing. He left Sol alone until he got out and then refused to accept Sol's fare.

'Welcome home Sol,' the cabbie said. 'You've been missed.'

•   •   •

Champions League Final 2006

'I think it just came down to little mistakes here and there as to why we didn't win the Champions League. I believe the Cup will remain elusive until something clicks; something changes and luck turns in our favour.'

SOL

He woke up early on the morning of the 2006 Champions League Final in the Hotel de Crillon in Paris. His mouth was dry. What time is it? He groped for his watch. One minute before the alarm was set. His timing was good. Let's hope it lasts the whole day. Before he showered, he knelt down on his knees by his bed and prayed. He heard it said that to try to pray *is* to pray. Sometimes it flowed, other times it was difficult. But that morning, the words flowed easily. He prayed as ever for his mother, for God to watch over the team, for strength that he would play his best. He got up feeling good, feeling strong. He had a shave and then a long hot shower. While doing so, he kept on repeating to himself, 'Today, I am going to make my presence felt.' It was going to be his last game for the club. He was moving on.

He had met with Dein and Wenger and told them he wanted to leave. 'I needed to get out of England, to get out of London to play abroad. At the time, I thought I had little choice.' He pauses and reflects on what he has just said. 'Maybe they should have made more of an effort to keep me. I knew my form had dipped and there were the other problems, which of course they knew about. But with me, they had quality and a player who had proved himself.' His tone softens. 'Perhaps they should have persevered in trying to change my mind. Not let me go. Like Alex Ferguson did with Ryan Giggs. He's a quality player, and there was a time he could have let him go to Inter Milan but he didn't, because he knew he would get out of his trough and that eventually his quality would come through.'

He still had two-and-half years remaining on his contract but it was agreed that he would finish with Arsenal at the end of the season and become a free agent. 'I think if I had a regret, it was that I should have stayed with Arsenal and let them find me another club. I don't think I needed the stress at that point in my life of becoming a free agent. But I was never sold by any club I played for. I think I'm the only player from the top league to have that.

'But there comes a moment on any journey when you're tired, and you just want to leave, however wonderful the place.'

'I supported him leaving Arsenal,' says Arsene Wenger, 'because I thought a fresh start abroad would help. I think the Arsenal-Tottenham transfer still shadowed him probably more than he realised. It was lasting far longer than any of us could believe. There would be none of that abroad.'

•   •   •

Sol is shaving methodically and looking at the strokes from the electric razor on his chin. He cuts himself, or could have sworn he cut himself but no blood emerges. No, it was sucked out long ago, he thinks. He feels the hangover from the season, the previous months. He knows he's only playing today because of an injury to Philippe Senderos; as they say 'through other's misfortune you get your chance.' He had played in the second leg of the Champions League semi-final. After Arsenal beat Villarreal 1-0 in the first leg from a Kolo Touré goal, in the return they drew 0-0 at El Madrigal. A last-minute penalty save from Jens Lehmann secured the two-leg victory. Sol remembers that moment as a sign he was truly back: 'No-one realised that when Jens parried it out, the danger was still on. But I did. I saw the danger before the penalty-kick was even taken. I'd worked out instinctively, call it what you will, that if the ball was parried by the keeper it would fall at the exact spot it did. If I hadn't been alert and kicked it out for a corner, then it'd be 1-1...'

Back in Paris, he finds his mind drifting towards thoughts of the final against Barcelona. 'It was with me all day, that this was going to be my last-ever game for Arsenal.' But few know this, certainly none of the players. He has told just two people that he is leaving: one his lawyer, the other is his mother. Not unlike when he moved to Arsenal in the first place. At times over the last months since his return from Brussels, he'd felt a little peaky, as if he was climbing a mountain and altitude sickness was setting in. But not this morning. He is feeling positively positive; the past cleansed, the present what he has worked for since kicking the ball against the wall as a little boy.

He has breakfast alone in his room: coffee with three slices of brown toast. Yes, he felt good, he felt strong and fit; a hundred per cent fit for the first time in a long while, since an injury sustained in training on the big toe of his left foot. 'Kolo Touré did a block tackle with his studs showing. It was a stress reaction, which at first was dealt with by a couple of injections. Maybe I should have let it heal and, when I got back to full fitness, start to try to get back in the side. But like most players, we want to continue, we want the games to flow. I wasn't twenty-one any longer. I suppose I was fearful I'd never get my place back.'

The team met downstairs. When he returned from his days in Brussels, he brought the players together and apologised for what had happened. 'He said he was sorry and we all moved on,' says Thierry Henry. 'I didn't approach him about what had happened. We spoke a lot, so I knew some of what he was going through. I thought if he wants to talk more, I'm here for him. What I truly believe is that Sol deserves happiness.'

The squad went for a walk close to the hotel on Place de la Concorde. The Parisians seemed oblivious to the group of football superstars marching down the street. As he walked, he found himself looking at his team-mates. *We have a good chance.* He felt relaxed. The team seemed relaxed. He studied the players and their movements. *Here we are, at the top of our game. Ready.* As far removed as you could be from the days when you're a rookie youth player called up for your first appearance for the first team; the nerves, the tension, the anxiety about not being ready. It had never been like that for Sol. He had always been ready. He was relishing the day. He loved competing at the highest level. It was his drug. He was also thinking if he played well today, another club would be interested.

When they got back to the hotel, they had a meeting to discuss more of the game, followed by lunch. They spoke about individuals for Barcelona. So many of their players were dangerous. Giuly, on the left, liked making runs into the central areas to try to split the right-back and centre-half, or sometimes if the centre-forward came deep, he would try to do a diagonal run in between the two centre-halves, to break the line, or collect a clever ball threaded through to him on the run. In that way he was similar to Freddie Ljungberg.

Ronaldinho had the ability to break the back line with the ball. He could thread the ball through as well as anyone, or chip the ball over the defence. Nothing with the Brazilian was predictable, other than he was going to do something very special. He had the ability to shoot from outside the box from twenty-five or thirty yards out. 'We were aware that Ronaldinho and Deco were dangerous with their shooting. If they got the ball outside the box, we had to lock them down and engage immediately. I would rather he tried to shoot when I was right in front of him, because I'm confident I've got his line. I can see from the shape of his foot where he's shooting. But I must not show my cards immediately, because the best players are quite likely to do a fake to get closer to the goal,' says Sol. 'We were aware that Edmilson would sit deeper in midfield as the other two moved forward. He was there as a safety net, to be in the right places so we didn't have much of a chance at goal. We knew Van Bommel would receive the ball and distribute it very quickly. He had a rather nasty way about him; always with the backchat. He was almost like a hatchet man, trying to hurt you. But he was good at it and he could certainly play football. We spoke of Van Bronckhorst, formerly of Arsenal. We knew he had a good left foot, so you couldn't allow him to have space diago- nally on the edge of the box. If he came into that danger zone, we had to watch him.'

When the Arsenal players went onto lunch, they felt confi- dent. They held no fear. They just wanted to get on with the game. Sol had chicken soup, some bread, followed by plain pasta. He drank apple juice. Afterwards he went back to his room to have a siesta. He slept for over an hour. He got up and did some stretching, went downstairs to have some tea and toast and then returned to his room to have his second shower of the day; a hot shower to loosen his muscles. Before leaving his room to meet the team downstairs, he took a bottle of water from the minibar and poured it, the neck of the bottle rattling against the glass. It resembled a bell in a boxing ring. Seconds out. *Yes, I'm ready. I've never been so ready.*

When he got downstairs, the team had a quick ten-minute meeting before boarding the coach. 'Bon chance!' the girls at the front desk shout and bystanders stare and wonder what fate may bring these players. And then it's off to the Stade de

France to play in the Champions League final in front of the world. 'Rock 'n' roll,' says Sol as he boards the coach.

'The atmosphere at the stadium felt like two warlords ready for battle. You have Catalan on one side, you have London on the other; ready to do battle out on a green cut field. It is beautiful to me. It's where I find peace.' The dressing room is louder than usual; players pacing, psyching themselves up; a feverish energy. Sol stretches out first his legs, and then arms. The yellow shirts seem to shimmer, although here there is no breeze. Is that plain yellow or is it a golden yellow shirt? He's never thought about that before. It's hardly important but the thought for a second is there. He's in his zone but his heightened awareness makes him observant of the smallest detail. Wenger says a few words before the team leaves the dressing room. The words were no longer important. They all knew what they had to do. Wenger nods his head at Sol. He has faith that the rock of his defense, the spine of his Invincible team, will not let him down.

In the tunnel, Sol looks at his opposition: Carlos Puyol, Ronaldinho, Samuel Eto'o... Some players like to look straight ahead towards the light but not Sol; he likes to take it in, feel gladiatorial. Although there are eighty thousand people a few feet away, he hears little sound except the crackle of movement from the players standing in line. The calm remains uninterrupted until he steps into the light... And then a roar explodes.

The teams line up in front of the main stand to the accompaniment of the Champions League anthem. 'There was a moment out there, and it happens with the England team during the national anthem, where I almost went into a daze. It's like I'm not there anymore. I don't notice the cameras hovering in front. I simply zone out for about ten seconds, into a deep meditation. It happens every time at games where the pressure is magnified. One, two and three, up to ten and then suddenly I come back and like that,' Sol snaps his fingers, 'I'm ready!'

•　　•　　•

Barcelona 2 Arsenal 1, Champions League Final, Stade de France, 17 May 2006

BARCELONA: Valdes, Oleguer (Belletti 71), Marquez, Puyol, Van Bronckhorst, Deco, Edmilson (Iniesta 45), Van Bommel (Larsson 61), Giuly, Eto'o, Ronaldinho. Subs Not Used: Jorquera, Motta, Xavi, Sylvinho. Goals: Eto'o (76), Belletti (80).

ARSENAL: Lehmann, Eboue, Toure, Campbell, Cole, Pires (Almunia 20), Silva, Fabregas (Flamini 74), Hleb (Reyes 85), Ljungberg, Henry. Subs Not Used: Bergkamp, Van Persie, Senderos, Clichy. Sent Off: Lehmann (18). Goals: Campbell (37).

Att: 79,500. Ref: Terje Hauge.

In a thrilling final, Campbell gives Arsenal the lead in the 37th minute with a bullet header, but only after the Gunners are reduced to ten men with the sending off of goalkeeper Lehmann after he upends an onrushing Eto'o. Arsenal are forced into a reshuffle and replace Pires, as Barcelona take control of the match in the second-half. The pressure finally tells, when Larsson plays in Eto'o for an equaliser, followed four minutes later by substitute Belletti's winning goal. A brave fight by Arsenal, but Barcelona are champions of Europe.

Thierry Henry could have twice given Arsenal the lead in the opening minutes. He turned brilliantly, only to be denied by the diving Victor Valdes from point-blank range, and from the resulting corner was again denied by the goalkeeper saving at the near post. Then the Lehmann sending off. 'I don't blame Jens. In the end he did save us from being a goal down early on in the match,' Sol says.

Barcelona duly built up the pressure, but it was Sol who scored. 'No-one picked me up. Barcelona seemed arrogant, like he won't be any trouble, or whatever. There was definitely a sense of that.' Wenger lifted his arms in delight. 'I knew it would be Sol. He was destined to score. It was Sol once again climbing to the occasion. He was immense that day. Immense.'

Henry had swung the ball in from a free-kick. 'It wasn't aimed for me but it went into the perfect area, where one of the big guys can get their head to it. If it misses me, it will hit someone else,' says Sol. He timed his run to perfection; just a few paces but those of a seasoned player. It isn't surprising how important goals from senior players seem to come from an accumulation of experience: where to position yourself, your actions, the movement off the ball, an instinctive feeling of what the opposition is going to do. He meets the ball hard with strength and twists his head to guide it in perfectly. Nothing was going to stop him meeting that ball. Nothing was going to stop him scoring one of the most important goals of his life.

'Once it left my head, I knew it was a goal,' he says. 'It hit a sweet spot. Even if the goalkeeper had been standing there, he wouldn't have saved it. I knew that the ball was heading straight into the net.' The goal gave Arsenal some breathing space but not for long. 'Samuel Eto'o turned me. He spun round and hit a shot against the post. He judged the spin right, and there was no way I could take him out. That's how quick football is. He didn't do it again. I learned. I had taken in the speed of his movement. I'm able to do that with strikers.

'Larsson coming on in the second half changed things even more. He's a fine player,' says Sol. But still, Arsenal had their chances. Freddie Ljungberg was denied by a superb save from Valdes and Henry had an opportunity but once again was denied by the goalkeeper. And then the two late Barcelona goals meant it was game over.

'We nearly won the game. Although we had ten men it didn't really matter; it was incredible how hard we fought. By the end we'd had enough opportunities to put the game to bed. You can't afford to waste chances against a side like Barcelona.' Sol was brave in the post-match interviews but felt pain. The disappointment was overwhelming. He knew he would never play in a match of such magnitude again. He still didn't tell anyone he was leaving the club. What was the point? The mood in the dressing room and around the camp was already downcast.

He wasn't going to add to the low. These were his team-mates; his friends.

When he left the Stade de France, he felt once again very alone. How defeat accentuates solitude. As the coach drove through the Paris streets, he never properly saw anything. Not unlike his mind at the time. *No-one really understands what I've been through, the struggle to get back to this point.* He lets out a sigh of submission. No-one hears it.

He thinks of his time as a young boy. He needed to regain that joy of playing football again, when he played for hours against the wall, and played with his mates inside the cage, a concrete area enclosed by a wired fence twenty feet high, where you had to learn to control the ball in that space or else you lost it, and spent your time chasing after it.

As the bus turned into Place de la Concorde he thought ahead about how difficult it would be to find a new club, the right club. He looked at his team-mates, heads down, slumped in their seats. They had become his friends on the field. Men who had learned to trust and respect each other. These same men had never lost their hunger and had always given a hundred per cent; now he would probably lose touch with many. At his most vulnerable time he was losing part of his family. He felt a flicker of worry. He saw the reflection of his face in the coach window. He was surprised to see his feelings showing. He was usually good at hiding that; one of the best. And then he thought of the goal he'd just scored. He was still good, still had it in him. And he felt better, and thought more positively, during a difficult end to the evening.

Juventus were interested. *Yes, that sounds good.* He had been told the negotiations were well underway. He'd be going to Turin soon to meet them. Turin? He knew little of the city but he had heard it was small and comfortable for a stranger.

He glanced at Robert Pires sitting a couple of rows ahead. Poor Robert, he had so looked forward to the game and yet he was the one to be sacrificed after the sending off. He remembered the look Robert had given him back in the dressing room at Highbury, the evening he left the ground and fled to Brussels. It now seemed such a long time ago. He convinced himself that he was a different person. He had changed and was now better. And yet he hadn't had any therapy after his return. The club did not offer, or suggest that he needed, some professional help. Wenger had never taken him aside and offered him any fatherly advice. 'That was not his style,' Sol says, as before. It was still a time when depression or any other form of mental illness, even in a club the size of Arsenal, was not acknowledged or fully understood. It is only now that players are beginning to talk freely about it, and clubs are much more aware of it now.

Those so unfortunate as to be suffering from clinical depression were seen as weak. In those days, there were seen to be two basic sides to the personality: the happy and the sad, the light and the dark. But if that's the case, have suicides in football been a tragic mistake, like a shot fired by someone so innocent that he's unaware of such a thing as a safety catch? When it happens, how could anyone know that he did not intend to kill himself? Things are better now, but much of the football world is still stuck in the dark ages. If you are slightly different, you are still looked upon as an oddity.

Much of what was happening to Sol in those days resembled a cloud that, like the moment itself, soon changes and passes, and is never to be repeated again.

• • •

When they got back to the hotel, there was food for the players and entourage. Sol was hungry, so he stayed to eat but he didn't want to talk. Ever since he was a kid, he was not the best company after losing a match, and it was the same that day. The dinner was full of polite, formal half-conversation, interspersed with the spasmodic rumble of thunder from the outside, threatening to break the warm weather. He ate quickly and excused himself from the table. He wanted to get to his room and pack for the flight home, which was set to depart later that same evening. He left the room with the hum of debate on what went wrong; the post-mortem on a dead match.

He shared the elevator up to his room with what looked like an affluent Arsenal fan. He looked like the sort of man who gets what he wants. There was a long silence until the elevator stopped on the fourth floor. Neither one moved. It was a mistake. The elevator doors closed and the fan gave a smile, as if to say he always pressed the wrong number.

Finally he broke the silence: 'Great goal, Sol.'

Sol mumbled a thank you. How he would change everything, even his majestic goal, just to have the European Cup in his hands.

'You know, we may have lost tonight but you did yourself and us good. I know what you've been through.'

They shook hands as the elevator stopped on the third floor. Just as the fan was getting out he said, 'It's an honour to have met you, Sol.'

As the elevator doors were closing, Sol heard the fan's resolution, said loudly enough that it probably woke up the whole hotel. 'We'll win it next year, no problem.'

The words pulsed in his head. Sol wanted to shout back, 'Not with me you won't!' but of course, he didn't. Instead, he looked up and watched the numbers of the floors as the elevator climbed slowly upwards.

ENGLAND

'When I put on the England shirt, I had a collection
of thoughts. It was like going into battle, fighting for
your team, your country.'

SOL

Passers-by stare and wonder how someone could be so lucky. But it can soon be forgotten, your name remembered by the few when only years before it would be difficult to walk down the street without a greeting or discreet nudge from one friend to another.

He had 73 England caps; the only player to have represented his country in six consecutive international tournaments. He was named in the official team of the tournament in both the 1998 and 2002 World Cups, and the 2004 European Championship. Aged 23 years and 248 days, he became the youngest England captain after Bobby Moore. He played under five England managers – Terry Venables, Glenn Hoddle, Kevin Keegan, Sven-Goran Eriksson and Steve McClaren – and scored England's opening goal in the 2002 World Cup in Japan. He had goals disallowed against Argentina in France '98 and against Portugal in Euro 2004, which would have changed his country's football history.

Sol Campbell's international career, virtually more than any other English footballer, encapsulates the expression 'Life is one long "if only"...' If those goals had been given, how life would have changed. In the way we all regard him. How we would remember him. Our hero? The man whose goals led us to glory? One of our best, most consistent international defenders, rather than a career that attracted enthusiastic interest for a short while, but has since been ignored or largely forgotten as new players have emerged.

Everything new is something old forgotten.

•   •   •

On 9 November 1996, Sol was picked by England for his first World Cup qualifier. He had made his international debut six months earlier against Hungary in a friendly. But against Georgia in Tiblisi, the second game of the qualification group, he would be starting for England for the first time. There would be no team sheet pinned to the wall like at school. He would be told while sitting in a team meeting. The full squad at long tables, watching the projector as the management went over the previous game; and then, without warning, the projector showing the team for the next game.

'At first I wasn't sure and then looked again.' Sol's name came into focus. 'Shit!' It was like someone creeping up from behind and bursting a paper bag right behind his ears. 'It was!'

He sat motionless. He didn't want anyone to notice how excited he was. His international future seemed all of a sudden, in an instant, to open up, with the realisation that he could really be part of the England setup. Even become a regular, a first pick.

He starts to go through in his mind the stretches and exercises he will need to do before going to bed. A mini-workout planned in seconds! Manager Glenn Hoddle continues to go through tactics. He listens but his mind is now elsewhere. *I need a good night's sleep. If I get to bed by nine, I'll be asleep by ten and up by seven. I must conserve all my energy. Pace myself.* Before going to sleep that night he prays the next day is good, and that he plays to the best of his ability. *I don't want to let anyone down.*

The next morning, he was at once wide-awake. In fact, he didn't so much as wake up, as sit up. 'Enjoy today,' he said out loud.

His mind speeds through his preparation until kick-off. Again, he repeats he doesn't want to let anyone down. He doesn't. England win 2-0. 'I made a good account of myself. I was nervous but confident. It was a nice and easy debut. It's always difficult playing away from home (it doesn't matter who you play) and to win was very satisfying.'

• • •

How suddenly life can change. England were defeated by Italy at Wembley three months later, on 12 February 1997. Zola scored in the ninth minute to win the game by a single goal. Sol learned a lesson that night in dealing with the press. It was only his fourth game, still just twenty-three and looking to become a regular in the heart of the defence. In international football, there is no room for sentiment; after the game, Sol and goalkeeper Ian Walker were blamed for the goal. 'I was naïve. I discussed openly with the press that it might have been my fault. Afterwards, I'd see captions in different magazines, blaming Walker and me for the loss. "Blame these two if we don't qualify," I glimpsed in one of the papers. You can imagine how I felt after seeing that.'

The reaction derailed any further admissions. He and the goalkeeper were being made scapegoats. He was learning that playing for England was different to playing for your club. The media inspection was more intense. He didn't mind, as long as they were fair. He noticed other players were guarded. 'I wouldn't be hiding, but I certainly wanted to protect myself in the future,' Sol says.

• • •

Italy 0 England 0, 1998 World Cup qualifier Group 2, Stadio Olimpico, Rome, 11 October 1997

ITALY: Peruzzi, Nesta, Maldini (Benarrivo 32), Albertini, Cannavaro, Costacurta, Di Livio, Baggio, Vieri, Zola (Del Piero 63), Inzaghi (Chiesa 46). Sent off: Di Livio (77).

ENGLAND: Seaman, Campbell, Le Saux, Ince, Adams, Southgate, Beckham, Gascoigne (Butt 89), Wright, Sheringham, Batty.

Attendance: 81,200. Referee: Mario Van Der Ende.

In a belligerent backs-to-the-wall performance, England get the draw they need to ensure their passage to the World Cup finals in France. The enduring image from the match is the bandaged bloodied head of Paul Ince after an elbow from Albertini resulted in several minutes off the pitch with the England man receiving stitches. The sending off of Di Livio with fifteen minutes remaining after a foul on Campbell is the final nail in the coffin for the beleaguered Italians.

After the Wembley defeat to Italy, England won their next three matches in the group. It would come down to their last qualifying game to see who got automatic qualification to the World Cup in France the following year. England had to go to the Italian capital needing just a point to qualify. Not so easy. No team had won a point there in fifteen attempts. It was a time when Italy were making the beautiful game even more beautiful: their glorious blue shirts, their players looking like silver screen stars, and Serie A probably the best league in the world. 'I just love the football mentality of the Italians. It's the reverse there [to England]. Defenders, midfielders and goal-keepers get the respect and adulation that here is only reserved for strikers. They are the stars.' So here is this young man from Newham, about to play against a team and country he respected, against legends such as Paolo Maldini who he admired, knowing millions of people back home would be watching. 'It was the ultimate!'

The England coach was escorted through the local traffic by police bikes and flashing lights to the north of the city. The streets were alive, with fans banging on the roofs of their Fiats, Vespas weaving through traffic like horses in blinkers; the Italians all gestures and gesticulations, a cacophony of sound. National colours hanging with pride from every conceivable vantage point showing that the Romans are resolute; this will be their day. England are in town. We beat them at Wembley, they are saying, now to the slaughter in Rome without a single lion needed. These times it is left to Cannavaro, Maldini, Zola and Vieri to slay the opposition.

Sol knew he would be playing on the Saturday. Any doubt he may have had was dispelled as soon as the pattern of play was worked on at the training ground, a few days before. He woke up nervous on the morning of the match. 'Not a bad thing as it focuses the mind,' he says. He sat towards the back of the coach. Three-quarters of the way down. He didn't want to be too near the front. That's where the management sits. Huge crowds were building along the route from the city to the stadium. Delays were occurring on every block.

'Get out of the middle of the road!' Fans are singing and dancing as the coach rolls by, crossing from the side of the street to get a closer look. There is a big match in Rome today. Sol watches the entertainment going on. The Carabinieri give orders for fans to disperse but they are slow in moving on. The Italian fans gaze up at the coach while the England supporters, on seeing their heroes, start a one-note chant.

'I remember, as we reached the stadium, I felt the butterflies inside my stomach begin to become a little more intense. I was excited. In the back of my mind, I was thinking I want to play the best game of my life. In a matter of hours, we could qualify for the World Cup.'

Paul Ince sat a few rows ahead in the coach. Sol looks at the player as he is talking to another team-mate. He thinks it was Ian Wright but he's not sure. He watches Ince's gesticulations. He had played in Italy, for Inter Milan. He had played for the best teams. He had experience. We will need that today, thinks Sol. More than ever. 'I think anyone would want Ince in their team because of his desire and his skill. He knew his position and he was an incredible tackler. He was not just a force. His anger motivated everyone around him.'

They get off the coach in silence, each player with their own thoughts and desires. Sol's mind is racing. He could not think quickly enough. He needed to calm down. On the outside, he looks assured for someone so young, but inside his heart is beating with an excitement, the will to win, a determination. The stadium is a block of concrete; grey and sullen, contrary to the player's mood of anticipation and excitement. It is pretty soulless on the inside too. 'There is no finesse about most of the international stadiums around the world,' says Sol, 'they tend to be very bland.'

Sol puts his bag down. Some of the players go to the massage room. Sol wants to get out and see the pitch as soon as possible, impatient like a schoolboy. It is something he does and will always do before a match. The stadium is virtually empty but the tension is still evident. There are England supporters around but the Italian fans, as is the norm in this country, tend to stroll in with minutes to go before kick-off.

He walks from one end of the pitch to the other. It is not only the players who are your opposition; it can also be the turf. He bends up and down like a bird feeling its texture, at first slowly and then shifting his hand along with greater pace and with concentration. He sees how long the grass is; it's different in every stadium. In some it's cut short, in others left long. The Italians liked their football to be a little slow, so the grass would be longer. By the time he walked from one box to the other, he knew it was a good pitch with no wet patches or particularly bad areas. That's good, he thinks, and now he is ready to pull on his England shirt and reap the rewards.

Back in the dressing room, he decides what studs to wear. He always liked longer studs, especially as a defender. His movement and style of play suited the longer length unless it was bone dry and then he would use moulds. He hardly ever wore just moulds, maybe only for pre-season friendlies. Towards the latter part of his career he would wear both, multi-studs (moulds and studs). He was one of the first footballers to do that. But today the longer studs will do. He gets down to business. He tightens his laces loop by loop, twice, and finishes off in a short bow, muttering, 'Okay, okay! Let's get out there.'

Glenn Hoddle was keeping his team calm. Quiet words to those he felt needed them. He had worked his team well and thoroughly. His preparations were complete. There was no need to panic. No, he'd done his job. This was his moment too, as a young international manager, to show the world, and he sensed his destiny. He gave the impression he had little doubt a result could be achieved. Sol was ready; as ready as he ever had been in his still brief international career. He had the look of a man focused for the coming hours. He felt relaxed and confident. Mature beyond his years. As he finished putting his white No.2 shirt on, he once again observed his team-mates. 'I looked at Shearer, I looked at Adams and thought, I've got winners here. Each one of us was ready to fight for our lives like an army going into battle. We were not going to be defeated.' He sat there, repeating to himself the mantra instilled in his psyche by his father: 'You have one chance. Grab it!' Yes, this was a game to take the chance and not look back. Paul Gascoigne knew it also. He stands, then strides around the dressing room. It is difficult to keep him calm. He is the opposite to Sol. This had once been his home ground, playing for Lazio at a time when he never attained full fitness and couldn't reach the heights he dreamed of. He could show the Italians today what they'd missed.

As the players prepared to leave the dressing room, Hoddle shook each one firmly by the hand, followed by placing his hand onto their chest just above the heart; it was meant to be a sign of reassurance. The players slapped each other on the back and knew what had to be done. Sol's heart was starting to pound hard. He didn't mind Hoddle's interest in the ethereal.

He thought it fitted neatly into his character. There were others who thought it was a little weird. But there was no thought of it now. They had a job to do. To win or draw. And then off to the World Cup. It sounded so simple.

•   •   •

The England team soaked up pressure from the very beginning. They were disciplined, with each player going in hard to disrupt the rhythm of the Italians. The English were playing like the Italians. Hoddle knew his team could beat them at their own game. There was Ince, wiping his forehead, a deep cut and a shirt splattered with blood, looking as if he'd been in a street brawl; then, returning to the pitch after a long delay with a white bandage, that seemed to belong more to a World War II movie, wrapped around his head. It encapsulated the day, the spirit. He was gone from the action for eight minutes and the English support filled in the space. The noise from the English fans drowned out the Italians. Ian Wright very nearly won it at the end, when he went around the goalkeeper and hit the post but immediately the ball was at the other end, for Christian Vieri to head just wide of the goal; he should have scored. The Italian bench groaned at the miss. The game was over. England won 0-0!

Sol met Vieri years later back in Italy, and with a shake of a hand they reminisced about the classic game. It wasn't the miss Vieri chose to remember; it was Sol's first tackle of the afternoon. 'I will never forget it,' he said, 'it was the hardest tackle of my career.' The compliment of a good tackle, Sol thinks, outweighs any goal.

For the English, it was as exciting a goalless draw as was ever seen. When the final whistle blew, Hoddle jumped up and down in excitement and, of course, relief. His coaching staff joined in the celebrations. Sol embraced his team-mates. They were going to the World Cup! Glory in the draw! Hoddle walked up to Sol to congratulate him. He shook him warm-heartedly and Sol saw a smiling face he recognised so well, and yet in the excitement it looked strangely unfamiliar. 'Yes!!' Sol shouted, 'we did it!!'

Sol has praise for Hoddle. 'His ideas were original, he was exciting to work with,' and, in what seems like an afterthought says, 'It's a shame he didn't maintain his career as an international manager. I'm convinced he could have gone a long way.'

He ran towards the England fans packed on the terraces chanting the theme tune of 'The Great Escape'. It was the first time the supporters had bellowed out the song from the famous war movie and its continual drone had driven the Italian fans mad; they were almost stunned into silence. 'We won on the pitch and we won on the terraces without a fist being thrown,' a fan who was in Rome proudly says, as if re-living that special moment. It was a memorable Saturday afternoon for the England team and its supporters. 'We deserved it. It's great for the nation. It's eight years since we qualified and now the hard work starts,' Hoddle said.

These were good days for Sol. He was a first-team regular for both club and country and he was just twenty-three. His confidence soared to new heights. He loved his football and now felt no-one could stop him reaching the very top. He had moved forward with his life and career. Everything worked. The deftness of his play seemed to be guided by a force that shadowed him in everything he attempted. Walking without fuss in one direction, and that was upwards. He was improving, getting better, and he knew it. It was one of those defining periods in one's life that we all crave for. 'When I put on the England shirt, I had a collection of thoughts. It was like going into battle, fighting for your team and your country. I would think that I'm playing against the best players in the world and would love that I could master them, control them and nullify them. Yes, I would love that.' He takes a pause and continues, 'I think international football played at the highest level is the best. Even if you played in a friendly and it's a mundane game, you just knew it meant a lot, not just to yourself and the team, but to the whole country.'

Eight months later, on 29 May 1998, prior to the start of the World Cup finals in France, Campbell was asked to captain England in a friendly against Belgium. The sides drew 0-0. 'It was a tremendous moment for me. I was the second youngest captain ever, and I was very proud.' And then he whispered, as if entrusting someone with a big secret: 'I was living the dream.'

•   •   •

The dream continued for Sol, and for his country. Having reached the finals in France, England's qualification from the group stage opened up the way to the last 16 and a potentially epic clash with South American giants, Argentina. The world held its breath.

•   •   •

Argentina 2 England 2 (aet; Argentina win 4-3 on penalties), World Cup 1998 Round of 16, St Etienne, 30 June 1998

ARGENTINA: Roa; Vivas, Ayala, Chamot; Zanetti, Almeyda, Simeone (Berti 91); Ortega, Veron; Batistuta (Balbo 68), Lopez (Gallardo 68). Goals: Batistuta (pen 6), Zanetti (45).

ENGLAND: Seaman; G Neville, Adams, Campbell; Anderton (Batty 96), Beckham, Ince, Le Saux (Southgate 70); Scholes (Merson 78); Owen, Shearer. Sent off: Beckham (46). Goals: Shearer (pen 10), Owen (16).

Attendance: 30,600. Referee: K M Nielsen.

In one of the most talked-about games in the history of England internationals, Glenn Hoddle's men come close to knocking out one of the tournament favourites despite Beckham's infamous red card following his kick at Simeone. England find themselves trailing to an early Batistuta penalty following a Seaman foul, only for Shearer to equalise in similar fashion from the spot.

Owen's memorable slalom through the Argentina defence leads to a wonder goal and a 2-1 lead for the men in white, but Zanetti's strike from a clever free-kick sees Argentina level at half-time. England put on a brave performance in the second-half with ten men to take the game into extra time and the dreaded penalties, where misses by Ince and, at the last, Batty, send Argentina through and England cursing their misfortune.

Before the game Sol had never felt such intensity. Everything seemed louder. The stadium was full of noise, which could have been disconcerting to someone who hadn't experienced such feral rivalry before. But Sol remained calm. He was just excited to be part of such a big game. He knew who he was about to face. He was prepared. He had learned his lesson about surprises from the Chilean striker, Marcelo Salas, who, with his two goals, had almost single-handedly led the England defence on a merry dance when the two countries played in a friendly earlier in the year; it would not be repeated.

The ground was packed on one side with the flags of St George, on the other with dancing, faithful Argentinians throwing confetti in the air and passing their national flag up and down from hand to hand, each man or woman grabbing the cloth as if it will bring luck. A shadow looms over a contest between two countries formerly at war. This is when football becomes political, however hard those in government, managers and players tell you that sport and politics have nothing in common. Try telling the Argentinians that it's simply a football match; try telling the English. 'The Falklands is always there. We were always reminded about it, even if we wanted to forget it. It was a real grudge match, as big as Germany. We simply didn't want to lose. It was the game that could be made into a movie. It was full of drama,' Sol remembers.

Before he shook the Argentinian players' hands he had a fleeting moment of unease. Just for an instant, and he is not clear why. Probably tension. The tension between the teams was so tangible that it infiltrated everyone on the pitch, in the stadium, those watching around the world. The build up to World Cup games is different to anything. It stirred emotions that had lain dormant for years. 'We are in the second stage of the tournament. Now anything can happen. If we beat Argentina, we play the Dutch and then ...Who knows?' The two teams pose for their photographs: Argentina in all blue, England in all white. Sol runs away in short sprints towards the box, taking small jumps, getting rid of the last remnants of nerves. He shouts out something to himself or his team-mates, or to anyone listening. There is a delay before kick-off. Deep breathing. The teams are facing up and ready to go. Television! Sol thinks. The wait goes on and on. The referee in red shirt hesitates and hesitates again, and then blows his whistle. The crescendo of noise is so great it becomes almost muffled. Sol will feel the crowd's interminable support; more aware of it than ever, when it is most needed.

His first touch doesn't come until the end of the second minute. He calmly intercepts a through ball and lays on the perfect pass to full-back Graeme Le Saux to start an attack. He will continue in the same vein. He will have a good game.

The scores are level at 2-2 after an explosive first half. Shortly after the restart, when David Beckham is sent off for a petulant kick on Diego Simeone, confetti, bottles and wrappers are flung into the sky and the lights fade from Beckham's first World Cup. 'We weren't angry with him, no-one in the squad was,' Sol says. 'We needed to get on with it, we had to. We were down to ten men.'

Nine minutes to go and with the scores still level, Darren Anderton sweeps in a corner. The ball flies over Shearer, and Sol meets it in full flight, heads it downwards. He watches the ball bounce off the turf and over the line. For one moment, everything comes to a standstill. Everything suddenly goes dizzy. He turns before the ball reaches the net, and runs to the English supporters in celebration. It is a team sport but he feels completely alone. He sees in the corner of his eye everyone from the bench jumping up and down. *What a time to score my first goal for my country.* His has to be the winner. Suddenly he sees the bench is no longer celebrating but signalling to him, hands and fingers waving to and fro. One of the substitutes yells, 'Get back! The goal's been disallowed.' Alan Shearer's flailing elbow on goalkeeper Roa is adjudged to have been a foul by the referee.

'It was a goal,' Sol says. 'Unless you are actually holding someone down, it is fair to challenge for the ball.' And he moves his fingers to show the position of the players: goalkeeper there, right-back there, Shearer there.

His celebration stops. Ecstasy swept away in an instant. And now he has to run full speed to the other end as the Argentinians are attacking. It is down to the man who took the corner, Darren Anderton, who runs the length of the field to perform one of the great lung-busting diving tackles, to save the day. 'The game would have been over if he hadn't made that tackle. People shouldn't forget it. It was one the greatest tackles I've seen on a football pitch.'

Extra-time is to be played. The golden goal rule is in operation. The first team to score in extra-time wins. Game over.

It had been a tough ninety minutes. One of the toughest Sol remembers. He lies on his back in the break. He drinks water, lots of it. His legs are rubbed down. Manager Glenn Hoddle is issuing instructions. He hears his assistant John Gorman trying to motivate everybody. Banging the palm of his left hand with the fist of his right. 'Come on!' Sol can't get the disappointment of his disallowed goal out of his mind. If only...If only. Shearer never fouled. *Come on, snap out of it! We still have thirty more minutes to play. I'm strong; I feel strong. Pass me another bottle of water.* Les Ferdinand comes over and whispers words of encouragement. 'I got stronger and stronger throughout extra-time,' recalls Sol. 'It was strange, I felt I could run forever.'

The game remained level after extra-time. Penalties. 'I wasn't chosen in the first five to take a penalty. After that, there isn't a set list, you are just randomly chosen. I think I would've been picked way down the line – probably number ten before David Seaman! So there was little fear that I'd have to take one.

I've seen over the years some ordinary players better at taking penalties than shooting in open play. Others fall to pieces when faced with the test in a high-pressured game. If I'd taken one, I'd have kicked it as hard as possible straight down the line, into the centre of the goal. Sounds easy but I never took a penalty throughout my career.'

England lost the shootout 4-3. The England villains could have been anyone. No-one misses a penalty on purpose and the pain of missing probably never leaves the psyche. Our heroes are, after all, mere humans. 'We all played well. We could have won...We *should* have won, even with ten men,' says Sol.

He showers and changes in silence. He suffers pain far worse than he has felt before. He feels cheated. *Come on. Relax. It will get better.* It has been a spectacular match; one of the best World Cup games in recent years. Better to be part of a match like that than not being part of it at all. Really? He is gutted. Those hours after the game are difficult to face. *Time to go. Time to get out of this stadium.* If only we could make ourselves inconspicuous. Some hope.

The team drift away from their dressing room, passing by people with wide smiles; faces incongruous to the England players' mood. A ball boy in a tracksuit looks at the English stars excitedly. He is tempted to ask for autographs but something tells him to wait for the Argentinians. Sol and the players are now joined by their families as they walk slowly, like a group of mourners, towards their team coach. It's parked next to the Argentinians'. Sol is about to experience 'one of the worst things I saw in my time in football.'

As the England entourage climb aboard their coach, a badly trained choir of Argentinian footballers are jeering, jumping up and down, banging the windows and swinging their shirts over their heads. If they had a wreath, they would have tossed it over. In the English players' eyes, it was the worst form of sportsmanship. It would not be forgotten.

'It was a disgusting display. I thought it was despicable. No class. Never seen it before or since. But it showed how much it meant to them.' And now there was a slight tut in Sol's tone. 'I was glad they were knocked out in the next round by the Dutch.'

• • •

England had departed the World Cup finals in France in glorious defeat. In adversity, they had shown spirit and togetherness. But when they returned, dark clouds began to gather.

After the World Cup, Glenn Hoddle said something stupid, which gave the press a chance to hang him. Once the Prime Minister started to criticise the England manager, the FA had no choice. Hoddle was gone within days. Sacked for nothing to do with football. The news of his sacking is followed by the name of one man. All we can see and read are pundits supporting their next sacrifice. Faces magnified, mouths opened wide as his name is repeated. This is a one-horse race.

The clamour had started. It grew in intensity, a fire being flamed by a strong wind. The fawning was overwhelming: 'He should always have been our England manager'...'The man's a winner.'

The clocks are ticking; spring is coming. Optimism is at its height.

Kevin Keegan was named as England's saviour. The former Liverpool and Hamburg star was making his name in management, and the FA called Fulham owner Mohamed Al Fayed, who graciously gave his permission for Keegan to leave Craven Cottage to manage his country. At the time, everybody won: Keegan was our new manager, the media and FA got their man, and Al Fayed got his best press for years.

Sol respected Keegan. He was still receiving general approbation for his playing career and now he was being acclaimed as a manager. Sol was disappointed that Hoddle had left but he couldn't have wanted for a better replacement. Players tend to get over the sacking of managers far quicker than some managers would hope. 'Keegan could get the best out of you. He could make you feel ten feet tall. I'd never experienced that before,' Sol says. 'He had a passion, a desire; and, he was a legend and enthusiastic. He would always back you up. A good manager always backs you up, always, through good and bad times.'

Sol repeats a story he was told by Keegan: 'When Keegan was at Hamburg, the manager was not happy with his team; they were not playing well and not working hard enough. So he got the squad onto the training pitch and told his players to run until he told them to stop. But he didn't tell them to stop; he just let them run and run until they started to groan, to falter and then the first one dropped out followed by another and then another until there were only three players left standing, or rather running, of which one was Keegan. The next season, the manager chose a team, with the three players who kept running the first on the team sheet. The rest he got rid of.'

And the moral of the story? 'Hard work defines the spine of your team. You build it up from players who can tough it out,' Sol replies. 'Keegan believed it and so did I.'

•   •   •

After all the hoopla, Euro 2000 was a 'washout' as Sol puts it. England scraped through to the tournament by winning a two-leg play-off with Scotland. In the actual competition in Belgium and the Netherlands, England failed to get through their group. Losing in the first game to Portugal 3-2 in Eindhoven after being two-up, things improved in the next match with a 1-0 win against a very poor German side in Charleroi. England then played Romania in their final group game. They lost 3-2, an 89th minute penalty knocking them out of the tournament. Sol played in all the games. He moves his hand around, like he's flaying at a wasp, when he says: 'We needed a draw in the final game and we just didn't get it.' His first reaction was self-pity, then frustration, followed by, 'We have to move on. These things happen.'

Sol returned home with as much confidence in his manager as he did going out. He remained optimistic that Keegan and the players would turn it round. He found the manager easy to work with and the atmosphere in the camp was good. There weren't any dramas, no back biting. Things remained upbeat even though the team was losing. Any initial negative reactions from the players had begun to recede by the time they landed back on home soil. Keegan, at the airport, seemed as positive on the outside as he did on the first day of the job. You have a good break, he told Sol, and I will see you soon. They shook hands. It will come good, he promised.

• • •

England had Germany in their qualifying group for the 2002 World Cup in Japan and South Korea. They were drawn to play them in their opening match. Sol was unfit for the game after his shoulder injury at Brentford in the Worthington Cup. He watched it from the stands. It was never a good experience to watch a game but that afternoon was particularly miserable. It was the last game to be played at the old Wembley stadium, a place of pilgrimage. It was going to be pulled down. Old Wembley had become a scrapyard of past glories; a relic of better days, standing on a past mourned with the help of old newsreels, technicolour film and iconic photographs. There was a lot of shouting and reams of paperwork about who should or would buy the stadium, but in the end even the journalists couldn't muster any enthusiasm for the idea that the new owners would be the FA. Nevertheless, this was the last hurrah to our national stadium, so the anticipation was keen; and, what better way to celebrate than to beat Germany in a World Cup qualifier?

It rained and rained. On that soggy October day in 2000, the once beautiful stadium emptied at full-time, a fan leaving a small bunch of wild flowers on a seat behind one of the goals, where once the crowd had stood in an explosion of colour and song. The gesture left a sense of loneliness in the vast expanse, but sometimes an action such as this can herald a new beginning. It needed to. It was a bad day all round. England had lost

1-0 to a Dietmar Hamann free-kick, struck well outside the box and sent skimming along the wet surface, past David Seaman. And yet it was just the beginning of the bad news.

As soon as the final whistle went, Sol left his seat in the stand to go to the dressing room. He didn't know why but he had a feeling of unease as he made his way down. By the time he reached the tunnel, the rumours were spreading. It was being said that Kevin Keegan had resigned. No-one was sure if it was true.

Sol dismisses it as gossip, suspecting someone has invented the story, looking for an angle on a miserable day by making it even more miserable. Soon the news gets louder, and now the manager's words have reached the ears of the footballing world.

'I'm out of here. I'm not up to it. I can't motivate the players. I can't get the extra bit out of these players that I need,' Keegan had said in typically honest fashion. He'd had enough and was going home.

Sol was disappointed. He had tremendous respect for this passionate man. He wanted to go up to him and help change his mind. Things will work out, he thought. No need to panic. He wanted to give him the sort of shove that children do, when pushing their parents towards their favourite sideshow at the funfair. But he didn't. He simply walked away from the stadium, head down, towards his car. The only thing comforting the fans on that day was how honourable and honest the manager was in the face of defeat. He had fallen on his sword.

Keegan had spoken to Sol a number of times about him taking on the role of England captain. But as Sol drove away from the stadium, those thoughts were far from his mind. No, instead he thought what a solitary job it was to be England manager. He's never given much time and is inevitably sacked, sooner rather than later. A stark but obvious realisation came to him: the only way we can keep hold of the same manager is to win a tournament. *It's possible! We had a bad day but we have good players. We have the makings of a good team. We can win the World Cup. We can certainly still gain automatic qualification from the group.*

As Wembley disappeared from view, Sol knew the press would wail at the death of their chosen manager and then begin to guess who would be the new one. A fresh surge of optimism would develop. He had seen it before. He didn't mind who they chose as long as the incoming man was someone who could inspire the players with new ideas and, above all, that they could believe in him.

•　　•　　•

Sven-Goran Eriksson was one of the most respected managers in Europe. A slim man with rimmed glasses, a receding hairline and a face that gave the impression he ate too much junket, the Swede was the sort who you would imagine getting off his deathbed to straighten the bottom sheet. He tended not to look a person straight in the eye; instead, he would glance down at his shoes, as if he was trying to work out if one of his feet was longer than the other. He had a voice that was a medley of head-master, airport announcer and librarian.

There was a suspicion about having a foreign England man-ager. 'I was intrigued,' says Sol. 'I had no problem with it, other than being disappointed that we didn't have an Englishman good enough at the time to step in.' Yet Sven carried around with him an aura that quietly intimidated and demanded respect from the English football fraternity. When he asked for some-thing, he usually got it. People would half-acknowledge him as he walked into the room, unsure whether to go up and introduce themselves. His Italian girlfriend, Nancy Dell'Olio, with her gregarious clothing and flashbulb *Hello!* magazine smile, did not make the personality any easier to understand. Still, an air of invincibility shadowed him, and there was a sense that he knew it too. 'He was always hammering on about respect,' Sol says. 'He showed us we needed to treat everyone with the same amount of courtesy, from the tea lady to the chairman.'

Sven's start was auspicious. The team began to win again. Qualification for the World Cup finals in South Korea and

Japan, which had at first seemed a long way off, turned into a series of celebrations, with England eventual winners of their qualifying group. The highlight was a 5-1 win against Germany in Munich. Under an overcast sky and on a damp pitch, England humbled their once-mighty rivals, with Michael Owen scoring a hat-trick.

We are converts now. We of little faith. Who needs an English manager? The Swedish demigod receives acclamation. Salvation! You win in football and our lives need no longer be 'If only... If only.'

The spirit in the camp was good. It had reached the point where the squad was beginning to overflow with confidence. 'We had a bloody good team. It was probably the best England team I played in.' Sol's relationship with his manager was also good. 'He was always charming. He wanted everyone to be included, to be involved, and wanted to get advice from his senior players, one of which I'd now become.' Sol pauses. 'He also had a very popular assistant.'

That man was Tord Grip, an accordion player who had been assistant manager to Sven at Lazio. 'He was a lovely man who I'd talk to after training. He always had time for you.' He had a sense of humour too. When he read that Sven's girlfriend Nancy Dell'Olio was telling the press she was a lawyer, Tord allegedly quipped: 'The nearest she's ever been to court is Wimbledon.'

Before the tournament, the manager found himself embroiled in a 'red top' frenzy, when he was caught having a fling with Swedish television presenter, Ulrika Jonsson. The story was too good to be true for the tabloids, especially as Eriksson was meant to be in a monogamous relationship.

When the England team went abroad, sometimes the morning papers would suddenly disappear. It was either the manager or the FA's decision. 'When I was in a tournament, I never read the sports pages. I'd avoid the television, too. Sometimes, I'd watch the football phone-in programmes on Sky for a few minutes and they would be talking about England, and when the show was finished I wouldn't feel so good about myself, or what I'd heard about my team-mates. Criticism, or even praise, brought up an equal amount of negativity in my head. Once you believe in your own success, that's when you're finished. Others in the squad were addicted to the stuff and watched all the time. I'd think, what are you doing? Why do this to yourself? But I suppose we're all different.'

There was no sniggering or whispers when the England manager walked by at the start of the tournament. There was no feigning of reading a broadsheet newspaper with a tabloid hidden inside. None of the squad took any pleasure in the tittle-tattle of gossip. 'Absolutely not...,' says Sol, pausing. 'Probably because we all thought we could be next.'

•　　•　　•

'Every time we reached the finals of a major tournament, our talisman got injured,' Sol mourns. Japan 2002 would be no different. Before the squad set off, David Beckham, the England captain, suffered a broken metatarsal during a Manchester United Champions League match against Deportivo. Sol felt as concerned as every football fan. 'My immediate feeling was of disappointment. I knew it was going to be difficult but I truly believed with all our best players fit, we had a good chance of winning the World Cup.'

The England build up was consumed with the usual 'will he or won't he be fit for the tournament?' saga. In the end the England captain travelled and posed with the England team, Eriksson and the FA chairman on the steps of their British Airways flight to Tokyo. Sol had done it all before. He understood the razzmatazz that goes with travelling with the England squad. 'It's quite funny really. Everyone pretends they don't care how they look on the aircraft stairs, but I saw a few hankering to find the best place and checking their hair before the click of the cameras.' He chuckles at the revelation.

Flights bore Sol. As soon as he boards, he wants to get there. He dreads the long and seemingly slow journey to reach the other side of the world. The plane is full. There is a large team of staff travelling. The full squad flies Club Class while the FA chiefs and manager fly First. Sol spends his time watching films to pass the hours away. And then, as the plane approaches Japan and the passengers are asked to fasten their seatbelts, he meditates on what is about to happen. That perhaps he is nearing his dream. Everybody who has ever kicked a football dreams that one day they will lift the World Cup. The future is golden. He knows he is in top physical, mental and emotional condition, in order to summon up all the forces necessary to win. The unique chemistry of mind and soul is ready. He's never been so ready.

•   •   •

It's England v Sweden, the first game in Group F, in Saitama. After 24 minutes, David Beckham whips in a corner and Sol rises like a dolphin leaping from the sea. GOOAALLLL!!! Poetry at any time. His first international goal! A great cheer went up to the heavens.

This time there is no question. The goal is given and Sol darts away, as if a cell door has suddenly opened. He is in intense celebration, and is followed by Rio Ferdinand clambering over his shoulders. The World Cup has truly begun. As the whistle blows to restart the game, his heart soars and he thinks not only has he scored his first goal for England but he has scored in the World Cup, the most important tournament on the planet. What makes Sol happy? This is what makes him happy! The pleasure of it lapped sweetly at his mind. His name was in the history books, and this time, no-one could take it away. 'The relief that I had actually scored for England was so powerful. I'd been waiting for that for a long time.'

The game eventually ended in a 1-1 draw. When he looked up at the scoreboard he felt a pang of regret that the team had not gone on to win. But in the World Cup, the cardinal rule is don't lose your first game, so things weren't so bad. There was a sense of relief that they were off and running. England had a great chance. Now it was on to Sapporo and a little matter of revenge.

• • •

Argentina 0 England 1, Group F, World Cup 2002, Sapporo Dome, 7 June 2002

ARGENTINA: Cavallero, Pochettino, Samuel, Placente, Zanetti, Simeone, Veron (Aimar 45), Sorin, Ortega, Batistuta (Crespo 60), Gonzalez (Lopez 64). Subs Not Used: Almeyda, Ayala, Bonano, Burgos, Caniggia, Chamot, Gallardo, Husain, Lopez.

ENGLAND: Seaman, Mills, Cole A, Ferdinand, Campbell, Beckham, Scholes, Butt, Hargreaves (Sinclair 19), Owen (Bridge 80), Heskey (Sheringham 56). Subs Not Used: Brown, Cole J, Dyer, Fowler, James, Keown, Martyn, Southgate, Vassell. Goals: Beckham (pen 44).

Attendance: 35,927. Referee: Pierluigi Collina.

Revenge is so sweet. England put the pain and hurt of St Etienne behind them with a stirring victory against their nemesis. And who better to score the winning goal than David Beckham? Michael Owen is tripped in the penalty area just before half-time and up steps the 'villain' of '98 to shoot emphatically past Cavallero from the spot. Spirited defending by Campbell and Ferdinand and a series of outstanding saves from Seaman keep the Argentines at bay, and suddenly the so-called 'Group of Death' looks a lot easier.

'When you put on that jersey, the name on the front is
more important than the name on the back.'
FROM THE FILM *MIRACLE*, 2004

It was on his mind, there was no denying it: the Argentines' truculent behaviour on their team bus four years before. 'We didn't exactly go around talking to each other about it, but those of us who were there carried it inside; it was unspoken. There was certainly a feeling of revenge. And of course, it was Argentina that drummed up an assortment of emotions.'

The draw in the first match made the Argentina game even more important. The Argentinians held no fear for Sol. The philosophy of facing strong opposition is simple. There is no foregone conclusion in any game of sport. There can be no competition without competitors, right? For the team to win, there must be a team to beat. Simple, right? Good, let's get on with it.

Sol and Rio Ferdinand were told to mark Batistuta. They did it well enough. He was substituted on the hour. Rio and Sol had forged a partnership that had grown stronger every time they played together. 'We were both good readers of the game. Maybe it's because we were both Londoners.' Sol shrugs his shoulders. 'I suppose it was,' and goes in search of a word. 'It was *natural*.'

The game began as if it was following straight on from the match four years before. Kily Gonzales had a wonderful chance but shot just wide from an exquisite set up from a Sorin backheel, and then Michael Owen broke free from a Nicky Butt long ball but hit the post. Beckham, minutes later, was virtually sliced in half but referee Pierluigi Collina played the advantage, only for the ball to fall to Michael Owen who was brought down in the box. Penalty! The guilty Argentinian shoos the bald referee away with the shake of his index finger but to no avail; Collina ignores his plea of innocence, and the ball is placed on the penalty spot.

Beckham steps forward for England. Who else? The captain. A world star. For God and country. These are the moments for the likes of him. He thinks about where he is going to strike the ball. So much strength and passion urging him to get it right. It comes from inside the stadium and from the other side of the world. A collective surge of spirit. He has to score and he does. Sol watches from just inside the Argentinian half, just in case the ball ricochets back and an attack is launched. 'I watched the ball hit the middle of net.' He then sprints over to the corner flag to join Beckham in celebration. One-nil to England. The main protagonists from the game four years earlier celebrate, if it's possible, more than anyone else. To all those critics with such little faith: we are England and for a beautiful moment we are the best team in the world.

The final minutes of the game ended with the inevitable onslaught from the Argentines. England had the chance to wrap it up with a Scholes shot and a Sheringham volley but failed to do so. A last-minute clearance off the line from goalkeeper David Seaman confirmed it was England's day. Many times that would have gone in, ruined everything, but this time it doesn't. The final whistle goes. Sol is ecstatic. 'We still had a chance to make the names on the pitch immortal. We were all beginning to believe.' Dreams were merging into reality.

England drew their next game with Nigeria 0-0 in Osaka. They only needed a point and without much trouble they got it. It was a game that seemed to be played in a half-sleep. 'We were getting tired. It wasn't just the weather, it was what goes on in here.' Sol points to his head. 'These tournaments are such a psychological grind, every part of you is tested.'

The draw left England second in the group and into the last 16 to face Denmark. But already there were regrets, that if they had beaten Nigeria they could have avoided a potential match against Brazil in the quarter-finals – assuming the Brazilians beat the Belgians. They did, 2-0. As for England against Denmark in Niigata, Ferdinand scored early from a Beckham corner and then Owen made it two. The match commentator was delirious: 'What an opportunity we have now!' not quite believing that we were heading to the quarter-finals. England scored again and it was 3-0 at the final whistle. On to Brazil.

•   •   •

'We were expecting Winston Churchill and instead got Iain Duncan Smith,' Gareth Southgate is famously alleged to have said about Sven's half-time team talk against the Brazilians. Sol says: 'I don't remember it being particularly inspiring but that wasn't his [Sven's] style. He sometimes took individuals to one side and gave them a talk but he certainly didn't with me that day.'

It rained the day before the match. Everything had cooled. As Sol walked alone in the hotel grounds, he prayed it would rain again the following day, *the* day. He was not alone, the whole squad felt the same. It would help. Brazil on the other hand prayed for the opposite. Hot and stifling.

Sol slept well. The small beds had now been exchanged for larger ones at England's home base. When the squad arrived in Japan, they found the hotel beds too small for the size of a typical English footballer. Replacement beds hadn't come straightaway and there was frustration but now everything was prepared, well organised.

Sol spent the night before alone in his room following dinner. He kept himself to himself a lot of the time. He accepted the fact that he would never get on with everyone. Not in life. Not in the England squad. It just doesn't happen that way. We are all different. Just because they happen to share a gift of being the best footballers in the land doesn't mean you have to get on. Many will consider themselves at best incompatible with, at worst superior to others, so that disputes are unavoidable. For his time abroad, Sol did not ally himself to any group or involve himself in any conversation that engaged in trivial debate or controversy. Sounds tedious? Perhaps, but he was simply more comfortable in his own company. He didn't play cards or play golf. He couldn't get into PlayStation. Martin Keown was part of the squad and Sol spent time talking with him. He was disappointed that he wasn't able to immerse himself in Japan's culture and surroundings. But he still enjoyed his time there. He enjoyed his football. When fit, he always enjoyed the games and the training. That was his fun. Playing in the best competition in the world against the finest players; he felt flushed with the freshness and sense of anticipation. When you're winning and playing well, it feels as if everything is under control.

Everything, of course, except the weather. As Sol woke the following morning and peered out of his window, he was greeted by blinding sunlight. The sky was as white as a shroud, which, as he watched, slowly turned blue. His heart sank. He knew that the heat would test the team.

The game at the Shizuoka stadium started well for England. Michael Owen scored in the 23rd minute, pouncing on Lucio's mistake; a pickpocket in action. But Brazil equalised through Rivaldo, from a perfect ball by Ronaldinho, which Sol was unable to reach, just minutes before half-time. Rivaldo turned in celebration, taking off his blue shirt and swinging it around like a giant wheel, revealing a yellow vest, licking his lips and enjoying the taste of the blood of the Englishmen. Just before half-time is thought to be the worst period to let in a goal. The team can feel exactly how the supporters do: deflated. Sol walked back into the dressing room looking at the positives. He could see the team was rattled but by the time they came out for the second half, they would be ready again. The break would give them the chance to re-energise. Change the pendulum back in their direction. Remain calm. Forty-five minutes left. Anything could still happen.

There seems to be a miscomprehension about a manager's team talk. The common belief is when a team walks in at half-time and they are losing when they should be winning, the truly great manager of the day will inspire the players with a coruscating speech. Sol doesn't see it like that. 'The manager's team talk doesn't really exist. Not one with words that can motivate us to win, not in my experience. Perhaps Keegan was the closest to that type of management. He spoke with passion. Wenger tended to let you relax when you first got into the dressing room. It isn't his style to come in and start immediately to motivate. He would let the players deal with the physical side first, and then if we needed a 'rocket' would let us know just before we went out again. It would be measured and well timed, so that his words were still spinning in our ears as we returned to the pitch.'

There was no speech from Sven that day. He said his piece and the players had their say. The feeling was collective that they could still do it. They were an established team now; a group of players who knew how to motivate each other. They spoke the same language. The fifteen-minute break, instead of feeling like a good rest, felt more like a catnap. It felt as if someone had tampered with the official watch. It felt as if time had started to act strangely. But as the team trooped into the heat again, there wasn't a player who didn't believe that victory could be theirs.

In the second half, Brazil went ahead 2-1 from a free-kick by Ronaldinho. It was over forty yards from goal. It caught Seaman off his line and left the English goalkeeper back-peddling in disbelief. 'It was a long way out,' says Sol. 'I don't think he meant to do it.' Whether he did or whether he didn't, England had to come back from a goal behind. Their task was made easier by the sending off of Ronaldinho for a late tackle on Danny Mills, just before the hour. Mind you, by the time he'd left the field, it was more like 65 minutes. But after that, the game petered out and England were unable to make their one-man advantage count.

Surely we could have won, couldn't we? We should have beaten Brazil, beaten Turkey in the semi-finals and then slaughtered Germany in the final. Hallelujah! England are world champs. The players' names are immortalised. The country celebrates for another fifty years. Oh God, if only...If only.

In the dressing room after the game, Sol feels parched. He drinks litre after litre of water. He washes away his sweat, his body pleading for rest. There is no more time for dreams. He can't see anything clearly at that moment. The disappointment is too great. He will only be able to truly register it when he returns to England, and catches the remaining games on the television. 'You know what, looking back I don't think we believed we could win,' he says. 'They were one man down and we still couldn't push, we were flat, all our bodies were spent, we were knackered. Michael Owen was half-fit, we had too many players not a hundred per cent.'

'Mind you,' he says, nearly as an afterthought,' if we had beaten Brazil, we would've been strong enough to play ten more games! Winning, more than anything else, gives you strength.'

• • •

Japan was in the past now. Could England put their hoodoo behind them and go the distance in the European Championships? They qualified for Euro 2004 in Portugal by topping their group one point ahead of Turkey. Sol played in four of the qualifying games, missing the others through injury.

But in the tournament itself, England gave a sigh of submission very early on. They lost their first game to France 2-1 in Lisbon after leading the game for 90 minutes. Zidane scored from a free-kick and, virtually with the last kick of the game, grabbed the winner from the penalty spot. The following match, England won 3-0 against Switzerland, with the night belonging to Everton's Wayne Rooney, who scored twice and became the youngest player in European Championship history. 'I'd put him in the same bracket as Paul Gascoigne,' Sol says. Two years earlier, Rooney, still only sixteen, had been introduced to the county's consciousness with a superb last-minute goal so cool, so unflustered, that it would skim past Sol's right foot and end Arsenal's 49-game unbeaten run. 'It was an exquisite shot but I had no idea he was a revelation. I've seen other young players doing extraordinary things, score wonderful goals. That's not the test. It's whether you can repeat it again and again over a long period that proves your greatness.' Rooney would score twice again in the last group game, England beating Croatia 4-2, the other goals scored by Scholes and Lampard. England progressed into the quarter-finals to face the favourites and hosts, Portugal.

Rooney, now the talisman of the England side and the media's darling, walked off injured as early as the 27th minute in Lisbon. But England had gone ahead in three minutes, from a Michael Owen goal after he intercepted a back pass from

Costinha. They held out for 80 minutes until Helder Postiga headed Portugal level, and the game looked as if it was going into extra-time. But not before we had another one of Sol's 'if only's'. If only referee Urs Meier had given the goal scored by Sol in the last minute of the game. 'It was an awful decision. Unjust. Worse than the disallowed goal against Argentina. If Portugal had scored, it would've been allowed. I have no doubt!' John Terry was adjudged to have fouled the goalkeeper, and a free-kick was given rather than a place for England in the semi-finals of a very open tournament. Another disallowed goal marked down on Sol's curriculum vitae and, once again, the prospect of being a national hero was snatched away.

In extra-time The Maestro, the attacking midfielder Rui Costa, scored the goal of the tournament, with a shot recorded at 91km/h. But Frank Lampard equalised five minutes later and the match was destined for penalties and yet another English disappointment. 'When we lost, I truly felt I couldn't go on like this. We had a very good team. We deserved to win. It felt as if a higher power had decided it wasn't to be. It had begun to happen too often for me to disregard other forces.'

Beckham missed his penalty by launching the ball into the top tier that, if it were the theatre, would have been the perfect moment to pull out the opera glasses just to watch it dart by. England's miss that decided the game was bestowed upon Aston Villa's Darius Vassell. His penalty was saved by goal-keeper Ricardo who promptly got up to take one himself and score the winner for his country. The hosts eventually played Greece in the final. The Greeks won 1-0, heralding one of inter-national football's greatest upsets.

•　　•　　•

In October 2005, Sol won his 66th cap and earned himself a place in the top twenty most-capped England players. His caps since Euro 2004 had dropped off due to injury, and the emerging partnership of John Terry and Rio Ferdinand. By the

Gunners striking gold. Sol celebrates with Ashley Cole as Arsenal clinch the 2002 Premiership title at Old Trafford after a 1-0 win against Manchester United.

On a lap of honour with the 2002 Premiership trophy at Highbury.

A champagne assist from Sol for the inspirational Thierry Henry.
'Sometimes we didn't have to talk, we knew how the other felt,' says
Henry. 'It reflected in the way we played our football.'

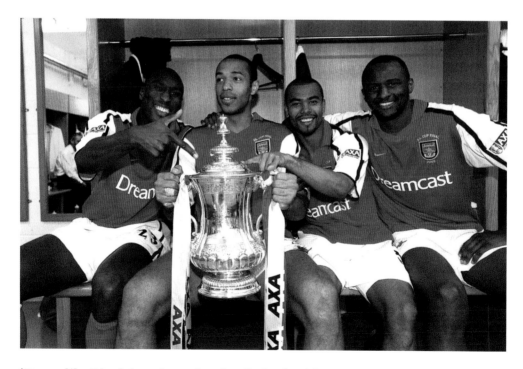

'It was like I had found another family.' Sol with team-mates Thierry Henry,
Ashley Cole and Patrick Vieira, and the FA Cup in 2002. In his first season at
Arsenal, Sol won the Double.

After his thank you speech to the fans at Islington town hall in May 2002.

Thousands lined the streets and rooftops of North London as Arsenal paraded the 2002 Premiership and FA Cup trophies in front of their fans. There was no happier man than Sol Campbell.

'Our time had come.' Sol with Arsenal's Invincibles as they celebrate their historic unbeaten record as Premiership champions in May 2004.

Sol soars above Oleguer to head powerfully home against Barcelona in the 2006 Champions League final, in what would be his last match for the Gunners before joining Portsmouth.

Linvoy Primus and Sol combine to stop Blackburn Rovers at Ewood Park in August 2006. The pair formed a solid centre-back partnership during Sol's first season at Portsmouth.

Portsmouth manager Harry Redknapp and his captain with the FA Cup.

Portsmouth beat Cardiff 1-0 in 2008 to clinch their first FA Cup in 69 years. Sol celebrates with David James, Sylvain Distin, Hermann Hreidarsson and Glen Johnson as FA Chairman Lord Triesman, to the left, looks on.

We can achieve anything. At least that was the promise made by Sven-Goran Eriksson when Sol posed with manager Ian McParland on signing for Notts County in August 2009. One match later, Sol was gone.

Sol, in his second spell at Arsenal, shimmies past Gareth Bale, against Tottenham at White Hart Lane in April 2010.

Challenging Manchester City's Emmanuel Adebayor in his only season at Newcastle, 2010-11.

Reunited. Sol with eight of his brothers
and a nephew at a family gathering.

On holiday in Italy.

Sol with his mother Wilhelmina and sister Pam.

Members of the Campbell family with the bride and groom after the ceremony.

Fiona and Sol on their wedding day, 17 July 2010. 'She's been my rock, a woman who gave me back my belief in life,' says Sol.

time the 2006 World Cup squad was named, Sol was no longer first choice. He made an appearance though, as a substitute against Sweden.

After the tournament, Sven said his goodbyes to the squad. His resignation had been accepted before the competition. He shook Sol's hand as they were about to board the flight home. Polite and comfortable, it was a civil goodbye. Little did either know then that they would be saying goodbye again five years later, but in a considerably different manner.

The process of finding a new England coach reached the heights of ineptitude. Promises of finding the best possible coach were acted out like a third-rate end of pier farce. The FA seemed hell-bent on pressing the self-destruct button. They initially chose Luiz Felipe Scolari but he quickly made it plain that they should look elsewhere. In the end they picked Eriksson's coach, Steve McClaren. Sol was promptly dropped from the England setup, along with David Beckham and David James.

There was no phone call, not even a letter. There was no explanation as to why he was being dropped. 'I got a text. ONE TEXT! That was all,' Sol says angrily, and then retreats into hesitancy. 'It just isn't right to treat someone like that. Also, it was shortsighted. You never know when you might need the player again.'

England started to lose. McClaren's team looked ineffective and unlikely to qualify for Euro 2008. The manager looked out of his depth. He was not ready for the job. The papers reported that McClaren was considering a recall for Sol. 'I knew the newspaper stories were coming directly from McClaren. It's how it works, a trickle of stories followed by a phone call.' His mobile rang. He knew who it was, even before looking at the screen. He was hesitant. *What should I do? Leave it? Let it ring forever?* The way he was treated by McClaren made him feel like he was in one of those dungeons in which you can't stand up or lie down. He felt incarcerated. Where were his good manners? Respect? It hurt. No-one knew how much.

His usual habit was to let calls go straight to voicemail. He thought for a moment and then reluctantly answered. It had taken McClaren a year to make the call.

'Hello Sol, it's Steve McClaren.'

'Yes, yes, yes,' Sol tutted down the phone while, half-sighing with his other voice.

He couldn't refuse the call-up. It was his country, after all. Anyway, he was happy to be back. He loved playing for England. Even when he was on the bench, however excruciating it felt, he was proud again to be part of the squad. McClaren said to the press, 'I always maintained that I was not closing the door on Sol. I know he won't let England down and I am very pleased to welcome him back...'

He played four more times for his country. His last game was against Croatia, which England lost 3-2 at Wembley. England didn't make the Euro finals and McClaren lost his job.

'England dropped me,' Sol says, miffed at the memory of his last years of international football. He believes he should have gone to South Africa in 2010. 'I was angry and disappointed not to have been picked for the World Cup squad in South Africa. I was playing well enough on my return to Arsenal and yet [England manager] Capello chose Carragher, who said he'd retired from international football, and Ledley [King], who was injured most of the season, ahead of me.'

He used to bump into Fabio Capello. They lived in the same area of London and went to the same coffee bar, just below Sloane Square in Chelsea. They would always greet each other formally; a hello, and sometimes a shake of the hand. One morning, Capello was with his assistant Franco Baldini. Sol spoke one to one with Baldini, making it clear he'd like to be considered for the England squad to South Africa. 'My form had been excellent for the last few months, I was getting better and I was getting stronger. I believed I was good enough to be picked. I wanted to make sure that they knew I was keen to be involved.' Baldini listened. He said they'd heard rumours from Liverpool that Jamie Carragher was considering a return to international football after he'd announced his retirement in 2007. 'There's him and of course Ledley King is still keen to be part of the squad, even through his injuries.' But he said that he would talk to Capello and see what could be done. He hurried away before his cappuccino got cold. It was one final aside before writing a loud 'THE END' and slamming the door on Sol's international career forever.

Meanwhile Capello's England tenure would last just two more years. He gave the visual impression that he couldn't wait to get out of the country. His body language exuded a need to escape; he might as well have said: 'The only worthwhile view of England is from the back window of a taxi heading for Heathrow!'

•　　•　　•

Sol ponders his entire England career with bicker and banter. From the moments before his debut against Hungary in 1996 to his tournament debut in Euro '96 as substitute against Switzerland and Stuart Pearce yelling, 'Get into your fucking position!!' when he first got onto the pitch; on what he expected it to be like; on what it actually was like as a player; and now, in retirement, on how it should have been.

It is the 'now' he finds himself thinking about the most. The hushed gossip of a hundred half-conversations, the absence of cries of 'Bravo!', the FA seemingly nervous to acknowledge and applaud in the wrong place. What went wrong? 'I'm acknowledged more around Europe than in my own country. It makes me sad. Maybe it's the English way,' he says. He finds it difficult when thinking of his international career to sit back, make himself comfortable and enjoy what he worked for and what was given back.

'I believe if I was white, I would've been England captain for over ten years. It's as simple as that,' he says without emotion. 'I think the FA wished I was white. I had the credibility, performance-wise, to be captain. I was consistently in the heart of the defence, and I was a club captain early on in my career.' He thinks the FA decided they couldn't have a black face fronting the full national side around the world on a regular basis. 'It's crazy!' he says. 'It's an indictment [of them] and I don't think it will change because they don't want it to, and probably the majority of fans don't want it either. It's alright to have black captains and mixed race in the Under-18s and Under-21s, but not for the full national side. There is a ceiling and although no-one has ever said it, I believe it's made of glass.'

He pauses. 'Are there elements in the FA who are [intrinsically] racist? Is the FA always the leader of football it should be? Is the FA as pro-active as it should be, or does it simply react to something long after a situation has developed? I have my views and others will have theirs.'

Take for instance the comments of previous FA chairman Lord Triesman, who, after leaving his post in 2011, was heavily critical of English football's governing body. 'It is more likely if he was white that he would have captained England on more occasions. I don't subscribe to the view that it [the FA] was consciously racist but I think there is an assumption of a type of person who should captain England.' Having said that, he continues, 'The team [selection] rests solely with the manager. I cannot remember anyone ever saying you should pick X or Y. Last time it happened was with Sir Alf Ramsey and he told the FA where to go. [In my time at the FA] I was a great enthusiast for Rio to captain England but it was Capello's choice for Terry and I left it at that.'

Sol contrasts his feelings on his full England debut against Hungary with those on gaining his fiftieth cap. 'I knew I was going to come on sometime during the game against Hungary. I was just waiting. But when I was told I was coming on, I felt so proud. What a feeling! I thought, this is what it's all about. I'm playing for my country. I remember thinking of Lilleshall. I'd progressed from there to the first team. I'd gone through the whole system and here I was, taking my first steps as a full international picking up my first cap.' He pauses and jumps ahead to when he won his fiftieth cap against Denmark in the 2002 World Cup in Japan. 'Do you know, the FA planned no recognition for me when I won that cap? They had prepared nothing. I was hurt and, again, disappointed. I complained to someone in the FA, and only then did they give me a memento, a few weeks after the World Cup: a collage of photographs from all the games, with no frame.'

Sol can't be angry. Instead he feels numb. He leans forward. 'Michael Owen was made captain ahead of me. I thought: what is going on here? I couldn't work out what was happening. The more caps I won, the further away I seemed to be pushed from becoming captain. I think the FA didn't want me to have a voice. I played well, acted honourably on and off the field, but there was little recognition. Owen was a fantastic forward but nowhere near being a captain. It was embarrassing. I kept asking myself: what have I done?

'I'll say it again. I don't fit the FA's image of an England captain. I'd done enough to be captain. I've asked myself many times why I wasn't. I keep coming up with the same answer. It was the colour of my skin. What's the point of having a bridge you can't access? I say, burn it, and build a new one so you can cross over. If I'm wrong, then I'm listening.'

DEFENDER

'He had the ability to read the mind of an opponent and the ability to read the game as good as anyone.'

ARSENE WENGER

If you scrutinise a striker close enough, he begins to reveal himself like the night sky, which at first seems starless, but on deeper investigation reveals more and more of its glittering charms. You can eventually see the way he uses space, his speed and movement, whether he is stronger on his left or his right side, and in which areas he predominantly moves.

Sol liked to study the opposition striker's pattern of play. Understanding each step, taking in different situations like whether he is trying to shoot, meet a cross or play with the ball close to his feet; a dance full of irrational surprises and variations. 'Every player has a set pattern of play, a frequency, unique to them, like a fingerprint,' Sol says. 'The very best may add certain patterns over the years, but generally these remain the same.'

Once Sol played an opponent, he never forgot their strengths or weaknesses. He remembered the subtleties of their movements. Certain patterns in different areas of the field. It was his job. He studied. His unrelenting work was a part of his longevity and success. He never took for granted the gift that helped his career soar. He worked every day to maintain it. 'I never feared playing against any individual. I had respect for them but always felt confident my game could meet any challenge.' And yet, some challenges proved more difficult than others.

Sol recalls a friendly between England and Chile in February 1988; a warm-up game for the upcoming World Cup finals against a South American side on a cold rainy night at Wembley. It was also Michael Owen's debut. Friendlies were always competitive at Wembley. Visiting teams wanted to win at the 'home of football'. Chile would be no different. They would pressurise and work hard. They had qualified for the World Cup and this was a chance to test themselves against European opposition.

Playing that night was Marcelo Salas, better known by the nickname El Matador. The River Plate striker was becoming well-known to English and European clubs, but Sol hadn't heard of him. He certainly would know him by the end of the night. 'He gave me one of my toughest games. It was early on in my England career, and I spent the night chasing him.'

Salas took early control. He made a mockery of Sol's talent. *Go and get him, chase him.* Experience would have told Sol to sit back, let him show his cards, but he was young. Salas surprised him at every turn. He scores a beautiful goal. A sublime left foot volley into the net. One of Wembley's best. Salas sings out, 'G-O-A-L!!!' like Pavarotti on an off-day. Chile are partying, it's as if they've reached their World Cup final early. The onslaught continues and Sol is being taught a lesson. Salas shrugs his shoulders, dips one way and then the other as Sol sticks out his right foot. Salas falls and Sol stands motionless for an instant, like a dummy before losing his footing. It is a definite foul in the box. Salas takes the penalty. Left foot, left corner. Goal. Two-nil. Salas' hand points to God.

When the final whistle blew, Salas exchanged shirts with Paul Ince. Sol found him soon afterwards and shook his hand. The striker had won that battle. *We will meet again and next time I will be ready.* He wouldn't face anyone ever again without first studying everything he could about them. He had to be ready for anything they could throw at him. But they never did play against each other again; it was the one and only time. Salas scored four goals in four games in the 1998 World Cup, following which he secured a transfer to Lazio for a reported £12 million.

• • •

Sol wanted to do little else but play with, and against, the best players in the game. He was always looking for a challenge when he went on the field, or when on the training ground facing his Arsenal team-mates. He threw down the gauntlet. He wanted to do little else. This was his passion.

But when he saw Thierry Henry on his first day at training he felt exactly like the Frenchman did: 'Thank God I don't have to be playing you anymore!'

'Thierry Henry was an organic machine,' Sol says. 'He had a lot of natural stamina, but he told me it improved when he got to Juventus. It seems he had a tough taskmaster there in Marcello Lippi. When you are lethal in front of goal and still, after eighty minutes, able to keep up the pace, it makes defending very difficult. As a defender, you have to maintain your attention. Never lose it for one moment.'

Sol practiced five and twenty-yard sprints in training, just to be able to turn quickly and challenge a striker with a burst of speed. He had to be on his toes as the ball was being passed to Henry, before it had even got to him. Sol may be a big man, but his ability to make quick turns was remarkable. He learned to adjust his body to different angles from a very early age; as young as six or seven he was playing bulldog, dodgeball and touch games in the school yard.

'With Thierry, as the ball was being passed I was already working out what he would do next. I always had to be a step ahead, to decide what he was going to do even before he had. I knew he was lightning quick and knew he loved his left side, but that was just the beginning. His range of skills and ideas were as expansive as anyone I ever faced.'

Sol found the quintessential English centre-forwards to be completely different challenges. 'Alan Shearer used me as a target to either jump across, or try and get behind. He was a classic centre-forward. He had the brain to bring people in and glide into areas, allowing him to shoot. With the ball coming across, he was also very good with his head. He had this habit that, when the ball dropped, he would use the defender as a buffer to give him space for a split second, so he could move in either direction. Early on in his career, he also had extraordinary pace.'

Some strikers could be quiet for most of the game and then suddenly morph into something completely different. 'I'd look on in wonder at how they'd suddenly change. When I was first picked for Tottenham and played against Mark Hughes, it was always a test. I was young and lacked experience. The leap from youth to the first team is huge. You're playing the best, the very best. You have to raise your game to another level. When Hughes chested down the ball and swivelled round it, it was virtually impossible to get it off him.'

He thought of each opponent as a type of animal. Some players would be leopard-like on the field, trying to be inconspicuous before striking. Others like Ian Wright were always shouting and hollering: 'I'm here, I'm big, I'm bad, I'm going to get you.'

'Wrighty was always in my ear. He once complained to someone, "I just can't get through to Sol. I'm shouting, I'm doing everything to distract him but can't get a reaction!" That was just me. Whatever the striker did, I just got on with my own game. I very rarely responded. I used to hate it when players chopped me down from behind and immediately tried to shake my hand afterwards, to say sorry. *Come on, let's get on with the game, with the battle. We can shake at the end.* For the ninety minutes, no-one on the opposing side was my friend. They were always my enemy.'

He would use the imagery of war in play; watching carefully the opposition's confidence and mood, and forming pictures in his mind, their swagger like a retreating army still stoutly singing their war songs. 'I had all these scenarios locked in, so when I needed to I could sense something before it happened. The coaches teach the form of the game, and I was good at listening and acting on their advice, but they always say really good defenders smell danger. You have to concentrate for ninety minutes plus; if you don't, that's when the centre-forward gets his chance and scores a goal. With someone like Rooney, if you try to shut him down he'll find another option; he has the ability to stop, turn, get around the other side and take a shot.'

Michael Owen also attended Lilleshall. 'He even remembers me going back there for rehabilitation when I first started to play for Tottenham. I made a speech and he was part of the audience at the Q&A we held afterwards. He was a lethal player. He could beat anyone at the right angle and with pace. I enjoyed playing with him, and enjoyed the challenge of facing him. At the beginning of his career, and when we first played together for England, his lack of fear combined with his pace made most defenders feel bamboozled. I saw terror in their eyes. Speed is truly frightening when it comes from the complete footballer. He was a young man loving the game. In the 1998 World Cup, he literally danced round people. How I remember his goal against Argentina, the way no-one knew what to do with this spark of energy sprinting towards them. I never got tired of seeing that. Unfortunately, injuries got him in the end.'

Through time, Sol could anticipate from sixty yards away where the ball would land, often in only a couple of places. This sixth sense on the pitch meant he would be first to the ball as a defender and could read the play in advance of his opposition striker.

Sol's hard work helped him to maintain his consistency over the years. There were naturally highs and lows in the course of the season, but he always knew he could rely on his football education if things began to go wrong. The only times on the field when he felt particularly vulnerable were when he was unfit. 'I needed to be consistent throughout my career and that's how I kept it fresh for twenty-plus years. If I felt tired with the game, I was able to replenish myself. I was comfortable in my own company because I dealt with things inside far better on my own. A lot of my football was in my mind. For me, it was more of a mind game than anything else. Before a game had even kicked off, I'd worked through most situations that could emerge in the ninety minutes.'

With England, Sol partnered a number of players. 'Rio [Ferdinand] and I shared some fantastic games together. Why it worked I'm not sure, perhaps it even went down to our upbringing, but our play complemented each other's. If he darted forward, I'd cover for him and vice versa. We had an understanding.' He teamed up with John Terry a few times – 'an accomplished player' – and Gareth Southgate – 'a steady eddie' – while others like Gary Neville 'worked hard at his game. Both he and his brother Phil were diligent and made the best out of the talent they were given.'

In club football, his respect for Martin Keown is boundless. 'He was a warrior who'd put his body on the line every time he played. I had faith that he'd never let the team down. I could see how much he loved his craft. He just loved defending.' Ashley Cole and Lauren were also quality defenders. 'Two of the best full-backs in Britain at the time,' says Sol.

When playing for Tottenham, he respected the famous Arsenal back four of Dixon, Adams, Bould and Winterburn, 'year after year bringing in top performances. They had a great understanding between them. Their consistency was masterly. I would include Martin [Keown] in that group. I think he played in more games with Tony [Adams] than Steve Bould did.'

Abroad, Paolo Maldini is the first name he mentions of all the defenders he played against. 'He had great awareness of where to play, positioning-wise. He sensed danger as much as anyone I ever encountered, and his timing of tackles was immaculate. They were always so crisp.' On the subject of tackling, Sol grieves its slow death in British football. 'Tackling is a beautiful part of football. It's sad to see the art form slowly disappear in this country.'

His conversation is full of movement, excited by the memory of his old adversaries and former team-mates. He suddenly pauses and reflects on his own game, his very own talent of defending. He speaks slowly, military-like. 'You'd have to do something special to get past me. I was ready for any challenge.'

PORTSMOUTH

'If you can get into Sol's head, you're doing a far
better job than I ever did.'

TONY ADAMS

Sol was like a person who had made a great decision and now expected the changes to come at once – *abracadabra!* – but he slowly realised even he had to wait for the days ahead to pass in their own time; that what could happen might take longer to arrive than he had expected.

His desire to play abroad never happened. He was to be disappointed. From what he heard, the deal with Juventus was very nearly completed (a three-year contract) until the manager, Didier Deschamps, pulled out. 'He didn't want me in the end. It was as simple as that,' Sol says, brusquely. 'So, once again through my own choice, I was on my own without the support of a club, looking for a new club.' There hadn't been many enquiries since Sol announced he was leaving Arsenal. Wenger said, when the news was released: 'Sol has been a giant for us but we respect his decision to move on and, of course, we are very sorry to see him go. His desire and presence have been instrumental to our success over the past five years.'

Sol believed the right team would come along. If it had to be in England, he was not ready to drop down a division. That was non-negotiable. But he wanted and believed he needed to go abroad, to get away from all the homegrown pressures.

Fenerbahce were interested. John Scales, the former Wimbledon, Liverpool and Tottenham defender, was helping him with the introduction. He had arranged for Sol to fly to Milan to meet Giuliano Terraneo and representatives from Fenerbahce. (Terraneo had left Inter as sporting director in 2003 and was now agenting deals.) 'I listened carefully to what they had to say but Turkey wasn't right for me,' said Sol. The language and culture would be too difficult, too distant from the life he knew. After the disappointment of Juventus, he had no idea where he would end up. He usually had a sixth sense, but this time nothing. He wondered where he would find fulfillment in the next phase of his career. Where he'd settle and find a home, like when he first joined Arsenal. He also hadn't given up hope of adding to his medal tally. Now where could he find a winning club that would give him peace and success? Not easy. In the end, it would be revealed in the most unlikely of places.

While he was away on England duty, Frank Lampard approached Sol. He had just sat down for some lunch. He was sipping a glass of water, thinking of how he had become better at assessing someone's true worth after a short acquaintance, even after a nodded hello. 'Hello.' Frank appeared across his line of vision. 'Can I have a word, Sol?' He noticed Frank had a look on his face that said he had something up his sleeve. He did. He had just been talking to his cousin Jamie (Redknapp) who had mentioned that his uncle, Harry Redknapp, was interested in talking to him. He immediately knew what for. Everyone knew Sol was looking for a club. In football, like everywhere else, contacts make the business go round.

'Tell Harry to give me a call,' Sol said.

Harry Redknapp was manager of Portsmouth. He had returned to the club late in 2005, and saved them from relegation back to the championship. With a new owner and the promise of 'loads of money', Harry got to work in assembling a concoction of players that would make the team a threat to anyone.

Harry called Sol; he called him twice. Sol had gone straight to Prague from playing with England, and was celebrating at a friend's stag do when he heard Harry's voice. They arranged to meet in London a couple of days later.

The venue was a small hotel off Chelsea Green. Sol felt relaxed. This was so different to when he signed for Arsenal. Then it was clandestine, collar pulled up to the ears and looking like a spy, a series of false decoys just in case anyone was watching. They were, but no-one found out.

Sol was there waiting. He'd already had his first espresso when Harry strolled in first, followed by Peter Storrie, Portsmouth's chief executive, a couple of steps behind. He immediately liked Harry. He had already met him, briefly, at son Jamie's twenty-first birthday, but that was simply a 'hello' and 'good to meet you' greeting. Harry was well-liked in the football community. He had the reputation of extending older players' careers and improving youngsters' discipline. He was the classic man-manager. He spoke so freely, and indeed easily, that you would consider joining him just to be in his company. The type who'd make you laugh at his jokes, although you may have heard them before. He was exactly what Sol needed personality-wise at this point in his life. Someone who he felt would manage him in a fatherly way.

The two had good patter. They did not interrupt each other, nor even once talk at the same time. They spoke with the pace of great salesmen, as if their lines had been rehearsed. Harry spoke of his plans and ambitions for the club. He told Sol that Portsmouth was 'a club going places, a good club to come to.' Storrie spoke about money. The deal was being negotiated across that table. It was an all-in-one package. Make the deal and sell the club, all within half an hour. Sol was about to say something like: 'You're exactly what I'm looking for.' But of course he didn't; that wasn't his style; never was, never going to be. A voice said, just listen to them and say you'll call them with an answer in a few days. Which is exactly what he did.

They did not know but there was no need to oversell; they were the only Premier League side interested in him. But they spoke with ambition and excitement. About the new owner, Alexandre Gaydamak, that he was young, had money and was keen to spend it. They spoke of potential signings just as

Wenger and Dein had done before he signed for Arsenal. David James, Kanu and Niko Kranjcar were names mentioned. As the bill arrived for lunch, Sol looked at his watch. He wasn't seeing what time it was; he was thinking, how long is it to the beginning of the new season?

After the meeting with Harry, Sol flew to Verbier to get together with his girlfriend, Fiona Barratt, an English interior designer who he had met earlier in the year. They say you meet someone romantically when the heart needs it most. The statement is true for Sol. He had been involved with Kelly Hoppen, also an interior designer, who had introduced Sol to her social world. To outsiders, they were a novelty; the black football star with the ambitious socialite. It was like they intruded onto the stage as complete strangers and acted out their relationship in front of an audience. The whispers began again around Sol's life; this time, on what he saw in her and the other way round.

'It was rare that I met someone who was successful in their own right,' Sol says. 'I was attracted to someone different who was independent, responsible, knew where they were going and were driven in a nice way.' They'd met at former Tottenham team-mate John Scales' wedding. They were sitting at the same table. They were attracted to each other and spent the evening talking. 'I think we were both intrigued by each other's worlds. In the beginning it was good, we travelled together and when I introduced her to the England setup, she was fine, she was well-connected. Becks was there and I think they were quite good friends. Some of the guys had heard of her. Gary Neville actually got her to do up his house in Manchester. Yes, we spent a good deal of time together.'

But then the relationship turned into the type that was forever ending. This is definitely it, and then the next day it started all over again, like a novel forever nearly ready but the deadline is constantly changing and moving further ahead. It also seemed to be discussed more openly by others and that did not rest easy. 'Even before I was told I was picked for the 2006 World Cup, Kelly told me she'd allegedly heard from Nancy

Dell'Olio that I was going to be in the squad. It all became very strange. It may have just been gossip, but I felt very uncomfortable with it even being discussed.'

Kelly visited Sol's family house in Stratford to see if she could help on the interior decoration. She went alone. 'Nothing happened in the end. Probably the meeting didn't go too well because I heard nothing more from either side! I also knew that by not going, it was a sign that it [the relationship] didn't really have a future. If it had, I would've gone with her.'

It was only a matter of time to see who got out first. When Sol got a bill listing all the money Kelly was owed (she was helping with the interior decorating of his house), under the miscellaneous column, 'flowers' were listed. When he checked what flowers she was talking about, he discovered they were the flowers she'd bought Sol for his birthday. The entry was immediately removed and the revised bill was paid in full. 'It was probably just a mistake,' Sol says. But afterwards they did not talk again.

•   •   •

Fiona Barratt's presence had given Sol his balance back. They had originally met in the Caribbean on the beach and then again, of all places, through Kelly Hoppen's office, where Fiona was working as head designer; she had worked on Sol's house. He liked her being around, enjoyed her company; he noticed that. He also noticed when he went to Kelly's office he hoped to see Fiona. His day naturally brightened. But nothing happened when she was still working for Kelly. No clandestine dates, no hidden kiss; simply a mutual attraction masked by hesitancy on both sides.

Six months later ('there was certainly no overlap,' insists Sol), they met again at a party. Fiona told him she was planning to leave her job and start a new business. They spoke to each other all evening. She is lovely, thought Sol. The chance meeting unsettled him. He called Fiona the following day; he still had her number from when she had worked on his house. He asked her out but at first she refused. 'She was wary of many things,' Sol says, 'past relationships, going out with a footballer, every-thing I brought to the table. It was frustrating because it seemed that she was using my public stature as an excuse not to get involved.'

They eventually met for dinner in Hampstead (a Greek res-taurant) and they started to date seriously until one afternoon, Sol suddenly disappeared. Not literally, because he was in the papers every day, but if he hadn't been, Fiona would not have known where he had gone. He simply didn't call, nor did he return calls. It was without explanation. 'I simply had to run away. It was getting serious and I didn't have the understand-ing to deal with someone who loved me in such a way. So I broke it up and then the mind starts to play games, like, did she really love me? What did she see in me?'

It was the week of his birthday, the anniversary of his father's death. It was a time since his death that had disrupted his life. 'The mind just started to explode leading up to the date of his death and beyond,' he says. It triggered a deluge of emo-tions, entailing a desire to escape those themes that unsettle, or dominate. He needed to be alone. But his solitude was well hidden from others at his club. He may have been sitting at the same table as his team-mates, but the conversation was dis-tant and his mind was elsewhere. If he hadn't had the anchor and responsibility of football, he would have gone abroad into deep hiding.

The silence continued for three months; harder for Fiona, dealing with someone in the public eye. The constant reminder when you least expect it: the mention of his name on the radio, the open pages of a newspaper in a coffee shop. Her heart was breaking and it got to the point where she would call him one final time and, if he was not prepared to take her call and discuss his fears and troubles, she would continue her life without him.

Sol was in Dubai. It was a training and team-bonding trip. He was preparing to go out for dinner when the phone rang.

He would miss going out with some of his team-mates; instead he would stay in his room. It was a phone call he would refer to later in his speech at his wedding to Fiona. It changed the course of his life. 'It just connected with me on a different level for some reason. It made me stop and think there was more to it. Does this girl really want to know me properly? Does she really love me, for me? If everything got stripped away, would she look at me in a different way?'

They met on his return and they knew they should be together. They loved each other and understood that fear should no longer be a part of it. 'I was always looking for that type of love. I didn't really understand it when I was growing up. It was tough love in the household. And then, growing up in football when I saw how things were extracted from players through bad relationships or bad marriages, it made me even more reluctant to trust and open my heart. None of my family has been married except for my parents and my sister in Jamaica, so in a way it was more normal not to be in a committed relationship.'

But it was different now. Sol had a friend and partner who would support him. Decisions would be easier. He could focus on his football while the other side of his life could have a peace that had never existed. He spoke to Fiona about the Portsmouth offer and before the week was out, he was back on the phone to Peter Storrie to finalise the deal. Yes, he was his own manager now and only had his lawyer check through the final wording. 'It wasn't straightforward. Storrie returned the contract five times, changing this and that before it was finally agreed.'

His working relationship with Sky Andrew had gradually petered out. They wanted different things. 'It was inevitable that we'd eventually take different roads,' says Sky. 'Our outlook on how to move things forward had changed. I knew he had to see things for himself. I was a hundred per cent sure he would come back as I'd always done right by him. If you do that, they always come back.' But Sol wanted to do things more his own way; to make his own decisions and not depend on Sky's advice. 'I felt comfortable enough to deal with my own affairs. I didn't need anyone. I was experienced and wasn't scared to negotiate. I like the business. I think I could've been a trader in a different life!' laughs Sol.

'It was almost like a younger brother going against his older brother's advice,' says Sky. 'If I advised on something, he would disagree. We had reached that stage of our friendship, our working relationship, and there is little you can do except wait until it passes.' Today they remain good friends and are involved together in Kids Go Live, an initiative that encourages inner-city primary school children to watch live sport. 'We will always be brothers,' says Sky.

•   •   •

On 8 August 2006, Sol completed his move to Portsmouth, signing a three-year contract. He was going to be well paid. He knew how much he was worth and expected his demands to be met. There was always a bottom line. He lived like many footballers of similar worth, in that, although he was highly paid, it wasn't going to last forever and before you knew it the career was over. Your pay packet would never be the same again. He had seen it with other well-paid footballers, who are now left with little. 'We don't talk about money in the dressing room or generally outside. It's a sort of no-go subject,' says Sol. 'With the older players in the Arsenal dressing room, I saw little change in their attitude, even though they were being very well paid. It's the youngsters who I sometimes see are affected. All of sudden, they can buy the best of things at a very young age. It's not good. Some prefer to be driving out of training in their new car, rather than putting in the extra hour to improve their skill.'

Everyone is different but it is fair to say that some find an excess of success, money, fame, etc, as difficult to handle as, if not more difficult to handle than, failure, poverty, or being a non-entity. But perhaps the theory is merely put about by the successful, rich, famous etc in order to keep the majority of the country in their place.

The way to handle money was instilled in Sol at a young age. Not by anything or anyone. It just seemed natural. One sight he couldn't stand was money falling into the hands of those who did not know how to use it. 'God sends chocolate to people who have no teeth,' is a proverb you can see played out at many a football game, where it is the people in the most expensive seats who seem to care least for the entertainment, strolling into the corporate boxes ten minutes late and wondering why the rest of us have had the audacity to start without them.

•   •   •

Harry Redknapp said about Sol: 'I think he'll give the place a real lift just coming in. He's a top, top player, a big character and I think he's a great signing for us. He's very strong. I think he's fine and looking forward to the challenge.'

Arsene Wenger said that he was surprised by his move to Portsmouth. He believed he'd left Arsenal to go abroad. He had, but the deal simply didn't go through. But there would be no explanation to Arsenal. These things happen and they would have to understand.

Tony Adams was restless. He was standing, pacing, sitting, squatting, and most other things. Sol was due to arrive that morning, and his former Arsenal skipper, now assistant manager to Harry Redknapp ('When we first met I'm sure Harry wanted me out of retirement to start playing again,' recalls Adams), knew how important the signing was going to be. 'Sometimes one signing can make all the difference,' says Adams. 'In Sol's case, he could organise the defence on the field and the players would look up to him. Wealth of experience is so valuable; once it's on the pitch, it can change virtually everything.'

Adams also knew that by having Sol at Portsmouth, his mere presence would encourage other players to join, with the 'If it's good enough for him, it's good enough for me' type of attitude. Yes, Adams knew this was a big signing.

Harry was now far calmer. The deal had been done. He knew there had been a bit of to-ing and fro-ing but now everything was agreed.

But Sol was late. Half an hour late. 'He isn't coming, Harry,' Adams said, looking at his watch.

'I'm telling you, he's on his way,' Harry replied.

Harry calls Peter Storrie just to make sure. 'Peter? Yeah... yeah...right.'

He turns to Adams. 'It's done. Stop worrying, he'll be here!'

Sol meanwhile was taking his time in his Range Rover, unaware of the slight panic going on. He was looking forward to a new start. He felt as good as he had for a long time. Portsmouth might not have been his first choice, might not even have been his second, but he liked Harry and thought they had the makings of a good team. He switched radio stations and listened to classical music and opened his window to let in the fresh air. By heading towards the coast, it gave him a sense of peace. He had a giggle about how life turns. He would never have believed he would be taking this drive only a few weeks before. *I will make an impact here.* Maybe greater things lay ahead. How lucky he was to be a professional footballer, a paid sportsman.

As he turned down the short driveway, the potholes brought him back to his senses. In front of him stood a portakabin. Sol let out a deep sigh. 'It was a throwback in time,' he says. Adams and Redknapp were outside waiting. 'I told you he'd be here,' whispers Redknapp, followed by wide smiles and firm handshakes. As he was being taken on a tour, more like a tour of inspection, Sol felt a hollow pit in the stomach. He felt the cell door slamming. The inside of the stadium, Fratton Park, looked like a relic from better days on the south coast. The bathrooms had the smell of cigarettes. *This is a shock. I may have made a big mistake.*

'People were saying, why is Sol moaning and groaning but I wasn't used to this; we were in the twenty-first century and I thought, what is happening here? This team was in the Premier League but the facilities gave the impression it was a non-

League side.' What he didn't understand was if the club was ready to pay millions for players, why the hell weren't they ready to put in a new set of showers? Water from the showers and washbasins trickled down the porcelain. 'Why wasn't buying a new training ground top of their agenda? Something not just for now but for tomorrow; something that would appeal to any potential buyer. Why didn't they invest and create a comfortable and stable environment to learn and improve the skill of the players? Believe me, I know it helps to have that in a club's makeup. And remember we were talking about a Premier League side at the time. Around that time, they had an opportunity to buy a ground right opposite Southampton airport. But they did nothing.'

By the end of the tour, he had, though, already noticed the warmth around the place. It had a sense of community, which was fed from the top. He felt a sense of relief, like if your train is going in the right direction, when you're convinced yourself you've got on the wrong one. 'There was a good atmosphere and Harry kept up the banter. He was good at that.'

•　　•　　•

'Portsmouth was like a church club. A number of the players believed in God and were vocal to the fact,' Sol says, 'That's maybe why we were winning!'

Linvoy Primus became a Christian in 2001. A pendulum in his consciousness had swung and finally rested in faith and the power of prayer. Linvoy prayed on match day. He was now in control of his life. He would habitually call the assistant club chaplain Mick Mellows an hour and half before the game. His team-mates were suspicious as he sneaked off the pitch to make calls. Some thought Linvoy was talking to his bookie. 'All I was doing was talking to God.'

Portsmouth at the time had eight players who were Christians. Soon a group had arranged to meet once a week for bible study. It was a quiet and private time at one of the player's or at Mick

Mellows' home. There they would pray and talk openly about their lives.

Six months before Sol arrived at Portsmouth, Linvoy went to Harry Redknapp to ask whether the group could pray before a game. Harry saw no problem as long as it didn't interfere with his team talk. They would meet in the laundry room, a small space that struggled to hold eight men. There was little difficulty finding a congregation. 'One time we had twenty-two crowded in there!' Linvoy says proudly. 'It was not just for players. We had a couple of stewards, the club doctor, members of staff. We also at times had members of the opposing team: players from Bristol City, Leicester City, Charlton, to name a few. Everyone was welcome.'

Sol did not go to church as a boy nor as a teenager. He seldom talked about religion. Not even at Christmas did the family attend the local church. 'It was as if my parents were so busy going to work night and day, maintaining the house, that they didn't have time to include it in their life,' Sol says. He remembers hearing his mum singing at the top of her voice hymns from television's *Songs of Praise* on a Sunday evening. He was also taught by his mother how to recite 'The Lord's Prayer' – and to always end it with a loud amen! He would pray kneeling by the side of the bed each night, before he closed his eyes and went to sleep. And saying his prayers remained important. Not out loud but to himself at breakfast or on a match day, and as he walked out onto the pitch. He felt God close; he felt his presence. And he thought to himself: *Prayers work. Believe it or not. So why don't I pray more often? Is it because I'm human? Or because I usually pray for the wrong things?*

After he had said a prayer, he quite miraculously did feel a bit better. He recalled the times when he returned from training with Tottenham youth on a Friday and would ride his bike from home to the local Chinese to pick up a takeaway. He did it once a week. It was his treat. The Chinese was next to a church and soon he found himself heading not only to pick up his Peking Duck, but while he was waiting for it to be cooked, he would head next door to stand at the gates of the church so that he could meditate and pray to God. It was comforting.

Linvoy told Sol about the prayer group at Portsmouth. The two had met before. They were both from Newham and had mutual friends. 'It was a unique time and we created our own community within the club; the likes of Sean Davis, Kanu, Benjani, LuaLua and others. It was a joy to have Sol join us. He was a massive figure in the club but in our group there was no hierarchy,' Linvoy says.

Sol took his prayers from the laundry room on to the pitch. He found comfort in the words he had heard. They resonated in his ears. He returned to his imagination of how armies prayed and took their prayers onto the battlefield. He liked that. He visualised it. He veered in and out of the fantasy, crossing the line from the past to the present. It was a place he had continually returned to throughout his career, seeking to recapture the spirit of battle. Ready for the start, for the whistle to be blown and finding relief that he was as prepared as he had ever been.

• • •

Towards Christmas 2006 Portsmouth were near the top of the league. Sol and Linvoy had formed a successful partnership in the centre of defence and helped them keep five consecutive clean sheets. Sol scored his first goal for the club in a 3-1 win over Sheffield United in late December and enjoyed playing at Fratton Park. 'The noise was extraordinary. It held twenty thousand but sounded like forty thousand,' Sol said. 'The singing did not stop. I'd never experienced anything like it.'

Andy Cole had joined Portsmouth at the beginning of that season. The former Manchester United and England striker found it difficult to nail down a regular starting spot, but was full of praise for Sol. 'He was one of the best centre-halves there's been in the English game. I think Sol was underrated. He was quick, strong and read the game as well as anyone I ever played with or against. We always got on. We are similar, in

that he is a very quiet person like me.' Cole's England career
spanned seven years, but during that time he won just 15 caps
and missed out on selection for the 1998 and 2002 World Cup
finals. 'For the quality he possessed in front of goal, he should
have got far more recognition in this country,' says Sol.

Sol knew his body was changing. He was beginning to feel
his age. The older you get, the more you feel it until there's a
point where you feel so much that the body tells you to give up,
to retire. The choice is made for you. He was not at this point
yet, but he knew his training routine had to change and
Portsmouth supported and encouraged him to pace himself.
Tony Adams knew how the process of an ageing footballer went;
he had been there. 'People forget in my last season at Arsenal, I
played thirteen times,' says Adams. 'I knew how it worked and
I encouraged Sol to pace himself. Monday, Tuesday, Wednesday
rub downs. Full training on chosen days.' Adams knew Sol
had to be very fit. 'We knew his fitness was paramount, as we
had Glen Johnson darting forward and we needed Sol to act as
cover. It was always an issue for us, but more often than not he
was fit and strong enough to deal with it.'

By the end of the season, Portsmouth had finished in the top
half of the league but failed by just one point to qualify for
Europe. 'It went right to the wire. We were very disappointed
not to get there but we knew we had a good team that could
only get better,' Sol says.

He was now living in a rented Georgian house near
Winchester, after spending the first months of his move at The
Four Seasons in Hook. He was feeling settled, that lilt of calm
which allowed him to drift into a sense of security. He slept
soundly, always. The now familiar creak of the countryside
brought him closer to a feeling of peace and freedom. And when
he woke up, he stayed under the shower for at least fifteen minutes without difficulty. He liked the freedom to choose how long
he bathed. The constant disruption in his bathroom when he
was a boy still rankled. There had never been a moment of privacy. But living in the countryside was the opposite of those

days. Nature made him happy. It reminded him of his time at Lilleshall. They were good days.

Fiona came to watch him play every week, and they were spending more and more time in each other's company. Not the night before a match, though. They once spent a Friday night together, and the next day Portsmouth lost heavily. This was not going to happen again. She bemoans the memory; he sees it differently. 'I saw it as a sign of how important football was in my life. I took it very seriously. I never lost my commitment on the field to any club I played for. This was my living and I never lost respect for it.'

•   •   •

There was nothing oblique about Harry Redknapp; he got straight to the point.

'I'd like you to be club captain, Sol,' he said to him one day.

'Sure Harry,' Sol replied, without a moment's hesitation. His time for caution on taking up the role had vanished years before, when he became Tottenham captain. Then he was young, still unsure of himself, but things were now different. He would lead from experience, not solely by his presence. At Arsenal, Sol had enough stress to cope with, without taking on the role. 'I probably thought he didn't need the added pressure of being captain after Patrick Vieira left,' recalls Arsene Wenger.

His second season with Pompey justified his move in football terms alone; they finished eighth, their best-ever position in the Premier League, and they won the FA Cup. 'To win the cup with a team like Portsmouth, when you see other teams up and down the country with better and deeper squads, was an extraordinary achievement. We weren't fashionable, we were no-one's favourites, and yet we proved to everyone and ourselves that a smaller club can achieve history,' Sol says.

Portsmouth started off their FA Cup campaign away against Ipswich, followed by a home tie with Plymouth and in the fifth round away to Preston. 'We needed a bit of luck against a number of lower league teams in the early rounds but we got through.' They were then drawn away to Manchester United in the quarter-finals. In football, motivation can be found in all forms. Manchester United hadn't even bothered to apply for their ticket allocation for the replay at Fratton Park. Why should they? They were going to win at home. It would be all done in time for a late lunch (it was an early kick-off). Sol used this experience to stir the troops. *Hold your head high. We are better than that. Let's show Manchester United.*

Before the game he walked as usual on the pitch; Old Trafford, one of his favourite grounds, the place of one his greatest memories and triumphs, when Arsenal won the League title in his first season. Now he leant down and touched the turf with his right hand. He could feel the freshly-cut grass; it was shorter than usual. He heard the Pompey chimes from behind the goal. There was no need to search for inspiration. It was here, right in front of him. He was back on the big stage. They could not lose. No-one believed they could win, but he did. Harry did. The team did. *Come on!*

It wasn't long, eighteen minutes to be precise, before Sol would pull off one of the most important and greatest tackles of his career. He talks about it as if he had scored one of his most memorable goals: 'There was a counter-attack and Rooney was heading in on goal. I said to myself, "Right, I've got to go!" We were overloaded and I ran to catch up, for I was the only one who saw the danger. I could see where he was heading, and what he was about to do.' Time stood still. It was as if a branch of his memory was reliving every little detail of the moment: the same tone and same smell of the ground, flicking up from his studs pounding against the turf. He ran from United's box straight down the middle of the pitch. He was passing everybody with a speed and force he thought he had lost some time before. 'For some reason, I just knew what was going to happen. I just ran and ran, straight ahead, with all my strength.'

Rooney had got to the point where he was one on one with goalkeeper David James. 'I knew instinctively what he was going to do,' Sol says. 'I was using that part of my brain that was able to calculate exactly what was going to happen. The formulation of everything I had learned or had taught myself; from the earliest days in the park, to all the coaches and managers who had trained and taught me. It all seemed to come together at that moment.'

It was like one of those silent movies projecting each frame inside one's brain in quick succession. 'I ran straight for the goal and when I saw David slide and try to parry the ball, I gambled and jumped over him, to cut round and be ahead of Rooney's charge on goal. I just knew that tackle was going to land perfectly. It was unbelievable! The ball fell to Tevez whose shot was headed off the line by Glen Johnson. Beautiful defending. It was a sensational feeling that's never left me. Everyone needs those moments in any sphere of life; when all the hard work pays off. You need your centre-forward to do something magical; and you need your defenders to be special too. That's how you win games of football.'

The atmosphere in the dressing room at half-time was tense. There was a chance here. It was still 0-0. Aspirations were alive, so alive you could virtually taste them. Sol had been through moments like this before. This was where he would help counsel the less experienced players. This is what Tony Adams talked about when Portsmouth signed him. All Portsmouth needed was one chance. That's all. Just the one.

That chance came in the 78th minute after United goalkeeper Kuszczak fouled Baros in the penalty area and was sent off. Baros had come on as a substitute for Kanu, a clever piece of management from Redknapp. 'We would never have been able to do that without money. Have someone like Milan Baros on the bench,' says Adams. Rio Ferdinand went in goal, but failed to stop the penalty from Muntari. Portsmouth went on to win the tie by that goal.

When Sol returned to the dressing room after the game, he took a deep breath and, as he exhaled, he started to cry. Real tears. Everything seemed to go into slow-motion. He watched his team-mates congratulate each other. He was asked whether he would mind being interviewed on television. Not right now. He was not the hero of today. His team was. Talk to them, each and every one. 'We had a good team. I was so proud,' he would say. 'No-one thought we had a chance in hell of winning. Manchester United and Portsmouth. Can you hear it? We went there earlier in the season and were beaten easily. Although we kept the score down to 2-0, we were played off the field. But that's the beauty of the Cup. You just never know!'

The semi-final was played at Wembley stadium and Portsmouth beat West Bromwich 1–0, thanks to a tap-in from Kanu. And so to Wembley again, but this time for the FA Cup final. Sol was never superstitious before a game. He wasn't going to start now. He thought for a moment, if he had done anything different in the quarters and semis, but laughed to himself that he might have put on his shorts first.

'The only thing I believe in first is God, not superstition. I've never been one to avoid walking under a ladder,' and he visualises it, not going out on Friday the 13th because it is considered by some to be unlucky. 'I'm determined never to shackle myself with the chains of superstition.' He looks over to Kanu and gives him a nod. He puts on his socks, shorts and then his blue shirt before putting on his boots, tightening his laces loop by loop, and muttering: 'We can't lose this game.' He repeats these words to himself, if only as a reminder that his strength is he can win anywhere and for anybody. Here he is on Cup final day, the most traditional of all football days, and he will be leading out Portsmouth. *I'm meant to be here today; this is what is written.* As he led his team onto the field he felt calm, as always before a big match. This would be no different. He would play his usual game. He would help guide his players. He would lead them with the fight of a general going into battle. He would lift the FA Cup.

•   •   •

Cardiff 0 Portsmouth 1, FA Cup final, Wembley, 17 May 2008

CARDIFF: Enckelman, McNaughton, Johnson, Loovens, Capaldi, Ledley, Rae (Sinclair 86), McPhail, Whittingham (Ramsey 61), Parry, Hasselbaink (Thompson 70). Subs Not Used: Oakes, Purse.

PORTSMOUTH: James, Johnson, Campbell, Distin, Hreidarsson, Utaka (Nugent 69), Pedro Mendes (Diop 78), Diarra, Muntari, Kranjcar, Kanu (Baros 87). Subs Not Used: Ashdown, Pamarot. Goals: Kanu (37).

Att: 89,874. Ref: Mike Dean.

In one of the most unpredictable of FA Cup tournaments in living memory, Portsmouth edge out Cardiff in the Wembley final to claim the trophy for the first time in 69 years. Kanu's first-half goal, scrambling the ball home after goalkeeper Enckelman fumbled a cross, gives Pompey's noisy fans plenty to celebrate, as well as presenting Harry Redknapp with his first major trophy in a management career stretching back 25 years. Winning the FA Cup means Portsmouth qualify for the following season's UEFA Cup.

It was an attractive game. Portsmouth started nervously and Cardiff were more comfortable on the ball. But once Portsmouth scored, from Kanu, just as he did in the semi-final, they took more of a foothold in the match. Attacking play full of chances for both sides characterised the second half, especially from Cardiff, but in the end Portsmouth deserved to win the trophy.

When the final whistle blew, Sol felt dissimilar to other moments when he had experienced that acute sense of victory. It just seemed different. He lifted his arms into the air and quietly thanked God. He hugged his team-mates and felt a happiness that, on reflection, was not only because of winning the Cup but because, as an old saying goes, 'most creatures are as happy as they make up their minds to just be.'

Sol was aware of everything, the smallest of details, as he began his long climb up the stairway to lift the FA Cup. He climbed the steps one by one. He was not going to be rushed and no FA official would come rushing out saying, 'Sol, do hurry up.' His mind was now filled with gratitude for where he was, and from where he came. Although there were thousands screaming and the world was watching, he felt an overwhelming sense of solitude. His journey was his own and nobody, however close, could possibly understand what it took to get here. Not just on the outside, but inside too. This wasn't a selfish emotion; it was an acceptance of how his life had mapped itself out.

As he walked towards the trophy, and now he was just metres away, he knew what an extraordinary moment he was experiencing. He didn't need the silver to focus his mind but as he took those last few steps, he started to stage-whisper a prayer to himself: 'I thank God for being part of my life and for leading me here.' He remembered how awkward the trophy was to lift up. He had done it before with Arsenal, but this time it was different.

He is the captain, the first to lift the cup for the team. Be mindful of its top. He's sure he has seen it fall with other captains. He looks down at his hands. The long fingers steady, the palms of his hands remarkably dry. He is calm and then has a moment's hesitation; will they fit? Will my hands fit round so I can lift it easily? He took the last few paces in longer strides. If he were still climbing stairs, he would be taking them in twos and a three. He takes a deep breath and shakes the hand of Sir Bobby Robson, followed by Lord Triesman, chairman of the FA. Together they present the cup to Sol, Bobby also gently patting Sol on his shoulder. He gracefully takes the trophy, kisses it and, with a Portsmouth scarf tied around his neck, turns to face the fans, who are singing the Pompey chimes... Then Sol lifts the FA Cup. He holds it aloft for just a second longer than is usual for a captain: 'Yeeessssssss!!!' he cries out, spellbound by an act that every kid in England dreams of; to be captain of a winning side in an FA Cup final.

Lord Triesman recalls the moment he handed the trophy to Sol. 'When a player approaches, I can see in his eyes a mania as if he is still on the field. For a man who is usually so cool, Sol seemed quite different as I shook his hand. "Congratulations," I said. "It's happened to a really nice guy." And he grinned back.'

When the team did their lap of honour, Sol thought he deserved this. Signing for Portsmouth, although at first there were doubts, had not been so stupid after all. 'When you're at the big clubs, you're expected to win the big trophies. I was no longer at Arsenal, I wasn't at Manchester United, nor Chelsea, but I made it work here at Portsmouth,' he says. 'I can win anywhere, I thought, and I liked myself for that.' And there's a hint of pride in his voice for being so honest with his emotions.

•   •   •

At Cheyne Walk Brasserie in Chelsea, Sol and the representative from Puma are having lunch. The restaurant is less busy at lunchtime than in the evening. There is enough room not to be overheard. The two have met before and are talking about a potential boot deal. Puma is one of the finest sports brands in the world. It has a history of representing the world's greatest footballers, such as Pele, Maradona and Cruyff.

Sol is keen. He likes the idea of working with them but negotiation is never easy when connecting a brand with a football star, indeed any star.

They order and the food arrives quickly. They talk about the latest results, nothing in particular, when the Puma representative asks a question.

'Are you gay?'

There is a pause for a split second. Sol is briefly surprised; maybe even a little shocked by the question.

'No,' Sol replies, cool, unflustered, honest.

The representative tucks into his food. 'Ah, that's a pity. We were hoping you were.'

'What?'

'Yup. We were keen to represent the first gay international footballer. We could sell many more boots. It would be a worldwide story.'

Sol shakes his head. He can't win.

When he first heard the homophobic chants from the terraces, he ignored them. He was used to the ignorance and the obscenities. It was part of the game. The ugly side. But the chants and then rumours spread like a virus. The whispering grew louder and louder, the murmur of people saying, 'You know he's gay.' 'He's gay, he must be.' His lifestyle enhanced the gossip. He wasn't seen that often in the company of women and his solitude made people suspicious that there must be something more going on.

'Because they didn't see me falling out of clubs or shagging in the alleys with different girls every week, they thought something must be wrong with me. I'm a footballer after all,' Sol says.

The Puma representative lets out a sudden sigh. He is clearly disappointed.

'I'm not gay. I'm not bothered by homosexuality,' Sol says. 'I'm not sure where the rumours began. Probably from my teammates at Spurs, who knows? I was brought up in a different way; I was very shy even with my mum and dad. And I was shy when it came to relationships, because I saw what happened when my brothers brought girls home. The way my parents treated them; it was a nightmare. The girls weren't allowed in the house when they turned up. They were told to go away or told to wait outside until my brother was ready. It was embarrassing. So I just kept my relationships quiet. Out of sight.'

Sol starts to wonder if the Puma representative is disappointed by the news that he is straight. Do other brands think the same? Is the gossip so convincing that everyone thinks it is the truth and there's nothing more to talk about? 'If there's one thing I can't tolerate,' says Sol, 'it's intolerance.'

They shake hands at the end of their lunch and the Puma man leaves the restaurant. The deal never happened. He never heard from him again. For whatever reason, it was not made clear. Their conversation stayed with Sol. But the rumours have now faded away, like a distant memory. 'The football world conveniently forgot that I was a human being who could do his own thing, rather than getting married in my twenties, settling down, and conforming to the stereotype,' says Sol. 'I like to think I ran my life according to the real world; I didn't find the need to boast to my football mates about going out with this person or that person. I was comfortable in my own skin.'

•   •   •

In the off-season, Villarreal had come in and made Portsmouth another offer for Sol. They had made their first a year before, but Portsmouth were keen to hold Sol to his contract. This time Sol was less tempted to leave. 'We had a team. We were becoming a very good side and if Portsmouth hadn't run out of money, they would have undoubtedly been challenging for the top four. It's a shame.' What he didn't know during the off-season was how little money was left. He might well have jumped at the offer had he known. Harry Redknapp sensed things weren't quite right. He kept saying to Tony Adams, 'I don't like this.'

In October 2008, Redknapp suddenly resigned and joined Tottenham. Sol heard the news with everyone else on the radio when driving back to his rented house. One day Harry was there, the next he was gone. But he wasn't surprised Harry had left. Only a few days before when Portsmouth were playing away at Villa, he said to Sol and Sylvain Distin after the game, 'If I was on my way, I'd definitely take you two with me.' The two laughed, thinking it was a bit of a joke, but Sol thinks Harry had already made up his mind that he was off. What Sol hadn't known was that he'd been feeling unsettled for quite some time. 'He obviously knew the state of the club's finances. He was just waiting for the right offer,' Sol says. Newcastle came in and Harry allegedly signed up but in the end couldn't uproot his family to go up north. Tottenham was impossible for Redknapp to refuse.

By coincidence, Tony Adams had handed in his own resignation twenty-four hours before. He'd had enough of being an assistant and wanted to be manager. Storrie hadn't had time to deal with it but instead asked Adams to be caretaker for the first match after Harry had left. 'Okay, but just for the one game,' Adams had said. Storrie agreed but after the game he brought Adams up to the boardroom to meet the owner, Alexandre Gaydamak. Gaydamak was talking to Sol at the time about the plans for the future. Adams thought Sol didn't know the full story; nor did he, but he knew more than most. The financial position was not good. Gaydamak asked Adams why he wanted to resign. Adams told him he wanted to manage a Premier League club. 'Stay here and manage us.' Adams thought about it. He knew the club had no money but he weighed up it was better to manage and possibly fail than be an assistant all your life. The opportunity might not come again. He accepted the job.

Adams had a torrid time and Sol is saddened by the memory. 'I think management chooses you. You can't force it. Some people have been great players but can't manage. Others have had no playing career and make some of the best managers of their time.'

He hesitates in talking about Adams; his shoulders up to his ears, eyebrows raised. He was his captain, coach and manager, and yet, Sol's words fall from his mouth like a series of unexpected snowstorms. 'Communication for Tony was very hard, which was strange because as a player on the pitch he communicated as well as anyone I played with.'

Adams never had a real fighting chance. A month after accepting the job he was called into the owner's office in Berkeley Square. He was told there was no cash left. Nothing. Gaydamak told Adams, 'I have sunk £180 million into this club and there is nothing left.' Adams shook his head.

'It's worse than that,' Gaydamak continued. 'If we don't get £6 million by the end of the transfer window in January, we will go into administration.'

'I'll have a whip-round,' Adams replied. He paused. 'I'm joking.'

•   •   •

West Ham had given Portsmouth the worst Christmas present of all: a 4-1 defeat at home.

Sol knew the New Year was going to bring in one, long struggle. Rules would have to change; we were talking about survival, which would become even more acute as the weeks went by. Adams had just completed his post-match interviews, where he told the press he had a good bunch of players who would work hard to get things right. He also said he hoped to hold onto his players during the transfer window. But what he said publicly was different to what had to be done.

The dressing room door flew open and Adams stormed in, tired and angry. Sol watched on as 'Tony lost it.' He put his face up close to anyone who got in the way and called his team a 'fucking disgrace'. It was a tirade of abuse. Before he made his final exit, Adams yelled: 'If anyone is up to it or wants to get out of here, come and see me Monday and I'll accept your transfer request!' Jermain Defoe was transferred the following week. Adams' plan had worked. He had walked into that dressing room hoping to save the club by forcing the hand of some of his players. It backfired a little bit when Defoe scored for his new club Spurs against Portsmouth, two weeks later in a 1-1 draw. In that game, Adams' respect for Sol grew even more when he saw, in his role as manager, the defender take on not just a good team but also an abusive crowd. Tottenham seemed to bring the best out of Sol and Adams says: 'It was extraordinary. He may have been directly involved in the action for say six minutes but everything he did was immaculate. I would say without hesitation that Sol Campbell was the most focused player I have ever played with. I wish I had played longer with him at Arsenal.'

Adams was sacked in February 2009; four months after his appointment and just sixteen games in charge in which his team picked up just ten points. They had also been knocked out of both the UEFA Cup and the FA Cup. 'In the end, it was a relief,' Adams says. The club, on the other hand, made a respectful statement. 'This has been a very difficult decision and Tony has worked tirelessly to arrest the slump in form. He is rightfully highly-respected within the football world, and played a major role in our FA Cup triumph last season.' Paul Hart was appointed caretaker manager until the end of the season and brought in Brian Kidd as his assistant. Kidd impressed Sol: 'I really think if it wasn't for Brian Kidd, we would've been in even worse trouble. He helped save us from relegation. He got us organised and installed discipline. He was enthusiastic and got everyone going. He is a very good coach.'

Sol did not for a moment think Portsmouth were going to be relegated. 'I wasn't going to let it happen. Mentally I kept everything going and being captain, I was going to push everyone on with the same attitude. I certainly didn't want relegation on my CV.' So basically, his style of play changed. 'I would do anything to clear my lines. Everything was basically about survival. I wanted to keep my job, roll up the sleeves to keep the club up.'

As well as Defoe, Portsmouth had been forced to sell Lassana Diarra in January. 'Jermain leaving killed us. When the man who scores the goals leaves, you're in deep trouble,' says Sol. 'We seemed to be losing a piece of our jigsaw every day. There was a suggestion in January for me to go, but nothing happened. I knew we were in big trouble and I'm glad I stayed. I needed to finish the season in the Premier League, with the team I won the FA Cup with. Portsmouth gave me one of my greatest memories.'

•　　•　　•

Sometimes a whole season can be determined by a bad decision, a glorious piece of play, a mistake, even the wrong words from the manager. When Portsmouth played Newcastle away at the end of April, they were still not mathematically safe from relegation. Heading that way, but not there yet. The 0-0 draw at St James' Park secured their place. They had read in the morning paper that Portsmouth was a game Newcastle expected to win. Three points added to three points from another game would mean safety for the Geordies. Sol knew Newcastle would get a surprise. 'I always like playing at St James' Park, although as a defender it's more difficult as there is a slope.' Some believe it is legend to motivate the Newcastle players with 'you are playing downhill in the second half.' But Sol insists it isn't his imagination. 'Newcastle prefer to play downhill towards the Gallowgate End in the second half so it's almost as if the ball gets sucked into the opposition goal – while their opponents have to huff and puff uphill! As a defender, playing against the slope, you almost have to play in zones, as your regular clearances and headers won't go as far. And if you're not careful, you can find yourself dropping deeper and deeper until the opposition are almost on top of you outside the penalty box.'

When the season ended, Portsmouth did not offer Sol another contract. They couldn't even if they wanted to. There was little money left. It was time to leave the club and so, not for the first time in his career, Sol was back on the market as a free agent. 'I enjoyed my spell at Portsmouth; it was like going back to a different time. Everyone up against it, mucking in,' he muses. 'I was sad to leave. When I first joined, although it looked from the outside to be in a bad shape, the club seemed to be full of promise. We had a rich young owner, Alexandre Gaydamak, who was full of ambition.'

In Sol's debut season for Portsmouth, the first team attended a press conference where they were shown plans for a big new stadium which was going to be built by the water's edge. Promises were copious. This could be very exciting, thought Sol. But soon he sensed they were false promises and empty dreams. 'I felt quite early on that something was wrong. I never realised how shallow the promises were, or even the perilous state the club was in, but I knew something wasn't quite right.'

After losing away to Wigan on the last day of the season, Sol packed his bags and left Portsmouth. He hadn't played his best that day. His mistake had led to the goal. He was disappointed he hadn't given a better performance, but he had captained the side to do its job and stay in the Premier League. In the end,

Portsmouth finished 14th. He felt good about that. Now the summer lay ahead and he was going to take a break. He was exhausted, both mentally and physically. He was going to get away from the pressure and see what turned up.

NOTTS COUNTY

'I think Sol is going to sign for Notts County!'

'Notts County?'

'Yes, from the sound of it they have more money than Real Madrid!'

Sol was out of a club. He was thirty-four years old and he was getting worried that his playing days were over. 'I was thinking of what I was going to do with my life. Perhaps it was time to start looking at a new career.'

He could have stayed with Portsmouth but would not be paid, so that was out. He had thought that maybe he would get into acting, but every script he received was not what he had hoped for. Also, he was being paraded around from meeting to meeting; told to be seen in Cannes and all the right places. Everything, though, was predictable. He always thought that the unexpected was often the most exciting and this was a new world to him, mixing with the film fraternity and shaking hands with the stars, but he wasn't really enjoying it.

The clock was ticking, and kept on ticking, but it was too early for him to be transformed into something new. He wanted to keep playing and still thought he had enough in him to play at the top level. The phone hadn't gone completely dead. FC Basle had made an offer but it wasn't for him. Young Boys were also interested but they played on a plastic pitch and he 'couldn't do that'. He spoke to Monaco but, in the end, nothing materialised. The dreaded word, which all sportsmen fear, was looming: retirement. He cursed the word metaphorically. It was not going to happen...Not yet anyway.

• • •

His mobile phone rang. He didn't immediately recognise the voice at the other end. It sounded like a monosyllabic tut; without intonation, without spirit.

'Hello?' It was his former England manager, Sven-Goran Eriksson. Sven had been in the news recently; Sol had read about it. He had taken over as director of football at lowly Notts County. There were reports that there was a 'shedload' of money about to be poured into 'The Project'.

Sven told Sol he was needed. He had his patter down to a perfect pitch: 'Sol, I want you to join us. We have big plans here. There is money to help build the oldest club in the football league to be the best. You would lead the line in helping to achieve our dreams. This is a fantastic opportunity.' Words to that effect.

Interesting, thought Sol. He was not an instinctive person who would immediately say, 'Yes, let's do it!' No, that was not his personality, as his other transfers had proved. He would digest what Sven had said. He liked Sven and trusted him. He enjoyed his time with him when he played for England. Yes, this could be good, he thought. 'It was almost reaching a time that if I didn't at least discuss it further, I wouldn't have a club for the new season.'

'I'll call you in a week,' Sven said, 'and see how you feel about everything.' The following week, Sol didn't give much thought to his potential move. He mentioned it to Fiona but just in passing. He was still hoping a Premier League club would come in. But there were no calls. He spent his mornings in his local Italian, making calls, drinking coffee and hearing the local gossip from Michele, the owner.

Then, virtually at the exact minute the phone had rung the week before, it rang again. It was Sven; resolute, punctual and persuasive. He repeated what he had said the previous week;

nothing too pushy, just carefully chosen words. Before Sol could answer or even ask a question, Sven ended the call, saying he would call the following week.

He does, again on the same day, the same hour. This time, it is decided that the two men behind the club who negotiated Sven's deal would drive down to London to have a meeting. 'They are very good and will be very helpful in explaining what is planned,' Sven says, and goes on to repeat his mantra of how exciting it would be to build a club from the bottom of League Division Two into a Premier League outfit. 'It will be our greatest achievement and we will do it together, Sol.' His pitch was near-perfect.

●　　●　　●

Chelsea Manor Street is used to seeing expensive vehicles purring down the road, but there was something in the way this particular Mercedes seemed to barge everything out of its way that made it different. For a side street, it has a surprising amount of activity, predominantly centred around a precinct of shops such as a newsagent, dry cleaners, health store and the restaurant La Delizia. This is where Sol arranges to meet the two men from Notts County, in his local Italian.

The black Mercedes didn't find it immediately. Just past the newsagents, they were told, but they missed it originally and had to double back. The car slowed like a hearse until it finally stopped directly outside the restaurant. The chauffeur got out and opened the door for the two men. Sol, punctual as ever, was already there, talking on the phone at a table on the pavement. It had been reserved but there was no need, as the restaurant was quiet. The two men were both large in size and heavy in weight. First Nathan Willett and then Russell King shook Sol's hand. Sol gagged the mouthpiece of his phone while doing so. He signalled for them to sit while he finished his call.

Russell King had a walking stick and something of a squint; the type that makes you wonder which of the two eyes is the

one looking at you. He leads the conversation but it becomes
clear he has the skill of someone expert in carrying on simulta-
neous conversations; ordering some drink while telling Sol their
dream of making the oldest club in the league the new power-
house of football. How they bought the club from the supporters'
trust and how they planned to put a fortune into it. They were
good at their job. They knew Sol was passionate about his initiative Kids Go Live; they talked about funding the project. They
talked about not seeing Sol as just a player; they saw him as
someone who could one day run the club, manage it, do whatever he liked with it. 'Play for two years and in this time we can
apply for your coaching badges. Then it will be for you to build
the team. Don't forget, we have the money. Not just millions but
billions!' Even Fabrizio, the Italian waiter, was salivating at
the numbers being mentioned. He went into the kitchen. 'I think
Sol is going to sign for Notts County!'

'Notts County?' the chef repeats.

'Yes. From the sound of it, they have more money than Real
Madrid!'

When Fabrizio returned to the table, he heard one of them
say: 'This is our dream. You and Sven are just the beginning.'

Sol was beginning to think that each time they opened their
mouths, he would doubtless be hearing the answer to a question in his mind. They were good, very good. 'They seemed to
know everything about me. They knew I wanted to play. And
they ticked a lot of boxes. I liked the idea of being part of the
renaissance of Notts County. I was ambitious for them. I wanted
to help move them up the leagues, play a couple of years, and
keep my playing days going.' By the time the bill was paid, Sol
had gone from being interested to wanting to sign. 'I really
thought they were kosher. They spoke of companies that they
had been involved in.' The men spoke of some of their deals and
the extraordinary profits they made. 'They spun the whole story
– new signings, new ground, everything new and with Eriksson's
involvement. I believed them and was excited. I thought I'd help
build the club.'

Within ten days, Sol had driven up to Nottingham to meet Eriksson face to face. It was best to see the city, take in the ground that could become home for three or maybe more years. When he walked into the stadium, he was struck by the quality of the pitch and stands. The dressing rooms, though, needed work, and a lot of it, but with all the money, it would be done probably within weeks of signing. 'The stadium on the outside was better than Fratton Park. It was Premier League standard.' The club trained at Nottingham University but much of what he saw or heard was about its future. Sol's, and indeed Sven's vision was the transformation of a near non-league club into one challenging teams in the Premier League and even in Europe – a miracle to behold.

He stayed at Hart's Hotel overnight. His room had views of the city. It was immediately comfortable and he thought it could easily be his home for the weeks before he found some-where more permanent. Eriksson, Willett and King, and for the first time Peter Trembling, the club's chairman, were waiting for him, for dinner next door in the restaurant. All were stand-ing with smiles especially wide to welcome the England international. This signing would signal their intention on the field. They were hungry, not just for the impending dinner, but also to close the deal.

They booked a table in the far corner. Sol ordered the fish, the others ordered as if they knew the menu by heart. 'Best in the city,' one whispered and they gossiped briefly about the owner having a degree at Oxford, or was it Cambridge? And his charming wife. 'I think she does the interior design,' another said. Very good work, thought Sol. They have taste. Sol looked around the restaurant and saw eyes moving with-out faces. The atmosphere distracted him. The conversation at the table seemed unintelligible, his mind seeming to drift like jetsam to another place. Only hindsight recognises he already felt uncomfortable with the company; someone blew his nose and Sol's senses were brought back to the table, to the here and now.

They all spoke the same language of optimism: Trembling, the most quiet of the quartet; Sven popping up with the occasional thought mainly about football and the players the club were interested in, like Benjani and Roberto Carlos who had been mentioned earlier the day in all the papers. This sounds good, Sol thinks. Sol mentions he knows players, friends who were out of contract and could be picked up for no fee. He talks about a couple of names. Sven listens carefully and recites each player's CV as if he knows them personally. Yes, let's make an approach. They all nod in excitable agreement. Sol tells them the sort of money they would be looking for. They tittered with excitement. Titters that amounted to, 'Is that all? We can raise that as quickly as...' And one snaps his fingers. Willett and King spoke again about the company Munto Finance and filled in any gaps in the story with more good news, this time about Nike who were keen to sign a ten-year deal. 'Everyone wants to be part of this extraordinary story. Well, who wouldn't be?' one asks. Again, they all nod in agreement. 'We plan to be in the championship within five years, with your help of course Sol, and then the Premiership.' They laugh at the audacity of the statement, followed by smiles, as if they had at least reached a comforting, if tacit, understanding.

'Promotion and the Premiership!' one of them toasts optimistically and they clink their glasses. Sol noticed Sven was a believer and part of the team. He raised his glass the highest. This was the key. Everything seemed too good to be true; which of course it was. There were clues all the time for anyone to expose the deception. Not least by the way the men engrossed themselves in earnest handshakes and unintelligible gabble that one should have been able to pick up on. But they chose not to, because they wanted a fortune and perhaps needed to believe that dreams can come true.

•   •   •

When Sol returned to his room, he looked out onto the city. He thought of what had been said. There was total silence except for the distant hum of the traffic. How he liked silence, he thought. He had never wanted to drop down one division let alone three, but this was different. He was egged on by the fantastic story he would be part of. He picked up his mobile to phone Fiona. He was going to sign. He had been seduced.

The financial deal was agreed; a very good deal. A bigger payday than Arsenal, more money than he had ever been paid before. *Sign here! Mr Campbell, the future is bright.* He signed. A five-year contract.

He drove back up to Nottingham a week later to face the press, to announce to the football world his signing. He shook hands with Peter Trembling with a firm grasp, and was given a warm welcome. Sol faced the press with the Notts County manager. He had been through all this before. He was not phased. This was going to be easy, compared to the day he signed for Arsenal. He outlined, with calm and clarity, his thoughts and aspirations: Notts County was the oldest club in the league and he wanted to be part of its heritage. 'This club has got great ambition,' he said, reciting the official line.

Press: 'Do you think this club is a well-oiled machine?'

Sol answers: 'It will be.'

Manager (*interrupting*): 'No, it is. This club is a professional football club. It is run from top to bottom like a Premier League club. Does that answer your question? Thank you.'

The manager seemed to have lost his cool. This was neither the time nor the place for this kind of emotion. They had met for the first time only minutes before and his name was hardly mentioned in any of the meetings. This guy won't last long, Sol thinks of the Scot sitting next to him. He was right. Ian McParland, who had been with the club for two years, was sacked after twelve games into the new 2009-10 season. What Sol didn't know at the time was that he would be leaving the club before McParland.

Sol and the manager went outside for their customary handshakes and lifted the black and white Notts County shirt between them with the name 'Campbell' and the number 32 printed on its back. The smiles were wide and confident. Peter Trembling glowed with pride. This is what he envisaged. What he wanted. To be chairman of a club going places. Notts County would be playing Real Madrid in no time. *We can achieve anything.*

•   •   •

'So I got there and thought, okay, right. Where's the money? It didn't seem anything was going on. All was quiet, nothing moving forward.' Within days, Sol still felt excited but also uneasy; an uncomfortable sensation. He remembered having a similar feeling many years back, when in his local park he had almost stepped on the nest of a bird and her chicks – though something told him this situation might involve a nest of vipers. 'Several voices inside me urged: "Get out of here, leave well alone, avoid that which harms you."' He instinctively wanted to take the first train out of there but he stopped himself. He certainly had reason to feel a little alarmed. The big-name signings weren't spoken of again. His suggestions had been ignored. *But I don't want to give up so quickly.* A pugnacious voice was constantly pounding away inside him. He should just relax, go with the flow and get fit. Stop stressing all the time.

There was something that Sol noticed, something that irritated him on his first visit to the ground: a broken window. A small matter, you would think, but something if you noticed it not being fixed, could get more and more irritating. When he first saw it, he looked round once, from left to right, from right to left, as if he was the guilty party. It was on the stairway, so it was difficult to miss. After the first week, it was still cracked. On this particular day it was raining and he could see the splashes of the rain falling through the crack onto the stairwell. Strange, Sol thought. They'll spend money on a hospitality room to entertain their guests but they won't fix a broken window...

He was enjoying the city of Nottingham, though. He was comfortable at his hotel and even started to make plans to buy a place locally. His friend Darren Caskey, who played with Sol at Tottenham youth and with the England Under-18s, was helping him find a place. 'The area was special. I think I would've been comfortable living there,' Sol says. But every time he tried to relax, his suspicion that all was not going as planned increased. Nothing seemed to be done. The crusade was not going as fast as he had imagined. The dressing rooms remained 'disgusting,' but he adds, 'still not as bad as Portsmouth.' Still, if they have the millions, sorry *billions*, they say they had, there should surely be a team of people working round the clock to make the place better? Remember, he thinks, we want to attract some of the best players to drop to the lower league and he knew small details could make the difference. Sven had also mentioned in passing that a number of the owner's investments were in North Korea. *North Korea!* Sol gulped. He quickly pulls himself together. He didn't want Sven to see what he was thinking. He wasn't ready to show his cards just yet. Remember, he is good at that. His thoughts stayed hidden until he was ready to share. Oh, God! He began to sense Notts County was not their first victim. He knew it already but was not yet able to admit that he may have made a *huge* mistake. And as he walked into his hotel, and this boy with wide eyes full of hope and optimism asked for his autograph, he thought: *Whatever you do, don't let them down. You can't treat the fans like this. They believe the future is full of potential.* This whole thought process was not helped by a visit to London when he ran into two friends who advised him to be careful. 'I've looked into them, they aren't honest,' one said. Sol was slowly waking up from his dream. He never tells anyone about his dreams or his prayers. They bore people. He wonders if he will ever be able tell anyone about all this. How excruciating it all seemed. It was beginning to feel like an embarrassment. 'It was dawning on me that I was being a mug,' he says.

•   •   •

It was nearing his debut. He looked as if he would be fit for the Saturday away game to Morecambe at Christie Park. First he had to play a final practice game at the Nottingham University ground. When Sol first saw the pitch, he could see that it was bad. He was never happy with pitches but when he inspected closely this particular one its condition was awful and he knew the surface could jeopardise his fitness. Best to see if there was anything better around, and there was. On the far side, there was a freshly cut pitch. He was going to ask Sven, who was at training most days, to deal with it; but as he was early this particular day, he'd do it himself. He approached the groundsman. 'Would it be possible,' he was being extra polite, 'to play on the pitch over there instead of this one as it seems in better condition?' The groundsman looked at him and gave a desultory wave of his left hand and covered his forced half cough with his other. 'Sorry Mr Campbell, but that one is for the University's first eleven.'

Sol swallows hard and lets the pain of what is happening disappear. Everything was becoming more and more emphasised. He tried to understand but it was becoming more and more difficult.

'Thank you,' Sol says. But the groundsman did not take a blind bit of notice. He was already deep in conversation with someone else.

•   •   •

The Lancashire coastal town of Morecambe had been in serious decline. Its West End pier had been partly washed away by a storm in 1977 and the Central Pier was demolished in 1992. There was a tragedy in 2004 when at least twenty-one Chinese cockle pickers were drowned in Morecambe Bay. It was as if the town had put its right hand over its heart: 'Why us? Why do we deserve such bad luck?' But Morecambe was slowly beginning to pick itself up again. Their football team was doing its best to revive morale. They got promotion to the Football

League in 2007 through a play-off final at Wembley and were spending their last season at Christie Park before moving to a brand new stadium, the Globe Arena. The town was full of fresh optimism; as was Notts County, never more so than that Saturday afternoon when Sol was seen in the team's strip for the very first time.

Sol walked onto the pitch with a face that presaged a northern storm. This was not Highbury but he was here now. *Come on! Things are good. We will win today!* he thinks optimistically as photographers follow his every step and the crowd's eyes turn unanimously in his direction. But County didn't win. They lost 2-1. As Sol is having a shower after the game he goes into full panic mode. *What am I doing here? I still haven't been paid and I'm not sure I ever will be.*

His performance would be instantly forgotten. 'I played average, and had a bit of muscle tightness,' he said. It did not help his mood. The whole day had been difficult, not because of the football but because he was now beginning to feel like a mug. Even then, his last thought of the day was positive: *Calm down. Tomorrow will be better.*

But it wasn't. He drove the following morning to the club ground for the team photograph. On the faces were smiles from the older players, lips tight, cheeks sucked in from the younger ones. There was no tension, just hope. Everyone at Notts County was still devouring the story. Positive and forthright conversations dominated the place. But the enthusiasm from Sol had all but evaporated. He was convinced he had been conned. He would stand for it no longer.

He called Sven early evening: 'What's going on? Nothing is happening!'

Sven was still toeing the company line. 'Give it time, Sol. Everything will be okay. I'm making headway with a few players...'

Sol's mood was becoming more and more obvious around the ground. His silence was becoming more acute. He was ready to have his say, not with a raised voice or the slam of fists.

He would give them one more opportunity to prove their intentions and take a decision from there.

•　　•　　•

He didn't know that this would be the day. But it was.

He drove to the University grounds for training but it was clear after a few minutes that his hamstrings, after his first full game for months, were tight and he needed a massage. He walked up to the manager and Sven, asking whether he could get back to the ground to get some treatment. They agreed and Sol set off in a tracksuit for his ten-minute drive. He hardly used the dressing room at the University. It was really just a room to change into your boots. 'To leave anything there didn't seem like the best of ideas,' he says cautiously.

When he reached the ground, it seemed deserted. It was as if he was walking into his own memorial service. He thought about the lack of activity; nothing had been fixed, virtually everything was the same as when he first walked in. *Damn it. I need to deal with this right now*. He decided to go straight to King and Willett's office.

'Well, then,' he said to himself before walking in, 'why not tell me simply and quietly what is it that is happening under my nose that is so up in the air that I cannot see?'

The office was small and a mess; half-opened files and books were piled in no particular order. The two were both on the phone leaning back in their chairs. One was moaning down the phone with more spirit than usual, while the other voice was cursing. They finished their calls simultaneously.

Sol wanted to concentrate on what had been said over the four weeks, what he had remembered from their first meeting in Chelsea. He wanted to hear from King and Willett that everything was about to change and that new players were joining at the end of the week. But, after a mere five minutes, it became clear: there was nothing. He warned them before he signed that if money wasn't forthcoming, he wanted to be allowed to walk.

He had no intention of going through what he had just experienced at Portsmouth all over again. 'Tell me...' he pleaded, 'tell me everything is going to be alright.' But again, there was nothing. The time of having that reverential look on their faces was in the past. 'I always remember their empty eyes,' says Sol. The relationship was over. They all knew. What was the point of prolonging the pain? None of that will happen here. They hadn't fulfilled their promises and Sol now knew they couldn't. He knew for absolute certain during those few minutes.

As he was about to get up, he noticed a contract on the desk. Not his, although he wished it was so that he could tear it up into a thousand pieces. He saw the signature at the bottom was that of someone who considers himself too busy for the full version, or someone who doesn't want his name recognised. This was not the time to talk about payment; that would have to be discussed later, probably between lawyers. He had a sense these guys didn't pay their bills. He would not be wrong. Eriksson famously said later that he knew things weren't going according to plan when he noticed a milk bill remain unpaid.

Then, his eyes returned to the two men. They said how disappointed they were. But nothing meant anything anymore. Strange, once you recognise a con everything seems so obvious. The hesitation in the voice, the softer tone, the way they want to make you feel special, the way they communicated suspiciously upright. The ever so slight touch of the elbow in greeting, giving you that sense of reassurance. The wide awake smiles and further hand movements, aimed at befriending you.

He left the office without a farewell handshake. What was the point? He was still in his tracksuit. His immediate thought was, shall I have a shower or shall I go straight back to the hotel and do it there? He chose the hotel. He needed to be out of there.

When he walks down the stairwell, he feels a breath of wind touch his face. He stops and looks upwards. He sees flecks of light squeezing through a dull autumn sky. It's the cracked window. It had still not been fixed. 'What have I done?' he says quietly to himself. As he leaves the ground, he passes what looks like an odd job man.

'Fix the fucking window, will you?'

The man looks startled.

'It's on the landing of the first stairway.'

•   •   •

He called Fiona. *I'm coming home.* He had a shower, packed and was in his car within the hour, heading down the M1 back to London. He texted his old school friend Jermaine 'Winston' Barclay who was living in the area: 'Sorry, can't make dinner tonight.' Winston already knew why. The story was beginning to break on Sky news.

Sol Campbell had left Notts County.

Peter Trembling made a statement: 'While we are disappointed that Sol felt he could not adjust to the long-term nature of the project underway at Notts County, we obviously wish him the best with the remainder of his career and hope that he is able to obtain a place where he can play at international level ahead of the 2010 World Cup.' It was a mollifying piece from the Notts County PR machine. The club offered to refund any shirt with Campbell's name on it with a voucher from the club shop.

Sven-Goran Eriksson said: 'I don't know the real reason he left but he didn't like the training ground or the dressing room...' He was certainly right about that, but Sven did not once call afterwards to check if Sol was doing okay or to apologise that he had brought him into the mess. 'Perhaps he was too embarrassed or maybe he never gave it a second thought,' Sol says, but is clearly very disappointed. He had trusted him and therefore trusted the others. Sven was the one who had persuaded him that everything would be fine and the one who had made the initial call, but even to his very last day at County he was defending them. Since then, he had vanished from Sol's life quicker than a body rotting in the tropics; scarpered with no admission of responsibility.

Sol had made a mistake. He was not alone in believing the scam but he was the most high-profile victim. He suddenly realised the whole episode had lasted a pitifully short time. He readily admits to being foolish. And if you're foolish, the media won't let you forget it, especially if money is involved. So the papers jumped onto the next instalment of the Notts County story, with reporters all scribbling manically. 'The star had left... His career was surely now over...' Sol knew what was coming. He had read it all before. He never minded the press as long as it was fair. But one story Sol thought was especially cruel. The headline was: 'Don't feel sorry for Sol, the most selfish man in Britain.' It was written by Piers Morgan. Here are some extracts: 'What about the day Sol was substituted at half-time, after letting West Ham run riot over Arsenal at Highbury, and reacted by throwing his toys out of the pram and marching off home, not playing again for a couple of months? A spineless, pathetic reaction.' And another: 'Arsene Wenger says Campbell is a strong man and that's why he tore up his County contract. With the greatest of respect Arsene, he's not. He's just a selfish git.'

'He didn't know the situation. He was too fast with his comments. Everyone was,' Sol says, as if he was anaesthetised by the continual onslaught.

BBC's *Panorama* ran an exposé of Russell King, 'The Trillion Dollar Con Man', and the whole Notts County debacle. Slowly, the truth of what had been going on came out and soon everyone knew about the fraud; Sol had simply seen it before most.

Like Sven, Piers Morgan never picked up the phone or wrote to apologise to Sol to say that he just may have made a mistake.

ARSENE

'You've seen me through so much and yet you still thought that I hadn't got it in me to come through this latest test. Don't you realise it's in my DNA?'

SOL

He needed a good night's sleep after his escape from Nottingham to be able to face the long day ahead. Just one night and then he was ready to go again; any sense of taking it easy was not possible let alone conceivable.

Under League regulations, Sol was unable to sign for another club until the transfer window in January but he needed to keep fit. 'I had no idea where I was going. I didn't have a job and really, for the first time, I truly didn't know what was going to happen.' He spoke with Tony Colbert, his former fitness coach at Arsenal. He asked whether he could join in some sessions. 'I need to be fit for January, Tony. Can I work with you?' Tony checked with Arsene Wenger who said, 'Of course.'

'I worked with the injured in order that I could get back to full fitness, so that was good for me,' Sol said. 'There were multiple sessions with balls, passes, cones, all on distance and timings, all measured.'

He was unfit. Far worse off than he had admitted or had been told. But he worked hard. He had made the decision that he was going to come back. Nothing, not even his age at thirty-five, was going to stop him. Within two weeks, his times began to improve, not slowly but rapidly. He was getting stronger and faster. The coaching staff were surprised. When they had first seen Sol, they thought he wouldn't come back. They wanted to tell him to forget any notion of playing at the highest level again. His physical condition was way off. But then their clocks started to tell a different story and his speed and times were improving. The coaches started to talk about it. 'Have you seen Sol's times?' Like the coach who looks at his stopwatch and shakes it to his ear to check it is working properly. 'I think we should tell Arsene something is happening here.'

Sol was being told how impressed everyone was and it made him more determined to get even stronger. But Wenger was not interested or simply not listening. He didn't re-sign players – end of. Never had and was not going to start now. But Wenger kept being reminded by his coaches: 'Arsene, some of Sol's times are as good as the twenty-one-year-olds. He doesn't seem to have lost it. He has the same skill as he always had.'

Sol kept on improving but still there was no murmur from the manager. Until, quite unexpectedly one day Sol got a message that the boss would like to see him work with the first-team squad. It is nice to be given a surprise, yes, but it is sometimes a little less nice to think how much more one could have enjoyed the surprise, if one had been forewarned about it! Here is a man who played over seventy times for England, played in three World Cups, scored in a Champions League final, played in high-pressure matches across Europe, won and lifted the FA Cup as a captain, won two Premier League titles and yet that morning he felt like a young footballer on trial for his career. He knew this was his chance. And his father's words rushed back into his conscience: 'You have one chance. Grab it!'

Wenger was not going to make it easy. Best to know if Sol still had it and if he didn't, then he could get on with his day without the continual nagging from his coaches. He arranged for some one-to-one sessions. Two full-sized goals, thirty seconds with the ball, and you take on each other, trying to beat your man and score in the allotted time. Wenger looks round his team. Who to choose? Who to put Sol up against? He thinks. There is a pause. Let me see now: 'Cesc! Get ready.'

Cesc Fabregas, the young Spanish midfielder who had been at the club since he was sixteen and was fast becoming one of the best-ever players to wear the Arsenal shirt. 'As soon as I saw Fabregas when he first came to the club, I recognised his talent. He had skill, balance, control, everything, but he also had an attitude and dedication that seems to belong to the best. I knew he would reach the top. I had no doubt,' Sol remembers.

Sol relishes the challenge of facing Fabregas. He feels fit. He feels good. *I'll show the boss. I'll show him what I can do.* And he does. Every thirty seconds testing every part of his fitness. 'It's very intense, pressing on all aspects of the game.' Sol trains as if back to the time when he was part of the Invincibles. Dennis Bergkamp said about training with Sol: 'You would test your pace and strength against Sol. He's your team-mate but if you can beat him, who couldn't you beat in the Premier League?'

Fabregas, like Bergkamp in his day, was as skilful as anyone in the league. Sol's knowledge of Fabregas' style of football, watching him grow from a teenager, wasn't going to help that morning. 'When you are good, you can just flip your play, do something different. Go to the left instead of right. Never predictable, never obvious.' He snaps his fingers. 'The great player simply unlocks his gift. I know some managers are very meticulous. Jose Mourinho has videos of every player his team is going to play. He has studied every single move. It's quite intense but you watch it. The centre-forward likes this. He studies the defender, the sides he doesn't feel comfortable with, whether he likes to pass to the right when distributing out of the box. Which direction he likes to head away at corners. The same works when the defender studies the striker. Does he move to the right? Does he like to shield the ball when the ball is about to be trapped? Does he like to tap the ball a fraction forward just before he shoots? You have to realise, when you come up against certain managers, that they have studied every move from every player. But if you have four or five geniuses on the pitch, you can study whatever you like and in the end it's worth nothing.'

After finishing with Fabregas and having a short rest, Sol sees Wenger send on another two players. It's as if he didn't want it to work. 'It was not that,' says Wenger. 'I was resistant to going back to a former player, an ex-champion. I had never done it before. How he left the club the first time weighed heavily on my mind; the stress that overwhelmed him during that time. I didn't want him to ever go through it again. I wasn't sure he really knew what he was letting himself in for. It wasn't times or skill that I was analysing; it was whether in his mind he had decided to go for it. Once I had seen he had, there was little doubt he would succeed.'

There was no denying it turned out to be a good session. Sol knew it. Wenger knew it. When it was over, coaches went over to offer their congratulations, but not Wenger. He walked away on his own, deep in thought. He has that habit of living as if to suck lemons and pretend they are not sour. Sol was neither surprised nor offended. That was Wenger's way. And whatever Wenger had just seen, he was still arguing in his mind that he simply didn't re-sign ex-players. It kept coming back to that fact. It didn't fit into his philosophy. There had been rumours in the summer that he was flirting with the idea of re-signing Patrick Vieira, but nothing happened.' It was just that: rumours. There was no truth in it,' says Vieira. A couple of the other coaches nudged Sol as he headed to the dressing room and in a stage-whisper said, 'You did good, Sol,' so Wenger, who was a few metres ahead, could hear. Wenger's assistant manager, Arsenal legend Pat Rice, gave him a smile, a slight nod. 'I always liked Pat,' says Sol. 'He wanted you to work hard but with it he had a sense of humour, and was always joking.'

Sol watched Pat catch up with Wenger. The manager was walking quicker now, as if he was hiding something. Pat walked as if he had seen something. They spoke. Sol knew Pat was part of Wenger's inner sanctum. He had been since Wenger arrived, since Sol first arrived. That's how it works. Wenger will consult those closest to him. Give each decision a sound hearing and then find the right conclusion.

When he drove home that afternoon, Sol was thinking that he's still at his best when he's under pressure. Again he recalled his father saying that you have one chance, so take it. He felt like a teenager once more. He had to prove himself. Well, *he* felt he did. *Now let's see what happens.*

Wenger kept Sol waiting. He was still trying to make up his mind, still unsure if it was a good idea to let Sol back into the Arsenal spotlight. Does he really need it? The image of Sol's face during that final season still haunted him. Meanwhile, Sol kept going, keeping up his times and continuing to train hard. 'I think he's going to speak to you today,' one of the coaches whispered but he didn't, and the days went by and still nothing happened. Sol wasn't going to approach Wenger and ask what was happening. No, although time was pressing, he would wait until Wenger was ready. He felt no fear of rejection. There was no time when he thought he would help hasten the decision; or beat Wenger to it by simply not turning up and playing hard to get.

Funnily enough, on the day it happened Sol wasn't even thinking about his future. Wenger approached him with forced ease and asked Sol to come to his office. The same office they had met in before he left the first time. The same office where he met Wenger to ask what was happening when he was dropped.

When he walked to his office he thought of the old adage, that in football you are only as good as your last game. And for Sol and Wenger, that was the Champions League final in Paris. Suddenly, he steps further back in time and remembers the games he played at Highbury; the glories and the few disappointments. The last game ever played at the old stadium, when Thierry Henry scored a hat-trick in a 4-2 over Wigan on 7 May 2006. How, at the end, he walked inquisitively from one end of the pitch to the other, like a schoolboy on a long train for the first time, insisting on seeing it all from the first carriage to the last. He thinks of the history of that day. He thought it was, until this moment, the perfect setting to end his Premier League appearances for the club. He recalls hours spent in the dressing room when he first arrived and was quiet, just listening to everything going on around him. It all seems a long time ago. Now, if he came back he would be the senior statesman; the player who would show the youngsters how to conduct themselves, play the game. He looked forward to taking on that role. He sensed the younger players needed his advice, his guidance. He had seen some of them disappear far too quickly after the training sessions, as if escaping something or other. He wasn't sure what the rush was, especially when he saw they all needed to work harder to improve their game.

He knocks hard on the door. He knocks again.

'Come in!'

He sits opposite Wenger. A man he has the upmost respect and loyalty for; surely the backbone of any good relationship. A man who dominated his thoughts over the last few weeks, far more than ever before. He knew that his destiny rested with him. There's a pause and then Sol is told that the club wants to sign him for the last six months of the season. They liked the way he had been training, improving every week. Wenger had been watching him carefully. There was still a bit of work to do, but he was confident that Sol would reach the standard that's needed. He starts mapping out the whole deal. You will be paid this if you play this number of games, etc. 'This is good for you and good for me,' Wenger says. He pauses and then slowly explains how he sees the coming weeks working out: 'To be the cover and teach the young players how to prepare and how to be professional.' He sighed. 'If you can do that as well, I'll be very happy, as it is needed.' Funny, thought Sol, I was thinking about that just before knocking on your office door.

This is good, Sol thinks. He is buzzing inside. He hasn't felt so excited since he first joined Arsenal. And now he's back and will be playing at the Emirates for the first time.

When he drove away from the training ground, he switched on the radio and felt contentment. The wounds that had scarred his final season with Arsenal had finally been healed in the last hour. He hadn't realised they were still open until that morning. Strange, how you can carry so much around and sometimes not notice it.

In the car, for a moment he reflects back to the point where he stood up, as the meeting with Wenger drew to a close, shook the boss' hand and said, 'I'm up for this!'

I've worked for this and now I've got it!

•   •   •

Everyone at the club felt that Wenger would eventually sign up Sol. The doubt as much as anything was that he hadn't done it before and it wasn't his style to start something he believed was fundamentally a retrograde decision. 'It is very unusual to bring a player back, but I always say you can never say never,' said Wenger.

Sol would be cover for Thomas Vermaelen and William Gallas. Philippe Senderos was loaned out to Everton for the rest of the season. The Swiss defender, who'd been heralded by Wenger as the future of the club – and had taken Sol's place in defence back in the day – was no longer needed.

It was officially announced on 15 January 2010 that Sol Campbell had re-signed for Arsenal. He would wear the number 31 shirt. 'It gives us an opportunity to have one more centre-back,' said Wenger. 'He's worked very hard and we've given him the opportunity to re-launch his career. For us, it is a good help until the end of the season. For him, it is a good opportunity to show he can play in the Premier League again. I think he showed he is motivated, he's happy to be back.'

The training became even more intense. Sol knew his time would come. He was living those weeks since agreeing the deal personally with Wenger with the certainty that he would have centre stage again, and a conviction that he would not let anyone down. He was in better shape than he had been for a long time; he thinks probably four years. His time with Portsmouth was disciplined but different in its intensity.

'Arsenal were in another league in the way they conducted their fitness. My weight just dropped off.'

For his first game back in the Arsenal team, he played in an FA Cup tie against Stoke. Arsenal lost 3-1 but Sol did not let his team down and kept up with the pace. The following Wednesday, he came on as a substitute for Vermaelen in the 35th minute of the 0-0 draw away to Aston Villa in the Premier League. His appearance made Sol only the third player up to that point to have played in all eighteen seasons of the Premier League since its inception in 1992 (Ryan Giggs and David James were the other two).

But it was his first game back at the Emirates that moved him far more than he anticipated; a 5-0 home win against Porto, which helped Arsenal advance to the quarter-finals of the Champions League. Sixty-thousand voices welcomed Sol back; he heard the cheers that night.

What a stadium, he thinks, as he runs onto the pitch. What a welcome. *I've worked damn hard for this and now I'm going to prove to all those doubters who had written my obituary how wrong they were.* The change in his character as he ran on the pitch appeared out of nowhere, with a precision and knowhow that spoke of years of experience on the battlefields of football grounds throughout the world. *'Be careful of quiet people, for there's nothing more deadly than the gentle pushed too far.'* If his career was reaching its final act, then he was ready. *Bring it on. It's showtime.* 'I was fully prepared for every eventuality. I heard later that Porto's pre-match talk was all about them "taking advantage of Sol Campbell, he's past it." Well, I was turning back into a Ferrari, thanks to the Arsenal coaching staff. Tony Colbert helped change that chapter of my life and I will always be grateful.'

Gallas' injury and Vermaelen's suspension meant Sol continued his run in the first team. The thought of playing just three games was quickly forgotten. He was important again, the main man in the centre of defence and his form was growing with each ninety minutes. Wenger said to Sol, after one of the early games: 'Hey Sol, you are looking like a footballer now.' His team-mates agreed. Andrei Arshavin ran up to Sol after training and said that he had his doubts when he first saw his movement. He had thought to himself that Sol had a long way to go. And yet, two weeks later, he had already been proved wrong. 'Huh,' Arshavin said, 'I will never doubt you again.'

You'd better not, thought Sol.

The players were able to see Sol more in the round than any previous squad. He cherished his role as the club's senior statesman, an experienced man on top of things. He was more vocal than he had ever been in previous Arsenal dressing rooms. The Lee Dixons and players from his first season at Arsenal would not have recognised him. They were bewildered by his silence, never convinced they would ever get to know the true Sol, a few either not bothered or unable to intellectually lift themselves into understanding someone different. Footballers aren't good at that. Lee Dixon tells a story that when he was in the coach heading to a game, Tony Adams asked how he was feeling. He answered that he was fine. When Adams openly said that he was feeling a little down, some players clustered nearby playing a game of cards gave each other a silent look, the lifting of the eyes. Most footballers aren't good in dealing with any sense outside the norm. But Sol was happier than he had been before in the Arsenal strip.

The intensity of the season was difficult for Sol's fitness. He lamented the passing of days when he could play on a Wednesday, followed by the weekend, without thought. But those days were over. He could play once a week. Now, when he left the pitch, he felt it. Felt every pull on every muscle. 'I couldn't play as many games as I wanted. It took too much out of me.'

He missed out on the Barcelona away game in the Champions League in April because of this schedule, and was very disappointed. He knew when he was picked for the Wolves game on the Saturday that he had no hope of making the game at the Nou Camp in the second leg of the Champions League the following Tuesday. Arsenal won the Wolves game with a goal in

added time by Nicklas Bendtner and kept their league title aspirations alive, but Sol questioned why he hadn't been kept for
the all-important Barcelona game. His disappointment was
well-hidden, he was good at that. He had been doing it all his
life. There would be no grumbling, no self-pity. He could still
revert to the Old Sol; the one no-one knew what he was feeling,
what he was thinking.

He sat on the bench and watched Arsenal get knocked out of
Europe, losing 4-1 after drawing the first leg 2-2 at the Emirates.
He couldn't have gone on, even if he had been called. Well,
maybe he could have dragged himself off the bench, but he
would have moved about like a rigid old tram.

A couple of days after they returned from Barcelona, Sol went
up to Wenger. Perhaps he should demand an explanation from
the boss. Their relationship had matured. He was better at com-
municating now. Sol asked his question and Wenger replied that
it was more important for him, and therefore the club, that he
played in the League game. 'We can still win the League,' he said.

They had one moderately large clash, when Wenger tore into
him after the Champions League first leg defeat away to Porto,
less than a month after his return to the first team for his
second spell with Arsenal. Sol back-passed a free-kick to his
goalkeeper, which was intercepted by Falcao, who scored the
winner in a 2-1 Arsenal defeat. 'After the game, he kept blaming
me when the goalkeeper should have just kicked the ball off to
the sidelines. He did not have to pick up the ball,' Sol says inno-
cently, accepting no responsibility. He felt Wenger was being 'a
bit harsh'. He had scored Arsenal's opening goal and thought he
had played reasonably well. But here was the same authorita-
tive voice he had heard for years. He had seen it all before.
That's what age and experience does. You've proved your talent,
succeeded or failed a long time ago. But it still irritates. Wenger
seemed to be making an example of him. He hadn't turned on
anyone else when the Arsenal performance was littered with
mistakes. Sol wanted to say, 'I think you're wrong.' Instead, he
remained quiet and, when Wenger finished his overlong tirade,

he turned away and walked to the showers. 'He *is* wrong,' he mumbled to himself.

•   •   •

The season ended with Sol making fourteen appearances for the first team. Arsenal finished third in the Premiership. The signing had been a success. No-one was sure it would be, except Sol himself. He never had a doubt. His focus, discipline and commitment, which people close to him recognised, had never left him even in the last acts of his career. He proved that in the years since he left Arsenal, he had regained his strength of mind. When he first left, it had been at its lowest; now it was strong again. It is sometimes easy to make yourself the hero of your own story, but over these few months he had rescued himself from a lack of fitness, shortage of matchplay and no club to play for, back to being one of the best central defenders in probably the best league in the world.

Arsenal immediately offered him a new contract. Sol began to negotiate but the two sides were unable to agree. And then, before negotiations could be continued, Wenger took off to South Africa to commentate on the World Cup. By the time they spoke again, Wenger had lost interest. He already had two names in mind for his defence, Laurent Koscielny and Sebastien Squillaci, both of whom he would eventually sign.

Wenger was straightforward: 'I feel you've moved on and so have I. I think it's best to leave it there...' He made the same decision with Thierry Henry a few years later. A champion needs to know when he should move on. 'Thierry came back, played again, and, like Sol, gained the respect of everyone. We had the opportunity to do it again and I said to him, let's not do this anymore. Let's finish on a high and that's what I wanted to explain to Sol. It's always difficult for great players to know when to stop. It's very difficult to lose, at a very young age, your passion, your fame and the money. Usually by your mid-thirties, you have to go in search of a new beginning.'

They agreed. Before Wenger said his goodbye he said: 'You surprised me last season, Sol. I never knew you had it in you.'

What a strange thing for Wenger to say, thought Sol. Those words stung. How could he even question his resolve and ability to succeed? This Frenchman who providence had chosen to be the most prominent manager of his career still didn't understand him. 'When he said those words, it really hurt. I thought, you've seen me through thick and thin, you've seen me sick, at my worst, at my best. You've seen me through so much and yet, you still thought I hadn't got it in me to come through this latest test. Don't you realise it's in my DNA? I can't get rid of it.'

Sol felt insulted. He felt underrated. Wenger is clear he was misunderstood: 'He misinterpreted what I said to him. What I wanted to say was that he had aged, and that I didn't expect as much quality from him as he had shown. I did not question his dedication, as I knew he had the fight in him, but I didn't expect him to be as good as he was. I thought he had lost some of his qualities; that was what I wanted to tell him. He was absolutely heroic and gained the respect of everyone.'

But Sol had not heard this. He switched off his phone, left his house and walked along the Embankment, immediately thinking of the old days; the days when he was considered by most as being one of the best defenders in the world. It is difficult for him to think in those terms; he doesn't like to think of himself as anything other than the hard-working professional he was. 'I recognised the cards I had been dealt and I've done my hardest to change them. I didn't have the best education and connections, but I worked every day to better myself, to prove myself.'

It is a warm afternoon and he is grateful for a sudden shot of cool air bouncing off the river. He passes a couple of tourists. One of whom says out loud, 'There goes Sol Campbell!' Sol hears what is said and walks on, a little faster than before. This is no time to stop. This is a time to be alone with his thoughts. He senses his career is coming to an end. Arsenal isn't going to work and Celtic, who had made an enquiry, didn't appeal. He wants to keep playing but for the right club. 'No more mistakes,' he says out loud. He had just proved he could get back to the top, whoever may have doubted it. He thinks of the England squad out in South Africa, and is irritated again he's not there. Such a wasted opportunity, he thinks. I could have done a good job for the country. Is this what happens? That outside forces choose when you get off the train? It isn't your own decision to say I won't play anymore, thank you, I'm getting off at this stop? No-one warns you how it can end. As someone once said: 'Play as long as you can because you are a long time retired.'

He keeps thinking. A thousand thoughts race through his mind, like cattle in a stampede. *Is there a man out there who understands me?* The 'off the cuff' remark by Wenger, which was surely meant to be a compliment, had sent Sol into a tail-spin. It had brought up thoughts of anxiety. He walked away from the Embankment to his favourite Italian, a sanctuary of sorts. It is the same one where he met those two men from Notts County but the memory has not soiled his fondness for the place. It is quiet, except for a wise-looking old man, who is devouring a large bowl of pasta. He eats quickly, as if late for an appointment. Sol is not in a hurry. He sits down at a table on the pavement and puts his head between his hands. He is quite alone thinking about his future. He looks up at the waiter. 'I'll have a coffee, please.' The waiter who would usually give a cheerful hello, this time does not. He senses Sol wants to be left alone.

•   •   •

He didn't know it then but he still had a year left of his career. He was asked by his friend Chris Hughton, who was managing Newcastle, to join him on a one-year contract. 'I wanted him at Newcastle for his presence and the experience he could bring to the team,' says Hughton. It seemed like the perfect move to finish his career. His soon-to-be wife Fiona was from the area, passionate about the club and they had recently bought a property 25 miles west of the city.

He made his Newcastle debut in the third round of the League Cup against Chelsea, and then in the Premier League on 3 October 2010 in a 2-1 defeat to Manchester City. Throughout his time at Newcastle he struggled for fitness, and six months after arriving, his friend Hughton was fired. He was very upset by the decision: 'He got sacked because they wanted to get someone else in. I couldn't understand why. He was doing well for them. He had got them promoted, and was maintaining the club in the top half of the league. He took that club out of the gutter, made it something, gave it dignity, gave it confidence and worked tirelessly throughout the time he was there. He gave everybody a hundred per cent. It was one of the more senseless decisions I witnessed in my career.'

Sol left the club when the season was over. It had not been the finale he had dreamed of.

•   •   •

The wise man orders a coffee as his plate of pasta is taken away. A boy plays keepie-uppie with a 1970s-style football by the side of the road. He plays with the ball with such deftness, it looks beautiful; he has everything ahead of him. Sol recognises contentment in the boy's eyes.

Where will Sol find tranquility now? Where was he going to find his hunger for contentment and peace of mind? In the past, if he ever lost his inner peace, he had always managed to rediscover it back on the football field. When times had been difficult, it was on the field with full fitness where he eventually reclaimed his equilibrium, and a sudden peace would flow through his body. His longing for that feeling would not have been so poignant, if it hadn't been for his childhood home and his escape into the streets and the nearby park.

Just as he was feeling as alone as he had been for a long time, he sees his future wife Fiona and mother of his children, walking towards him. It reminds him of when he was a little boy, looking out of the window waiting for his mother to return from work. His father would be asleep upstairs or be downstairs, paying no attention to his youngest son; his mother representing the comfort and affection he was so in need of. As Fiona is about to reach the table, he recognises that she is someone who does understand him. Probably knows him better than anyone has ever done. Perhaps better than himself; his sins, his needs, his desires. Someone who will keep him company in the days ahead and is able to understand those chapters he found difficult to talk about. 'She's been my rock, a woman who gave me back my belief in life, and an ability to trust in people again. I was falling out of love with a lot of things. I shut down and withdrew into a shell – perhaps as a form of self-preservation, not wanting to be exposed to hurt – but Fiona found a way to open me up, showed that it was safe to emerge, and taught me how to love again.' He needs her.

And, although his playing career was nearing its close, he saw, like the kid playing with the ball, the possibilities for his future were endless.

EPILOGUE

'The real paradises are the paradises lost.'

MARCEL PROUST

When Portsmouth played Tottenham at White Hart Lane on 28 September 2008, the abuse from some Spurs fans not only shamed the club but shamed common decency. 'They were chanting about what I had supposedly contracted, about lynching me and about my sexuality,' Sol says. The hideous one-note chant, which sounded like the braying of inebriate Nazis, was not made up while they were in the ground watching the game; it had been composed and worked on. During the game, Sol hadn't heard it in its entirety. He had heard the odd line. It had not affected his game, although at times when he hears abuse it is like being burnt slowly, in the way an effigy is held up by a marauding crowd outside an embassy. There is a photograph taken of Sol that afternoon. Arms stretched out as if he was being crucified, pain lashed over his face, mouth wide open shouting something indistinguishable, lost in the hiss of the crowd. The so-called fans standing gormlessly, staring open-mouthed into the dank dark, trying to confuse Sol further, upset him, push him towards such disconcertedness with what is going on, both in his head and all around him, that he gives up playing, maybe even causes harm to himself; is that what they want in the game they play from the terraces? Do they possess a thing called conscience?

Someone in the dressing room (he doesn't remember who) told him afterwards that reporters had strung the words together of what the Spurs supporters were shouting. It was different this time, something more wounding than they had heard before. Be warned, a couple of team-mates said, you are going to be asked about it. And when he heard what was being sung, he thought at first, *What is all this? Why is it still going on?*

At home that night, he started to digest what had happened hours earlier. What goes through these people's minds? He felt spat at. Fathers standing next to their sons, some as young as pre-teens, encouraging them to join in. Ignorance, insecurity or bigotry? Or all three? Isn't it time to move on? Am I still the villain in their lives? Who do they think I am? It doesn't matter how I may feel; appear to feel. What I may think; appear to think. What pain my friends and family are suffering; appear to be suffering.

The silence in his house made the chanting from earlier even more palpable. He needed space in which to be able to address his thoughts, prepare himself for unexpected developments, some of which might have serious consequences for those who probably, at that moment, were just living their own ordinary lives, unaware that they would soon be marked in some degree forever. He could hear them. He could hear every word now. When he was playing he caught the odd line but he was too focused, buzzing from adrenalin, to hear everything. Now he could debate what to do. The afternoon had given him the chance to bring out those figurative skeletons from the cupboard. Yes, put them in the middle of the stage of our fear, and see them for what they are: pitiful piles of dried bones! This malice had been tracking him for far too long, and in truth, he had dealt with it internally when he played and came face to face with it, but not on the outside. I'm older now, he thinks. It's time to have my voice heard. Future players shouldn't have to take this anymore.

Sol rang Sky Andrew and asked him if he could get on BBC Radio 4. 'I've had enough of this. I want to talk. I'm tired of the FA. I'm tired of them ignoring the racism and homophobia in the stadiums. They have done nothing. *Nothing.* It needs to be dealt with; it's got to stop.'

In his interview he said, 'We can all take the booing or light banter, but when it gets to the realms of verbal abuse, it's a bridge too far. This is a human rights situation, where professional sportsmen want to do their job professionally and people are abusing them verbally. If this happened on the street, you'd be arrested.' Within hours the story grew. The police received an official complaint and an investigation was launched. The club and manager were wholly supportive. 'This kind of thing has no place in football, no place in life,' said Spurs manager Harry Redknapp. 'Someone has got to do something about it, somebody has got to make a stand, and if Sol wants to do that, we are right behind him.'

Aside from that 2008 game at White Hart Lane, Sol has had to deal with racist and then homophobic chants throughout his career but two incidents stand out, even today, that make him shiver at the memory. 'I was playing for Tottenham against Sunderland at Roker Park, and every time I picked up the ball or took a throw-in, the monkey chants were deafening, overwhelming. I had never heard anything like that noise before. I looked at Gary Bennett, a black player who was the Sunderland captain at the time and thought, how can you play in an atmosphere like this? I didn't understand it.'

In another game, again when he was playing for and captaining Tottenham, he laments a moment in his life, when he felt ashamed to be playing football. He kept a bottle of water inside his goalmouth, so he could grab a quick drink whenever he was thirsty. Against Northampton in a third round League Cup tie, there was a lull in the game and Sol walked over to the goalmouth to take a drink. As he swigged his water, what must have been a thousand home supporters standing behind the goal started making monkey chants, within spitting distance from where Sol was standing. Sol stood motionless, immobilised by a mass of contorted faces making racist noises.

'That's enough, that's enough!' he shouts but the chants get louder and the faces get more ugly, so ugly they turn into foul beasts with ridges and creases. Until he catches sight of one face.

He notices it because it is the only face that looks about nervously, with an expression that looks different to all the others. A woman in her thirties has shame marked on her forehead, her eyes pleading an apology. Her delicate features, so feminine in this crowd of bigots, snap him out of his stupor. He calmly puts the bottle of water down and continues his game. Is one's turmoil truly less if expressed? Sol doesn't show any emotion. Spurs won the game 3-1 and Sol scored. The date was 27 October 1999, seven months after Spurs had won the League Cup.

Three weeks later, he received a handwritten letter in blue ink from that same woman, expressing her sorrow, her embarrassment. 'Dear Sol, I am the woman who you saw at Northampton last month and I was appalled by the behaviour of people standing beside me and I am writing to apologise...'

As for the Portsmouth-Tottenham game, a total of eleven fans of all ages were arrested and four men pleaded guilty to racist and homophobic chanting in January 2009. They received a three-year football banning order and a fine.

Another chapter of his abuse had closed.

•   •   •

Sulzeer Jeremiah 'Sol' Campbell. Is there a finer English footballer over the last fifty years who has been eyed so suspiciously? Has his silence, or lack of understanding for the average football fan, heightened the intense speculation about everything that goes on in his life? Does his desire for solitude, together with his innate shyness, in such contrast to his role as a professional footballer, make him even more difficult to fathom? Are the rumours and suppositions that followed each chapter of his career unjust? Remember, conspiracies in the football world extend to every corner of the globe. Our curiosity for the famous will not die. Perhaps the curious maintain it long after the final whistle.

•   •   •

SULZEER JEREMIAH 'SOL' CAMPBELL

Born: 18 September 1974
Birthplace: Plaistow, East London
Height: 6ft 2in
Playing weight: 13st 8lb–14st 2lb
Playing strengths: Powerful frame, athleticism, quick feet, resolute attitude

CLUB CAREER

Tottenham 1992-2001

Appearances: 315 (11 as sub)
Goals: 15
Honours: Worthington (League) Cup 1998-99
Managers played under: Doug Livermore-Ray Clemence (joint), Ossie Ardiles, Gerry Francis, Christian Gross, George Graham, Glenn Hoddle
Central defensive partners: Gary Mabbutt, Colin Calderwood, Ramon Vega, Chris Perry

Arsenal 2001-2006

Appearances: 197 (2 as sub)
Goals: 11
Honours: Premier League title 2001-02, 2003-04; FA Cup 2001-02, 2004-05; Community Shield 2002-03

Manager played under:
Arsene Wenger
Central defensive partners:
Tony Adams, Martin Keown, Kolo Toure

Portsmouth 2006-2009

Appearances: 111
Goals: 2
Honours: FA Cup 2007-08
Managers played under: Harry Redknapp, Tony Adams, Paul Hart
Central defensive partners: Linvoy Primus, Sylvain Distin

Notts County 2009

Appearances: 1
Manager played under:
Ian McParland

Arsenal 2010

Appearances: 14 (1 as sub)
Goals: 1
Manager played under:
Arsene Wenger

Newcastle 2010-11

Appearances: 8 (3 as sub)
Managers played under:
Chris Hughton, Alan Pardew

ENGLAND CAREER

England Under-18

European Championship winner 1993

England Under-21, 1994-96

Appearances: 11
Goals: 2

England B, 1994 and 2006

Appearances: 2

England 1996-2007

Appearances: 73 (6 as sub)
With: Tottenham 40, Arsenal 29,
Portsmouth 4
Record: W40, D19, L14 (Lost 3
drawn games in penalty shoot-outs)
Goals: 1
Captain: 3 times (2 under
Glenn Hoddle, 1 under
Sven-Goran Eriksson)
Other managers played under:
Terry Venables, Kevin Keegan,
Steve McClaren
Central defensive partners:
Tony Adams, Gareth Southgate,
Rio Ferdinand, John Terry

PLAYING CAREER HIGHLIGHTS

1992

September: After being part
educated at the FA School of
Excellence at Lilleshall, and having
a brief association with West Ham
United, Campbell signs professional
forms for Tottenham as a central
midfield player.

December: Makes his debut, aged
18, as a 63rd minute substitute
and scores in a 2-1 defeat by
Chelsea at White Hart Lane – his
only appearance in the senior team
that season.

1993

July: Wins the European Under-18
Championship with England, who
beat the defending champions
Turkey 1-0 in the final with a
penalty by Tottenham club-mate
Darren Caskey at the City Ground,
Nottingham.

August: Plays his first full match
for the club on the opening day of
the new season – a 1-0 away win
over Newcastle.

1994

March: Makes his first appearance
for the England Under-21 side in
a 1-0 win over Denmark in a
friendly international at Griffin Park,
Brentford.

May: Ends his first full campaign
at Tottenham with 27 full
appearances, many of them at full-
back, and a further seven as a sub.

June: Scores his first goal for the
Under-21 team in a 2-1 win over

Belgium in the Toulon Tournament in Berre L'Etang, France.

1995

May: At the end of a season in which Campbell continues to cement his place in the side, Tottenham finish seventh in the Premier League – the highest position during his time at the club.

1996

May: Wins his first England senior cap as a 65th minute substitute for Paul Ince in a 3-0 win over Hungary in a friendly international at Wembley.

June: Included in Terry Venables's squad for Euro 2006 in England as defensive cover for Tony Adams and Gareth Southgate. Comes off the bench in the 85th minute of the 2-0 win over Scotland at Wembley to replace Jamie Redknapp.

August: With Gary Mabbutt nearing retirement, Campbell becomes the central defensive cornerstone of Tottenham's defence.

November: Makes his first England start in a 2-0 World Cup qualifying victory over Georgia in Tbilisi.

1997

May: Completes an ever-present season for Spurs, playing in all their 38 Premier League matches.

1998

May: Aged 23 years and 248 days, he becomes the youngest England captain since Bobby Moore. England lose 4-3 on penalties after a goalless draw against Belgium in the King Hassan International Cup competition in Casablanca.

June: Starts all four England matches at the World Cup finals in France. In their second round game against Argentina in St Etienne, with the score 2-2 after Michael Owen's sensational goal and David Beckham's red card, Campbell has a goal disallowed for a foul by Alan Shearer and England lose 4-3 on penalties.

1999

March: Captains Spurs to a 1-0 victory over Leicester City in the Worthington (League) Cup final at Wembley. It is Campbell's one major trophy with the club.

May: Finishes the season as the club's third highest scorer with six goals behind Steffen Iversen (9) and Chris Armstrong (8). Also scores twice in the League Cup in the most prolific campaign of his career. Named in the PFA Premier League Team of the Year.

2000

June: Starts all three matches at Euro 2000 in Belgium and Holland in which England fail to qualify from their group after losing 3-2 to Romania in Charleroi.

2001

April: Limps out of his final match for Tottenham, a 2-1 defeat by Arsenal in an FA Cup semi-final at Old Trafford, with an ankle injury.

July: Campbell makes a controversial move to Arsenal – Spurs' biggest rivals – on a Bosman free transfer.

December: Scores his first goal for Arsenal in a 2-1 victory over Chelsea at Highbury on Boxing Day.

2002

May: Finishes his first season with a double success as Arsenal beat Chelsea 2-0 in the FA Cup final at the Millennium Stadium, then claim the Premier League title, seven points clear of Liverpool.

June: Scores his first – and only – England senior goal with a header from David Beckham's corner in their opening match of the World Cup Finals against Sweden (1-1) in Saitama, Japan. Campbell starts all five games and is the only England player named in FIFA's 'All Star' squad at the tournament. England lose 2-1 to Brazil in the quarter-finals.

August: More silverware as Arsenal defeat Liverpool 1-0 in the FA Community Shield at the Millennium Stadium.

2003

May: Banned for four matches after being sent off against Manchester United and misses the FA Cup final win over Southampton. Also ruled out of the season's run-in when Arsenal finish five points behind champions United. Included in the Premier League Team of the Year.

2004

April: Campbell and Arsenal make sure of regaining the title in a 2-2 draw at White Hart Lane – in front of the Spurs fans who criticised his move from their club.

May: Arsenal's 'Invincibles' complete their 38-match programme without losing a game. With Campbell forming a rock-solid central defensive partnership alongside Kolo Touré, Arsenal concede just 26 goals and Campbell is named again in the Premier League's Team of the Year.

June: Has a goal disallowed for a foul by John Terry with the score 1-1 in England's Euro 2004 quarter-final against Portugal in Lisbon, which ends with a 2-2 scoreline and a 6-5 defeat on penalties. Starts all four of England's games of the tournament in Portugal and is named in UEFA's 'All Star' squad, together with Ashley Cole, Frank Lampard and Wayne Rooney.

October: Arsenal concede a controversial penalty when Wayne Rooney falls over Campbell's outstretched leg, Ruud van Nistelrooy converts it and their 49-match unbeaten Premier League run is ended in a 2-0 defeat by Manchester United at Old Trafford.

2005

May: Campbell collects another FA Cup winner's medal as an unused substitute at the Millennium Stadium, where a goalless draw is followed by a 5-4 penalty shoot-out win against Manchester United.

2006

May: Heads in Thierry Henry's free-kick to give Arsenal the lead in the Champions League final against Barcelona in Paris. But goalkeeper Jens Lehmann is sent off and they lose 2-1. It proves to be his final game for the club.
June: Campbell is third choice behind Rio Ferdinand and John Terry at the World Cup finals in Germany, but becomes the only England player to feature in six successive major tournaments when replacing Ferdinand after 56 minutes of the final group game against Sweden (2-2) in Cologne. It's his only appearance at the tournament in which England lose 3-1 on penalties to Portugal after

a goalless game in which Wayne Rooney is sent off.
August: Seeking a 'fresh challenge,' he joins Portsmouth under manager Harry Redknapp.
December: Scores his first goal for his new club in a 3-1 victory over Sheffield United at Fratton Park.

2007

May: Leads Portsmouth into the top half of the Premier League and almost into the UEFA Cup.
November: Wins his 73rd and final England cap in a 3-2 defeat by Croatia at Wembley which results in the team's failure to qualify for Euro 2008.

2008

May: Captains Portsmouth to a 1-0 victory over Cardiff City in the FA Cup final at Wembley – the club's first triumph in the competition for 69 years.

2009

August: After leaving Portsmouth at the end of his contract, Campbell joins Notts County, where former England manager Sven-Goran Eriksson is director of football.
September: After playing one match for the League Two club, a 2-1 defeat at Morecambe, Campbell has his contract cancelled by 'mutual consent.'

2010

January: Returns to Arsenal on a short-term deal after training with the squad and scores against Porto in a 2-1 defeat in the first leg of the Champions League's first knock-out round.

July: Joins Newcastle on a one-year contract, his final club in a career in which none of his moves cost a penny in transfer fees.

October: Comes off the bench in a 2-1 defeat by Manchester City to maintain his record of playing in every Premier League season since its inception in 1992.

2011

March: Makes his last appearance as a player in Newcastle's 4-0 defeat at Stoke in which he is substituted after 66 minutes.

May: Released by Newcastle manager Alan Pardew.

2012

May: Brings down the curtain on a distinguished career by officially announcing his retirement.

INDEX

ACKNOWLEDGEMENTS

There are a number of people I want to thank. First and foremost, Sol Campbell, for his honesty, openness and resolve to put his life out in the public arena. To those who granted me interviews during the course of writing this book. My deep gratitude goes to Michael James for his words, quotes and guidance. To Michele for the table, chair, coffee and water every morning, from the first to the last day of summer 2013. To all those who devoted many hours in producing this book, thank you. And last but certainly not least, to my publisher, I am truly grateful.

Simon Astaire

SOL'S THANKS

To my mother Wilhelmina, who has always been there for me. My wife Fiona Barratt-Campbell, my love, a special human being, and to our beautiful children. My father Sewell, who was extremely tough on us, but I forgive you. My brothers and sisters, who in their own way showed love and compassion in the difficult earlier years – I honour you and forgive you all, because life has a strange way of turning upside down, and actions which you can't explain back then, are only seen in their true light later on.

To all the coaches, players and teachers, past and present, who positively contributed to my life. My friends who I grew up with from Stratford, East London – you know who you are. My biographer Simon Astaire, who showed great patience when, at first, I wasn't ready to tell my story. My publisher, who has been on hand when things were turning and twisting all the way through the writing of this book. Thank you all for being a part of this journey.

Finally, to all my foes, who made me stretch myself to see how far I could go, even when sometimes it was too much. At least I found out a lot about myself and the landscapes through which I was navigating, and I ultimately grew as a person.

PICTURE CREDITS

The publisher would like to thank the following for permission to reproduce photographs:

Action Images, Brandon Malone / Stuart McFarlane, Arsenal Football Club / Blue Pitch Media / Colorsport / Getty Images, Shaun Botterill / Getty, Michael Regan / Sky Andrew / Action Images, Darren Walsh / Action Images, Tony O'Brien / Roger Price Photography Ltd / Action Images, Tony Henshaw / Action Images, Andrew Boyers, Livepic / Kieron Doherty, Reuters / Bob Thomas Sports Photography / Mattias Pettersson / Adam Butler, Press Association Images

All other photographs are courtesy of Sol Campbell and Fiona Barratt. Thanks to Sol Campbell for his back cover design input.

The publishers have endeavoured to contact all copyright holders to clear permissions, but where omissions have been made, it will rectify on notification.